Robert DiYanni is Director of International Services for The College Board. Dr. DiYanni, who holds a B.A. from Rutgers University and a Ph.D. from the City University of New York, has taught English and Humanities at a variety of institutions, including NYU, CUNY, and Harvard. An Adjunct Professor of English and Humanities at New York University, he has written and edited more than thirty-five books, mostly for college students of writing, literature, and humanities.

Twenty-Five Great Essays

Twenty-Five Great Essays

Third Edition

Edited by

Robert DiYanni
New York University

PENGUIN ACADEMICS

New York   San Francisco   Boston
London   Toronto   Sydney   Tokyo   Singapore   Madrid
Mexico City   Munich   Paris   Cape Town   Hong Kong   Montreal

Senior Vice President and Publisher: Joseph Opiela
Senior Sponsoring Editor: Virginia L. Blanford
Senior Marketing Manager: Sandra McGuire
Production Manager: Savoula Amanatidis
Project Coordination and Text Design: Elm Street Publishing Services, Inc.
Electronic Page Makeup: Integra Software Services, Pvt. Ltd.
Cover Design Manager: Wendy Ann Fredericks
Cover Photo: Copyright © IPS Co., Ltd./Beateworks/Corbis
Manufacturing Buyer: Roy Pickering, Jr.
Printer and Binder: R. R. Donnelley and Sons Company—Harrisonburg
Cover Printer: Phoenix Color Corporation

For permission to use copyrighted material, grateful acknowledgment is made to the
copyright holders on pp. 197–198, which are hereby made part of this copyright page.

Library of Congress Cataloging-in-Publication Data

Twenty-five great essays / edited by Robert DiYanni.—3rd ed.
    p. cm. — (Penguin academics)
  Includes index.
  ISBN 0-205-53556-9 (alk. paper)
  1. College readers. 2. English language—Rhetoric—Problems, exercises, etc.
3. Report writing—Problems, exercises, etc. 4. Essays. I. Title: 25 great essays.
II. DiYanni, Robert III. Series.

  PE1417.O56 2008
  808'.0427—dc22

Please visit our website at www.ablongman.com.

For more information about the Penguin Academics series, please contact us by mail
at Longman Publishers, attn. Marketing Department, 1185 Avenue of the Americas
25th Floor, New York, NY 10036, or by e-mail at www.ablongman.com.

ISBN-10: 0-205-53556-9
ISBN-13: 978-0-205-53556-9

    7 8 9 10—DOH—10

For Michael Hogan
Cherished Colleague and Friend

Contents

Preface

Twenty-Five Great Essays is one volume of a three-book series designed to provide college students and teachers with an outstanding collection of essays for use in university writing courses. The other volumes are *Fifty Great Essays* and *One Hundred Great Essays*. All three volumes are based upon the conviction that reading and writing are reciprocal acts that should be married rather than divorced. Because reading and writing stimulate and reinforce one another, it is best that they be allied rather than separated. In learning to read and respond critically both to their own writing and to the writing of others, students mature as writers themselves.

Twenty-Five Great Essays offers a compendium of the best essays written during the past four hundred years. Readers will find here essays by the great early practitioners of the genre, Montaigne and Bacon, as well as numerous examples from the centuries that follow, both classic and contemporary. Taken together, the essayists whose work is anthologized here offer an abundance of nonfiction that takes the form of autobiographical and polemical essays, observations and speculations, reminiscences and sketches, meditations and expostulations, celebrations and attacks. Overall, the selections balance and blend the flamboyant and innovative with the restrained and classically lucid.

Each of the essays in *Twenty-Five Great Essays* can be considered "great," but is not necessarily great in the same way. Montaigne's greatness as an essayist is not Franklin's, nor is Bacon's essay writing matched equivalently by Swift's. And Orwell's greatness, inspired by a political animus, differs dramatically from that of E. B. White, whose inspiration and emphasis derive less from grand social issues than from personal observation and experience. Yet however much these essayists and essays differ, two aspects of greatness they share are readability and teachability. Whether classic, modern, or contemporary, and whatever their styles, subjects, and rhetorical strategies, these twenty-five essays are worth reading and teaching. They have served students and teachers of reading and writing well for many years.

The second edition of *Twenty-Five Great Essays* deviates only slightly from the first two editions. The introduction to reading and writing essays and the format for the collection of great essays remain the same. The changes occur in the anthology of essays, with five essays from the second edition being replaced by five new selections. The new essays are provided with the same apparatus—author biography, essay headnote, and questions—just as the selections carried over from the second edition.

This collection should be of great value to university instructors who are teaching writing courses both introductory and advanced. They will find here an abundance of outstanding writing to serve as models for their students–models of style and structure, models of thought and feeling expressed in, with, and through carefully wrought language.

Students will find in this valuable collection a source of ideas and models for their own writing. They will also discover here writers who will serve as inspiration and influence as they develop their own styles and voices. In studying these essays as models of good writing, students will profit from analyzing not so much what these writers say, but as how they say what they do.

Writers, too, can benefit from reading the essays collected here and studying the craftsmanship they embody. Montaigne's ease and elegance, and his quirky individuality, while not easily imitated, provide an example of how the familiar material of everyday life can be artfully blended with the exploration of ideas. Bacon's pithy prose exemplifies ideas expressed with aphoristic acuteness. And while these early stars of the constellation of essayists may shine more brightly than others, writers who read with care the contemporary pieces collected here will learn new tricks of the trade and discover unexpected surprises and pleasures.

The heart and soul of *Twenty-Five Great Essays* are twenty-five outstanding essays that span seven centuries. The essays provide a rich sampling of styles and voices across a wide spectrum of topics. They range in length and complexity—some more accessible, others more challenging—all worth reading. These twenty-five essays provide excellent opportunities for readers to meet new writers and to become reacquainted with writers and essays they already know. General readers, both those who have completed their formal education and those still in college, will find in these excellent essays promises and provocations, ideas to respond to and wrestle with, and sometimes argue against.

The Introduction to *Twenty-Five Great Essays* provides an historical overview of the essay from antiquity to the present. It traces developments in the ways writers used essays to entertain readers as well as to inform and persuade them, and it describes the wide range of interests that writers of essays have pursued over the centuries. The Introduction also includes discussion of various types of essays and the pleasures that readers find in them.

Guidelines for reading essays are identified and exemplified with a close reading of a contemporary essay—Annie Dillard's "Living Like Weasels." Readers are provided with a series of guiding questions, commentary about the essay's style and voice, as well as its structure and ideas. The guidelines for reading essays are supplemented by guidelines for writing them. A discussion of the qualities of good writing is complemented by an approach to the writing process, which includes consideration of three major phases or stages—planning, drafting, and revising.

In addition to a set of general essay writing guidelines, the Introduction provides an approach to writing about reading, with a sample from the text of Susan Sontag's essay "A Woman's Beauty: Put-Down or Power Source?" The approach to writing about Sontag's essay takes the form of strategies for blending critical reading and writing, including annotating, freewriting, using a double-column notebook, and writing a summary. A further set of guidelines linking reading with writing focuses on observing details, making connections, drawing inferences, and formulating an interpretation. Throughout the discussion of writing and the sample demonstration, the emphasis is on analysis, reflection, and deliberation— on considering what the essayist is saying, what the reader thinks of it, and why.

Students should be interested in the Introduction's advice about how to read essays critically and thoughtfully. Other readers may be interested in the historical overview of the essay's development. And all readers can practice their reading skills by reading Susan Sontag's essay

"A Woman's Beauty: Put-Down or Power Source?" along with the commentary that explains and explores the writer's ideas.

Each essay in *Twenty-Five Great Essays* is preceded by a headnote, which includes a biographical sketch along with an overview of the essay's key ideas. The biographical information provides context, while the commentary provides a starting point for consideration of the writer's ideas and values. A brief set of questions for thinking and writing follows each essay. All in all, *Twenty-Five Great Essays* should provide readers with many hours of reading pleasure and numerous ideas and models for writing.

Patient and persistent work with *Twenty-Five Great Essays* in the classroom and out will help users understand the qualities of good writing and discover ways to emulate it. With the guided practice in critical reading and essay writing that *Twenty-Five Great Essays* provides, students will increase both their competence and their confidence as perceptive readers and as cogent and able writers. Through repeated acts of attention to their own writing and to the writing of others, students can be expected to acquire a sense of the original meaning of "essay": a foray into thought, an attempt to discover an idea, work out its implications, and express it with distinctiveness. Readers and users of *Twenty-Five Great Essays* should come to see the essay as a way of enriching their experience and their thinking while discovering effective ways to share them with others.

ROBERT DIYANNI
New York University

Twenty-Five Great Essays

Introduction: Reading and Writing Essays

History and Context

The essay has a long and distinguished history. Its roots go back to Greco-Roman antiquity. Forerunners of the essay include the Greek writer Plutarch (46–120), whose *Parallel Lives* of noble Greeks and Romans influenced the art of biography, and who also wrote essays in his *Moralia*. The early Roman writer Seneca, a philosopher, dramatist, and orator, also wrote essays in the grand manner of classical oratory, on topics that include "Asthma" and "Noise." These two early western writers of essays are complemented by a pair of Japanese writers: Sei Shonagon, a court lady who lived and wrote in the tenth century, and Yoshida Kenko (1283–1350), a poet and Buddhist monk, whose brief, fragmentary essays echo the quick brushstrokes of Zen painting.

In one sense, the modern essay begins with Michel de Montaigne in France and with Francis Bacon in England. Both writers published books of essays at the end of the sixteenth century. Montaigne's first two books of essays came out together in 1580 and Bacon's first collection in 1597. Each followed with additional volumes, Montaigne in 1588, Bacon in 1612 and 1625. With each later volume, both writers revised and expanded essays previously published in the earlier volumes as well as adding new ones. Both writers also wrote longer and more elaborate essays from one collection to the next.

Generally recognized as the father of the essay, Michel de Montaigne called his works "essais," French for attempts. In his essays, Montaigne explored his thinking on a wide variety of subjects, including virtue and vice, customs and behavior, children and cannibals. Although Montaigne's first essays began as reflections about his reading and made liberal use of quoted passages, his later essays relied much less on external sources for impetus and inspiration.

The power of Montaigne's essays derives largely from their personal tone, their improvisatory nature, and their display of an energetic and inquiring mind. In his essays, Montaigne talks about himself and the world as he experienced it. He repeatedly tests his opinions and presents an encyclopedia of information that sets him thinking. Amidst an essay's varied details, Montaigne reveals himself, telling us what he likes, thinks, and believes. The openness and flexibility of his essay form make its direction unpredictable, its argument arranged less as a logical structure than as a meandering exploration of its subject. But what is most revealing about Montaigne's essays is that they reveal his mind in the act of thinking. The self-revelatory circling around his subject constitutes the essential subject of the essays. Ironically, in reading him we learn not only about Montaigne but about ourselves.

Another Renaissance writer credited with an influential role in the development of the essay is Francis Bacon—statesman, philosopher, scientist, and essayist. Unlike Montaigne, who retired from active political life early to read, reflect, and write in his private library tower, Bacon remained politically active and intellectually prominent until the last few years of his life. His life and work exhibit a curious interplay between ancient and modern forms of thought. Coupled with a modernity that valued experiment and individual experience was a respect for the authority of tradition. Bacon's scientific and literary writings both display this uneasy alliance of tradition and innovation.

Bacon's essays differ from Montaigne's in striking ways. First, most of Bacon's essays are short. Second, his essays are much less personal than Montaigne's. And third, many of Bacon's essays offer advice in how to live. Their admonitory intent differs from Montaigne's more exploratory temper.

Eighteenth-century America included a profusion of essayists writing in a variety of nonfictional forms. Thomas Paine wrote essays of political persuasion in the periodical *The Crisis.* J. Hector St. John de Crèvecoeur wrote his essayistic *Letters from an American Farmer.* And Benjamin Franklin compiled his *Autobiography* and his *Poor Richard's Almanack*, which is a loosely stitched collection of aphorisms, including "haste makes waste," "a stitch in time saves nine," and "Fish and visitors stink after three days."

During the eighteenth century, more and more writers produced essays, along with their work in other genres. Among them are Samuel Johnson (1709–1784), whose philosophical and moral periodical essays appeared regularly in his own *Rambler, Idler,* and *Adventurer.* The gravity and sobriety of Johnson's essays were complemented by the more lighthearted and satirical vein mined by Joseph Addison (1672–1719), and Richard Steele (1672–1729), whose essays in their *Tatler* and *Spectator* periodicals, which they jointly wrote and published, were avidly awaited when they appeared, as often as three times a week. Jonathan Swift (1667–1745), best known for his satire, *Gulliver's Travels,* also wrote a number of essays, including what is perhaps the most famous satirical essay ever written (and the essay with one of the longest titles): "A Modest Proposal for Preventing the Children of the Poor People in Ireland from being a Burden to their Parents or Country; and for making them beneficial to their Publick."

The nineteenth century saw the rise of the essay less as moralistic and satirical than as entertaining and even a bit eccentric. Among the most notable practitioners were Charles Lamb (1775–1834), whose *Essays of Elia* and *More Essays of Elia* are constructed to read less like random assortments than as books centered on characters, and whose stories form a loose plot. Among these essays is his "A Bachelor's Complaint," in which Lamb, himself a lifelong bachelor, takes up a list of grievances he holds against his married friends and acquaintances. Complementing the playful essays of Charles Lamb during this time are the passionate and highly opinionated essays of William Hazlitt (1778–1830), a friend of the English Romantic poets William Wordsworth and Samuel Taylor Coleridge. Hazlitt's "On the Pleasure of Hating" is written with his customary "gusto," a characteristic he brought to his writing from his life and one in synch with the Romantic poets' emphasis on the importance of feeling.

Nineteenth-century American essayists include the powerful twosome of Ralph Waldo Emerson and Henry David Thoreau. Emerson's essays grew out of his public lectures. He was at home in the form and wrote a large number of essays in a highly aphoristic style that contained nuggets of wisdom served up in striking images and memorably pithy expressions. A few quotable examples include "hitch your wagon to a star," "trust thyself," and "give all to love." Much of Emerson's writing focused on nature, which he envisioned as a divine moral guide to life.

Thoreau, a friend and protégé of Emerson, was another New Englander who limned the natural world in prose. Like Emerson, Thoreau wrote essays on a variety of topics, but mostly about nature. Thoreau's most famous essay, however, is political—his "On the Duty of Civil Disobedience," in which he argues that each individual human being has not only the right but the obligation to break the law when the law is unjust or immoral. Thoreau's "Civil Disobedience," a much cited essay, has also been an influential one, affecting the stances of peaceful nonviolent political resistance taken up by both Mahatma Gandhi and Martin Luther King, Jr. But it is Thoreau's *Walden* that contains his most beautifully crafted essays in his most artfully composed book. Who can forget the matchless prose of sentences such as "If a man cannot keep pace with his companions, perhaps he hears the sound of a different drummer. Let him step to the music which he hears, however measured or far away."

If in one sense the Renaissance can be considered the beginnings of the modern essay, in another, the modern essay is synonymous with the twentieth-century essay, a period in which the essay developed into a literary genre that began to rival fiction and poetry in importance. George Orwell (1903–1950), best known for his satirical *Animal Farm* and *1984*, is equally eminent for the four thick volumes of essays and letters he produced. Orwell's "A Hanging" and "Shooting an Elephant" are modern classics of the genre, as is his "Politics and the English Language," perhaps the best-known essay on language in English. Another English writer better known for her work as a novelist, Virginia Woolf (1882–1941), like Orwell, left a splendid set of essay volumes, including her "Common Reader" series, in which she presents her views on a wide range of authors and works of literature in a relaxed, casual style. "The Death of a Moth" is deservedly among her most highly regarded essays.

On the twentieth-century American scene E. B. White (1899–1985) stands out as a modern master of the genre. White, too, is best known for his fiction, in his case the books he wrote for children, all gems with the diamond among them the ever-popular *Charlotte's Web*. White published many of his essays in *The New Yorker* and a number of others in *Harper's* magazine. "Once More to the Lake," his best known and oft reprinted essay, is also among his most beautifully written, and some would argue, among his most enduring contributions to literature.

Along with White, who rarely wrote about social issues per se, there is James Baldwin (1924–1987), who wrote almost exclusively about race, particularly about race relations in America and about his place in society as a black man and a writer. In fact, Baldwin's consistent theme is identity, his identity as a black writer, who became an expatriate, living in Paris, in part to discover what it meant for him to be an American. A third modern American essayist is James Thurber, a humorist who published satirical cartoons, humorous stories, and parables, as well as journalism. His "The Secret Life of Walter Mitty" and "The Catbird Seat" are two comic story masterpieces. His *My Life and Hard Times* is a classic of American autobiography, and his *Is Sex Necessary?* a spoof on pop psychology.

At the beginning of the twenty-first century, the essay is continuing to thrive. Essayists of all stripes and persuasions continue to publish in magazines and anthologies and in books of collected essays. The annual series, *The Best American Essays,* has recently celebrated its twentieth anniversary. Other annual series of essays have joined it, notably *The Anchor Essay Annual.* These essay volumes are joined by others that are not part of any annual series, but which, nevertheless, come out with great frequency and regularity. The essay, in short, is alive and well in the new millennium.

Pleasures of the Essay

But why has the essay been so well regarded for such a long time? What attracts readers to essays? And what attracts writers to the form? Why has the essay endured?

One answer lies in the wide variety the genre affords. There are essays for everybody, essay voices and visions and styles to suit every taste, to satisfy every kind of intellectual craving. There is variety of subject—of topic—from matters of immediate and practical concern to those of apparently purely theoretical interest; from essays of somber gravity to those in a lighter more playful vein; from easy essays on familiar topics to complex and challenging ones on subjects outside the bounds of most readers' knowledge and experience.

An essay can be about anything. And essayists have written about every topic under the sun, from their own lives and experience to what they have read and observed in the world, to their speculations and imaginings. All of these are available, for example, in Montaigne's little essay, "Of Smells." In fact, to list just a handful of the more than one hundred essays Montaigne alone wrote is to convey a sense of the essay's bewildering variety. In addition to "Of Smells," Montaigne wrote "Of Friendship," "Of Sadness," "Of Idleness," "Of Liars," "Of Constancy," "Of Solitude," "Of Sleep," "Of Fear," "Of Age," "Of Prayers," "Of Conscience," "How We Cry and Laugh for the Same Thing," "Of Moderation," "Of Thumbs," "Of Cannibals," "Of Names," "Of Virtue," "Of Anger," "Of Vanity," "Of Cruelty," "Of Cripples," "Of Glory," "Of Presumption," "Of Books," "How Our Mind Hinders Itself," "That Our Desire Is Increased By Difficulty," "Of the Inconsistency of Our Actions," "Of the Love of Fathers for Their Children," and "That to Philosophize Is to Learn to Die." A similarly wide-ranging list of topics could be culled from Bacon's essays, expressing an equally strong interest in the human condition.

For all his essayistic variety, Montaigne did not write much about nature. Many others, however, have written about the natural world, including Ralph Waldo Emerson in "Nature," N. Scott Momaday in "The Way to Rainy Mountain," Annie Dillard in "Living Like Weasels," Mark Twain in "Reading the River," and Virginia Woolf in "The Death of the Moth." In each of these essays the writer describes an encounter with nature and explores his or her relationship to it.

When not writing about themselves or about nature, and when not speculating on one or another aspect of the human condition, essayists often write about the social world. Joan Didion's "Marrying Absurd" is about Las Vegas weddings; James Thurber's "University Days," about college; and Pico Iyer's "Nowhere Man," about living in multiple places and being a member of no single social group.

Identity, in fact, is a frequent topic among contemporary essayists, with writers exploring their roots and their relationships in essays that touch on race and gender, and on broad social and cultural values. James Baldwin explores what it means to be a black man in a white world. Frederick Douglass writes about his struggle for literacy as a black slave; Judith Ortiz Cofer writes about her dual cultural and linguistic identity; Martin Luther King, Jr., writes about racial prejudice and injustice, and what must be done to establish and ensure racial equality, and why; and Jamaica Kincaid writes about finding and valuing her Caribbean Antiguan identity under the seductive influence of British colonial culture.

Issues of gender are equally important for essayists. Gretel Ehrlich writes about what it means to be a cowboy who cares for animals as an integral part of his life, and of how cowboys, if they are to be good at what they do, need as much maternalism as machismo, if not a good deal more. Maxine Hong Kingston writes about the power and place of gender in traditional China by telling the story of a man, Tang Ao, who visits the land of women, was captured, and was transformed into a woman. Another strong woman who appears in an essay is N. Scott Momaday's Kiowa Indian grandmother, who reflects the cultural values of her tribe and its Native American tradition.

Besides a wide variety of topic and a broad spectrum of human concerns, including gender, race, culture, and identity, essays appeal, too, because of their style, the craftsmanship and beauty with which they are written. And just as there are many essay subjects, so also are there many styles. There are as many styles, in fact, as essayists, for each essayist of distinction develops his or her own style, finding a voice and tone appropriate to the topic, audience, and situation that occasioned the writing of each essay.

E. B. White's "Once More to the Lake" is written in a style at once easy and elegant, familiar and formal, in a splendid blend of language that is as easy on the ear as it is on the eye. For the sheer beauty of language, it begs to be read aloud. George Orwell's "Shooting an Elephant" is less lyrical but no less memorable, written in a style that seems to be no style at all—as clear as a windowpane. Amy Tan's "Mother Tongue" is written in a mixture of styles, an indication that she speaks more than one brand of English, as she describes the worlds of English both she and her Chinese mother inhabit. Langston Hughes uses a simple and direct style in his "Salvation," which tells the story of his religious "anti-conversion." Martin Luther King, Jr., writes in a style that appeals to thinking people, as he develops his own arguments and rebuts the arguments of others about the right of African Americans to protest against racial injustice.

Types of Essays

The word "essay" comes from the French "essai" (essay), which derives from the French verb "essayer"—to try or attempt. The word "essay" suggests less a formal and systematic approach to a topic than a casual, even random one. In this sense, an essay differs from other prose forms such as the magazine article, whose purpose is usually to inform or persuade, and the review, which evaluates a book or performance. Essays, to be sure, may also evaluate, and they often inform as well as persuade. But their manner of going about offering information, making a case, and providing an evaluation differs from those less variable genres.

The essay can be compared with the short story in that some essays, like short stories, include narrative. But the short story is fiction, the essay fact. And fiction works largely by implication, the essay mostly by expository discursiveness. Essays explain what stories imply. This is not to say that essayists don't make use of fictional techniques and strategies. They do so often, particularly in personal or familiar essays, which include narration and description.

The essay can also be linked with poetry, particularly with the more discursive poems that explain as well as image ideas that tell straightforwardly rather than hint or suggest in a more oblique manner. Essayists, on the other hand, typically say what's on their mind fairly directly. They explain what they are thinking. Poets more often write about one thing in terms of another (they write about love, for example, in terms of war). And they prefer implication to explication, which is more characteristic of the essay writer.

Kinds of essays include, broadly, personal essays and formal essays. Personal essays are those in which the writer is amply evident—front and center. Employing the personal pronoun "I," personal essays include opinions and perspectives explicitly presented as the writer's own in a personal, even idiosyncratic, manner. Formal essays, by contrast, typically avoid the pronoun "I," and they omit personal details. Formal essays include expository essays, analytical essays, and argumentative, or persuasive, essays. Expository essays explain ideas and scenarios, using standard patterns of organization, including comparison and contrast, classification, and cause and effect. Analytical essays offer an analysis and interpretation of a text or performance, typically breaking that text or performance into parts or aspects, and presenting both an evaluative judgment and the evidence on which it is based. Argumentative, or persuasive, essays advance a thesis or claim and present evidence that is organized as part of a logical demonstration, utilizing the modes of deductive and inductive reasoning, and including support for the argumentative claim in the form of reasons, examples, and data as evidence.

Most essays, even the most personal ones, are composites and blends. They may tell personal stories rich in descriptive detail to provide evidence to support an idea or claim to persuasion. They may use traditional patterns of expository organization such as comparison and contrast in the cause of developing a logical argument. And they may include information and explanation along with personal experience and argumentation. More often than not, the most interesting and memorable of essays mix and match what are typically thought of as distinct essay types and the conventions associated with them. Contemporary essayists, in particular, cross borders and mix modes, as they write essays that break the rules in a quest to be engaging, persuasive, and interesting.

Reading Essays

Reading essays is a lot like reading other forms of literature. It requires careful attention to language—to the words on the page and to what's "written between the lines." Reading essays involves essentially four interrelated mental acts: observing, connecting, inferring, and concluding. Good readers attend to the details of language and structure of the essays they read. They note not only the information that writers of essays provide, but also how that information is presented, how any stories are told, how arguments are made, and evidence presented. Good readers of essays look for connections among the details they observe—details of image and structure, argument and evidence. And good readers draw inferences based on those connected observations, inferences that prepare them to make an interpretive conclusion from their inferences.

Good readers are also engaged by what they read. They respond with questions that echo in their minds as they read. They make their reading an active engagement with the essay text, an involvement that continues after their actual reading of the words on the page has been completed.

Reading in this manner—observing, connecting, inferring, concluding, and questioning—alerts readers to nuances, to things rendered but not explained or elaborated by the writer. Active, deliberative reading of this sort involves both intellectual comprehension and emotional apprehension, a consideration of the feelings essays generate as well as the thinking they stimulate. This reading process requires that readers make sense of gaps in texts; that they recognize linguistic, literary, and cultural conventions; that they generalize on the basis of textual details; that they bring their values to bear on the essays they read; and that they do all these things concurrently and simultaneously.

Reading Annie Dillard's "Living Like Weasels"

We can illustrate this kind of active, engaged reading by looking at the opening paragraphs of Annie Dillard's "Living Like Weasels," an essay printed in full on pages 62–67.

> A weasel is wild. Who knows what he thinks? He sleeps in his underground den, his tail draped over his nose. Sometimes he lives in his den for two days without leaving. Outside, he stalks rabbits, mice, muskrats, and birds, killing more bodies than he can eat warm, and often dragging the carcasses home. Obedient to instinct, he bites his prey at the neck, either splitting the jugular vein at the throat or crunching the brain at the base of the skull, and he does not let go. One naturalist refused to kill a weasel who was socketed into his hand deeply as a rattlesnake. The man could in no way pry the tiny weasel off, and he had to walk half a mile to water, the weasel dangling from his palm, and soak him off like a stubborn label.

First, a few questions. What strikes us most about this passage? What do we notice on first reading it? What observations would we most like to make about it? What questions do we have? What feelings does the text inspire? What expectations do we have about where the essayist is taking us?

Next, some observations. The first sentence is abrupt. It announces forcefully the key point that a weasel is wild. But what does it imply? What do we understand by the word "wild"? How wild? In what way is the weasel wild? The second sentence is a question, one that invites us to consider what a weasel thinks about. (Or perhaps it suggests that we shouldn't bother because we simply cannot know.) "Who knows what he thinks?" How we take this sentence depends on how we hear it, which in turn, affects how we say it. Here's one way: Who knows what he *thinks?* Here's another: Who knows *what* he thinks? And still another: Who *knows* what he thinks? Whichever way we prefer, we recognize the possibility of alternative emphases and thus, alternative ways of understanding what the writer is saying and suggesting about weasels.

Dillard's next two sentences provide information—that weasels sleep in dens where they can remain for up to two days at a time. There's nothing really surprising here. But what about that other little bit of information—*how* the weasel sleeps: with his tail draped over his nose. Whether factual or fanciful, that draped tail is a lovely surprise, a gratuitous image offered to engage and entertain as well as inform.

The fifth and sixth sentences of the opening paragraph reveal the weasel as hunter—stalking prey, killing it, dragging it to his den, where he eats it and then, presumably, sleeps. When we are told that the weasel is obedient to instinct and are shown exactly how he kills—by splitting the jugular vein or by crunching his victim's brain—we remember the opening sentence: "A weasel is wild." And we begin to understand in a new way just what this means. Although we "understood" before, on first encountering the sentence, that vague and general knowledge is now particularized. We have since acquired specific information that we can understand intellectually and respond to emotionally. Now, we know more fully what it means to say that a weasel is "wild."

It is here, in the middle of the paragraph, that we perhaps register our strongest emotional response. How do we respond to Dillard's details about the weasel's method of killing its victims? Are we amazed? Engaged? Appalled? Or what? That question about response is directed at our experience of the essay. We can also ask a technical question: Does Dillard need that degree of detail? Suppose she had diluted it or perhaps even omitted such concrete details entirely. Or conversely, suppose that she had provided an even fuller rendition of the killing. How would such alternatives have affected our response?

Dillard's opening paragraph concludes with an anecdote about a naturalist bitten by the tenacious weasel. The anecdote makes a point, to be sure. But it does more. The image impresses itself on our minds in language worth noting: the verb "socketed"; the comparison with the rattlesnake; the image of the stubborn label. To make sense of Dillard's opening paragraph, even a preliminary kind of sense, is to make such observations and to wonder about their significance. And it is to wonder, too, where the essay is heading, where the writer is taking us. What *do* we expect at this point? Why?

Once we read the second paragraph of Dillard's essay, we can consider how it affects our understanding of and response to the first. How does it follow from the opening paragraph? What does it do rhetorically? That is, what effect does it have on us, and how does it advance Dillard's point about the wildness of the weasel?

Here is Dillard's next paragraph:

> And once, says Ernest Thompson Seton—once, a man shot an eagle out of the sky. He examined the eagle and found the dry skull of a weasel fixed by the jaws to his throat. The supposition is that the eagle had pounced on the weasel and the weasel swiveled and bit as instinct taught him, tooth to neck, and nearly won. I would like to have seen that eagle from the air a few weeks or months before he was shot: was the whole weasel still attached to his feathered throat, a fur pendant? Or did the eagle eat what he could reach, gutting the living weasel with his talons before his breast, bending his beak, cleaning the beautiful airborne bones?

Our questions at the beginning of this second paragraph of Dillard's essay necessarily invite our responses, both intellectual and emotional. In asking what strikes us about the details or the language of this paragraph, we move from subjective responses to objective considerations. On the basis of the details we notice and relate, we form inferences. We move backward, in a way, from our initial response to a set of observations about the essay's rhetoric. We might observe, for example, that the second paragraph begins with an image very much like the one at the end of the opening paragraph. The tenacious weasel holds on fiercely, in one instance to a man's hand, and in another, to an eagle's throat. And we might register the justness of this pair of images, the more striking image of the eagle following and intensifying the first image of the weasel socketed to a man's hand. We might also observe that the second paragraph begins with statements—with declarative sentences—and ends with questions. We might notice, further, that it includes a reference to another written text (did we notice that this occurs in the opening paragraph as well?). And, finally, that the writer speaks personally, using the personal pronoun "I," revealing her desire to have seen the amazing thing she had only read about.

In addition, we should note Dillard's profusion of precise, vivid, strong verbs, which contribute to the power of her prose. We should note, too, the image of the eagle gutting the living weasel, bending his beak and cleaning the weasel's bones of its flesh—an image brought forward and elaborated from the previous sentence, where it exists as a pair of adjectives and corresponding nouns: "his feathered throat, a fur pendant." Dillard actually brings the dormant image to life in that string of participles: *gutting, living, bending, cleaning.*

The repeated words in this second paragraph create a litany of eagle and weasel, their rhyming sound echoed again in "*eat*," "*reach*," "*beak*," and "*cleaning*." We should notice, as well, the alliterative b's of the final sentence: "his talons *b*efore his *b*reast, *b*ending his *b*eak, cleaning the *b*eautiful air*b*orne *b*ones." And further, we might see how the paragraph's monosyllabic diction is counterpointed against both the polysyllabic name of the naturalist, Ernest Thompson Seton, and the continual yoking and re-yoking of the animals, eagle and weasel always coming together. To hear the remarkable sound play of Dillard's prose, including its subtle yet muscular rhythms, we must read it aloud.

We can make some observations about the overall structure of Dillard's complete essay. We have described how the first two paragraphs present facts about weasels, especially about their wildness and their tenaciousness. This introductory section of the essay is followed by a section, paragraphs 3–7, that depicts Dillard's encounter with a weasel and their exchange of glances. The middle paragraphs of that section—4 through 6—set the scene, while paragraphs 3 and 7 frame this section, with an emphasis on Dillard's and the weasel's repeated locked glances. Paragraph 5 is of particular interest in its mix of details that contrast wilderness and civilization. They exist, surprisingly, side-by-side, one within the other: beer cans coexist with muskrat holes; turtle eggs sit in motorcycle tracks; a highway runs alongside a duck pond.

Dillard's next large section of the essay, paragraphs 8–13, provides a crescendo and a climax. Dillard describes the weasel in detail, emphasizing the shock of their locked looks and the shattering of the spell. She also laments her unsuccessful attempt to re-forge the link with the weasel after the spell had been broken. The section ends with Dillard and her readers pondering the mysterious encounter she experienced.

In her concluding section, paragraphs 14–17, Dillard speculates about the meaning of her encounter with the weasel. She contemplates living like a weasel—what it means, why it appeals to her. She explores the implications of what a weasel's life is like, and how its life relates to the life of human beings like her own. She concludes with an image from the opening: an eagle carrying something that is clinging fiercely to it, not letting go, holding on into and beyond death. The image brings the essay full circle—but with the important difference that we, Dillard's readers, have taken the weasel's place.

We are now poised to consider the ideas, the meaning, of "Living Like Weasels," though, clearly, it is necessary to read the essay in its entirety at least once for the following remarks to be completely comprehensible.

What begins as an expository essay that outlines facts about the wildness and tenacity of weasels turns into a meditation on the value of wildness and the necessity of tenacity in human life. By the end of the essay, Dillard has made the weasel a symbol and a model of how human beings might, even should, live. And her tone changes from the factual declaration of the essay's introductory section to speculative wonder, and finally to admonition. Dillard encourages her readers to identify their one necessity, and then, like the weasel, to latch on to it and never let it go.

Dillard also suggests that there is between human and animal the possibility of communication, of understanding. She opts for a mystical communion between woman and weasel, by necessity a brief communion, one beyond the power of words to describe. The experience for Dillard stuns her into stillness and momentarily stops time. In linking her mind even briefly with the weasel, Dillard undergoes an extraordinary transforming experience. But it's an experience that, as much as she wishes it to continue, she cannot prolong because her own consciousness, the distinctive human quality of her thinking mind, which enables her to appreciate the experience in the first place, prevents her, finally, from staying at one with an animal.

There seems to be, thus, in Dillard's essay, a pull in two directions. On one hand, there is the suggestion that human beings can link themselves with the animal world, and like the weasel, live in necessity instinctively. On the other hand sits an opposing idea: that human beings cannot stay linked with the weasel or any animal, primarily because our minds prohibit it. We are creatures for whom remembering is necessary, vital. The mindlessness of the weasel, thus, can never be ours, for we are mindful creatures, not mindless ones. Our living as we should is necessarily different from the weasel's living as it should. And although we can certainly learn from the weasel's tenacity and purity of living, we can follow it only so far on the way to wildness.

Writing Essays

Reading actively and with critical judgment is a necessary adjunct to writing well. In reading carefully and critically, we learn about suggestiveness, about allusion, about economy, about richness. We learn about rhetorical and stylistic possibilities for our own essay writing.

The Qualities of Good Writing

But what constitutes good writing, the kind of writing expected of students in college courses, the kind expected of professional employees on the job? Writing, essentially, that is characterized by the following qualities: (1) clarity; (2) coherence; (3) logical organization; (4) accuracy and correctness; (5) sufficiency; and (6) style.

Good writing is *clear* writing. Readers can follow and understand it easily. This is harder to accomplish than it sounds because what is clear to the writer may not be clear to the reader. Writers need to remember that the entire context of their thinking is not readily apparent to their readers. Readers can determine what a writer is saying only from the words on the page.

Good writing is *coherent* writing. Coherence refers to how a writer's sentences "hang together," how those sentences relate to one another sensibly and logically. We can think of coherence, first, though not exclusively, as a quality of paragraphs. Good writing allows readers to determine the focus and point of every paragraph, and to determine, further, the relation of one paragraph to another. This aspect of coherence reveals a writer's inescapable concern with essay organization overall.

Good writing is carefully *organized* writing. A well-written essay has a discernible beginning, middle, and ending (a clearly identifiable introduction, body, and conclusion). Each of these three main parts of an essay need not be baldly announced, but each should be readily discernible by a careful reader. But the organization of an essay requires more than including these three broad aspects. Of particular importance is how the essay unfolds, how its information and evidence are deployed, how each aspect of the writer's idea leads into the next, how the paragraphs that make up the middle, or body, of an essay exhibit a logical structure.

Good writing is also *accurate* and *correct* both in terms of information included, and in terms of its language. Grammatical accuracy is essential. So is accurate spelling and punctuation. These elements of good writing can be assisted through the use of grammar and spell-check features of word processing programs, through the use of a good dictionary, and through keeping a good handbook, such as *The Scribner Handbook for Writers*, nearby.

Good writing is also *sufficient* to the scope of its subject and the limits of its topic. Short essays may be adequate to discussing highly focused aspects of a topic, while broader and more inclusive topics require longer, more detailed writing. Sufficiency, of course, is a relative concept. But it is important for a writer to include enough evidence to support an idea persuasively, enough examples to illustrate a concept clearly, a sufficient number of reasons to support a claim in developing an argument.

Good writing, finally, has a sense of *style*. Every writer needs to develop his or her own way with words. Paradoxically, one of the best ways to do this is to observe and imitate the style of other writers. Good writers attend to how other successful writers structure their essays, shape their sentences, and select their words. One of the reasons to develop skillful habits of reading is to glean, from that attentiveness, strategies and techniques for good writing.

An Overview of the Writing Process

These six qualities of good writing require patience, persistence, and practice. Good writing can't be rushed. It requires planning, drafting, and revising.

Planning

In the planning stage of the writing process, it is important to take notes and to make notes. Taking notes involves mostly marking or copying passages, which you might use in your essay. It also involves summarizing and paraphrasing what you read—putting it into your own words. Making notes refers to the act of thinking about what you have marked, copied, summarized, or paraphrased. Writing out notes about what you think about your reading, beginning to formulate your own thinking about it, is an active and reflective process that provides an important step toward drafting your essay.

Planning your essay requires making notes to yourself in other ways as well. You can make lists of observations from your reading or lists of aspects or elements of your topic to consider in your essay draft. You can jot down questions, and you can do some freewriting to jumpstart your thinking. These and other preliminary planning strategies are necessary for all but the most informal of writing projects. Time spent on them pays off later during the drafting stage.

Drafting

A draft is a first take, one that provides an overview of your essay, including some kind of beginning and ending, and much of the body or middle, with its examples and evidence to support and develop your ideas. First drafts of essays are often called "rough" drafts, and for good reason. The preliminary draft is not meant to be worried into final form. The first draft is not intended to be a finished product, fit for public display. It is, rather, an attempt the writer makes to see where the topic is going, and whether there are sufficient examples and evidence to support the idea. The idea too, may very well require adjustment and revision, more often than not.

In drafting an essay, it is important to consider your purpose. Are you writing to provide information? To convey an experience? To amuse and entertain? To present an idea for your readers' consideration? To persuade your readers to see something your way? Being clear about your purpose will help with decisions about other aspects of writing your essay, including how to begin and end, as well as choices of language and tone.

Your draft should also make a good start toward providing the supporting evidence necessary for making your ideas persuasive. In marshalling evidence for your ideas from your reading of primary sources, such as works of literature (including the essays in this book), and from secondary sources written about the primary sources, keep the following guidelines in mind:

1. Be fair-minded. Be careful not to oversimplify or distort either a primary or secondary source.
2. Be cautious. Qualify your claims. Limit your assertions to what you can comfortably demonstrate.
3. Be logical. See that the various elements of your argument fit together and that you don't contradict yourself.
4. Be accurate. Present facts, details, and quotations with care.
5. Be confident. Believe in your ideas and present them with conviction.

After writing a draft of an essay, put it aside for a while—ideally for at least a day or two. When you return to it, assess whether what you are saying still makes sense, whether you have provided enough examples to clarify your ideas and presented sufficient evidence to make them persuasive. Read the draft critically, asking yourself what is convincing and what is not, what makes sense and what doesn't. Consider whether the draft centers on a single idea and stays on track.

If the first draft accomplishes these things, you can begin thinking about how to tighten its organization and refine its style. If, on the other hand, the draft contains frequent changes of direction, confusions of thought, multiple unrelated ideas, incoherent paragraphs, and more, you will need to decide what to salvage and what to discard. You will need to return to the planning stage—though now with a clearer sense of your essay's possibilities, and begin the process of drafting your essay again—a second attempt in a second draft. This scenario, by the way, is not uncommon. It simply represents the way first efforts often begin: in some degree of confusion that is eventually dispelled. This common scenario, moreover, argues for leaving enough time to do a second (and, if necessary, a third) draft.

Revising

Revision is not something that occurs only once, at the end of the writing process. Redrafting your essay to consider the ordering of paragraphs and the use of examples is itself a significant act of revision. So, too, is doing additional reading and even rereading some materials to reconsider your original idea. Revision occurs throughout the entire arc of the writing process. It requires you to reconsider your writing and your thinking not once, but several times. This reconsideration is made on three levels: conceptual, organizational, and stylistic.

Conceptual revision involves reconsidering your ideas. As you write your first and subsequent drafts, your understanding of the topic may change. While accumulating evidence in support of your idea, you may find evidence that subverts or challenges it. And you might decide, if not to change your idea dramatically, at least to qualify it to account for this contradictory or complicating evidence. On the other hand, as you write your various drafts, you might find yourself thinking of additional ways to develop and strengthen your idea, to support it with additional evidence, examples, and reasons.

Organizational or structural revision involves asking yourself whether your essay's arrangement best presents your line of thinking. You might ask yourself questions such as these: Is the organizational framework readily discernible? Does it make sense? Have you written an introduction that identifies your topic and clarifies your intent? Have you organized your supporting details in a sensible and logical manner? Does your conclusion follow from your discussion, and does it bring your essay to a satisfying close? However you choose to end your essay, your conclusion should answer the question "So what?" for the reader. Even though you may have presented details, reasons, and examples to support your idea, your readers will still expect you to explain their significance, and in ways that they themselves will want to see as interesting and valuable.

Stylistic revision concerns smaller-scale details, such as matters of syntax or word order, of diction or word choice, of tone, imagery, and rhythm. Even though you may think about some of these things a bit in early drafts, it is better to defer critical attention to them until your final draft, largely because such microscopic stylistic considerations may undergo significant alteration as you rethink and reorganize your essay. You might find, for example, that a paragraph you worked on carefully for style in a first draft is no longer important or relevant, and thus disappears from the final draft.

Focus on aspects of style that may require revision with the following questions:

1. Are your sentences concise and clear?
2. Can you eliminate words that are not doing their job?
3. Is your tone consistent? (For example, you need to avoid shifts from a formal to an informal or colloquial tone.)
4. Is your level of language appropriate for the subject of your essay?
5. Are there any grammatical errors? Any mistakes in spelling or punctuation? And, finally, before letting an essay go public, be sure to proofread it to check for typos and other unintended mistakes.

Writing from Reading — An Example

In order to write essays about what you read, it is always useful to work through some preliminary, informal writing en route to preparing a more formal piece, whether a short summary or a longer, full-fledged essay.

Earlier, some types of preliminary writing were mentioned. Here they will be illustrated with a short excerpt from Susan Sontag's essay, "A Woman's Beauty" (pp. 152–155).

We begin with annotation.

Annotations are brief notes you write about a text while reading it. You can underline and circle words and phrases that strike you as important. You can highlight passages. You can make marginal comments that reflect your understanding of and attitude toward the text. Your annotations might also include arrows that link related points, question marks that indicate possible confusion, and exclamation marks to express surprise or agreement.

Annotations can be single words or brief phrases; they can be written as statements or as questions. And depending on how extensively you annotate a text, your annotations may form a secondary text that reminds you of the one you are reading and analyzing. Annotations used this way serve as an abbreviated guide to what the text says and what you think about it.

As you read the following passage, notice the various types of annotations, and, if you like, add additional annotations of your own.

Here, first, for convenience, is an excerpt from Sontag's essay.

Excerpt from Susan Sontag's
A Woman's Beauty: Put-Down or Power Source?

Is beauty really
essential? Seems
exaggerated.
Society defines
norms of beauty.
Women are pushed
into *over*concern
with their
appearance.
Contrast: men *do*
well; women *look*
good.

To be called beautiful is thought to name something essential to women's character and concerns. (In contrast to men—whose essence is to be strong, or effective, or competent.) It does not take someone in the throes of advanced feminist awareness to perceive that the way women are taught to be involved with beauty encourages narcissism, reinforces dependence and immaturity. Everybody (women and men) knows that. For it is "everybody," a whole society, that has identified being feminine with caring about how one looks. (In contrast to being masculine—which is identified with caring about <u>what one *is* and *does*</u> and only secondarily, if at all, about how one looks.) [. . .]

It is not, of course, the desire to be beautiful that is wrong but the obligation to be—or to try. What is accepted by most women as a flattering idealization of their sex is a way of <u>making women feel inferior</u> to what they actually are—or normally grow to be. For the ideal of beauty is administered as a form of <u>self-oppression</u>. Women are taught to see their bodies in *parts,* and to evaluate each part separately. <u>Breasts</u>, feet, <u>hips</u>, waistline, neck, eyes, nose, <u>complexion</u>, hair, and so on—each in turn is submitted to an anxious, fretful, often despairing scrutiny. Even if some pass muster, some will always be found wanting. [. . .]

In <u>men, good looks is a whole</u>, something taken in at a glance. It does not need to be confirmed by giving measurements of different regions of the body; nobody encourages a man to dissect his appearance, feature by feature. As for <u>perfection</u>, that is considered trivial—almost unmanly.

Annotations in left margin:

Contrast: *desire* for beauty versus *obligation* to be beautiful. Sontag politicizes the issue—beauty as means of oppression. Women + beauty = body parts.

Doesn't author exaggerate here about perfection? Nice distinction here on beauty and the sexes.

Freewriting

Your initial impressions of a text, which you can record with annotations, will often lead you to further thoughts about it. You can begin developing these thoughts with freewriting. As with annotating, in freewriting you record ideas, reactions, or feelings about a text without arranging them in any special order. Freewriting is free-form writing. You simply write down what you think about the passage, without worrying about logical organization. The point is to get your ideas down on paper and not to censor or judge them prematurely. Freewriting, in fact, provides a way to pursue an idea and develop your thinking to see where it may lead.

Both annotation and freewriting precede the more intricate and deliberative work of analysis, interpretation, and evaluation. Annotation and freewriting also provide a convenient way to prepare for writing essays and reports. These two informal techniques work well together; the brief, quickly noted annotations complement the more leisurely paced, longer elaborations of freewriting.

Here is an example of freewriting about the Susan Sontag essay excerpt annotated earlier. Notice how the freewriting includes questions that stimulate reflection on the passage.

Example of Freewriting

Interesting questions. Women do seem to think more about their looks than men do. But since it's men women wish to please by looking good, men may be responsible (some? much?) for women's obsession with appearance. How far have women bought into the beauty myth? How much are they responsible for obsessing about beauty? How about money and profit? And at whose expense?

Why don't men *need* to be beautiful? To please parents—employers? To attract a mate? To be considered "normal"? Sontag says beauty is irrelevant for men—men judged by different standards—strength, competence, effectiveness. She doesn't mention power, money, status—leaves out intelligence and moral qualities—kindness, decency, generosity? How important?

Distinction between *desiring* to be beautiful (perhaps to be desired or admired) and *needing* to be. Nothing wrong with women wanting to be attractive, to look good. Problem is when desire becomes *obligation*—a waste of women's talents—minimizes them, keeps them subservient.

Parts and whole—are women concerned with *parts* of their bodies—certain parts? Their overall appearance? Their sense of self? Silicone breast implants? Face lifts? (But men have nose jobs, pec implants.) Men are concerned with *some parts* of their bodies more than others—like women? Or not?

What about the words for good-looking women—and men? Beautiful women, but handsome men. Foxy

lady—gorgeous woman (guy?) attractive girl. And what
of men? Handsome, good-looking. Pretty boy? Hunk—
derogatory for men. A real "he-man."

Double-Column Notebook

Still another way to develop your thinking about what you read is to make entries in a double-column notebook. To create a double-column notebook, simply divide a page in half. One half is for summarizing and interpreting what you read. Use this side to record your understanding of the text. Use the other side to respond to what you read, to think about implications, and to relate it to knowledge gleaned elsewhere.

The advantage of a double-column notebook is that it encourages you to be an active reader, to think about your reading, and to make connections with your other reading and with your experience. You can use the double-column notebook to think further about your earlier reactions and thoughts recorded in your annotations and freewriting.

Here are, first, a generic look at how a double-column notebook page appears, and then an example based on the Sontag essay excerpt.

Double-Column Notebook Page

Summary	*Comments*
Summarize the text.	Respond to your summary.
Interpret the author's ideas.	Reflect on the author's ideas.
Explain the ideas succinctly.	Consider your agreement or disagreement.
Identify important details.	Raise questions about those details.
Relate details to central idea.	Relate main idea to reading & experience.

The following sample page details how a double-column notebook page might look based on Sontag's essay excerpt. But it's not an attempt to comment on every aspect of her essay.

Double-Column Notebook
for Sontag Essay Excerpt

Summary

Sontag argues that women's beauty is more dangerous than beneficial. Their beauty and their concern with it hurt women by distracting them from more important things, such as intellectual pursuits and political opportunities.

Sontag claims that women are seen as superficial and frivolous because they occupy much of their time with attempting to improve their appearance.

She criticizes a society that relegates women to a form of second-class citizenship in which beauty counts less than brains, and in which obsessing about appearance instead of devoting time and energy to power and status allow women to be dismissed as superficial and decorative.

She sets the standards and ideals for women's beauty over and against those for men, and she finds the standards for men's appearance more sensible, reasonable, and meaningful.

Comments

Sontag's agenda here seems genuine. She values women as intelligent people with a contribution to make to society. She seems genuinely angry by their being forced to be overly concerned with their appearance.

Sontag implies that women are damned if they do and damned if they don't. Women have to look their best in a world that expects nothing less of them. If women neglect their looks they are criticized for it; if they labor to be beautiful, they are equally criticized. It's a no-win situation for them.

In blaming society for women's beauty dilemma, is she really blaming men? Isn't it men who continue to rule the world and set the standards and expectations? Or is she blaming the consumerism and commercialism that dominate contemporary culture?

Writing a Summary

A summary is a compressed version of a text in which you explain the author's meaning in your own words. You summarize a text when you need to give your readers the gist of what it says. A summary should present the author's text accurately and represent his or her views fairly. You build your summary on the observations, connections, and inferences you make while reading. Although there is no rule for how long or short a summary should be, a summary of a text is always shorter than the text itself.

Writing a summary requires careful reading, in part to ensure that you thoroughly understand what you are reading. Writing a summary helps you respond to what you read by requiring careful analysis and consideration of its details.

Writing a summary requires essentially two kinds of skills: identifying the idea of the text you are summarizing, and recognizing the evidence that supports that idea. One strategy for writing a summary is to find the key points that support the main idea. You can do this by looking for clusters of sentences or groups of paragraphs that convey the writer's meaning. Because paragraphs work together, you cannot simply summarize each paragraph independently. You may need to summarize a cluster of paragraphs to convey the idea of a text effectively. It all depends on the length and complexity of the text you are summarizing and on how it is organized.

Here is an example of the process applied to the essay excerpt by Sontag.

Sample Notes toward Summary

General idea of passage: Women are seen as superficial and trivial, concerned with surface beauty rather than with deeper qualities of character. Women are viewed as beautiful objects, valued for how they look rather than for who they are and what they have achieved.
Key supporting points:

- Women's preoccupation with their beauty is a sign of their self-absorption.
- Women's concern for beauty is a form of enslavement to appearances.

- Men are less concerned with appearances, especially with perfecting their appearance.
- Women are objectified in connection with parts of their bodies.
- Women are deemed inconsequential and frivolous.

To create a smooth summary from these key-supporting points, it is necessary to expand and elaborate on them a bit. It is also necessary to put them in a logical order, and to create introductory and concluding sentences for the summary paragraph. Transitions also need to be provided.

Here is an example of such a summary. This one avoids direct quotation from Sontag's text, though quoting her essay is certainly permissible in a summary. Opinions and judgmental words and phrases are avoided, and the writer and text are identified in the opening sentence.

Sample Summary
Sontag Essay Excerpt

In her essay "A Woman's Beauty: Put-Down or Power Source?" Susan Sontag explains how women's need to appear beautiful trivializes them, making them sound superficial and identifying them as creatures preoccupied with how they look rather than with who they are and what they have achieved. Sontag suggests that women's preoccupation with physical beauty is a sign of their self-absorption and triviality. Through being taught to see themselves as mere body parts, women become both objectified and ridden with anxiety that their parts may not measure up. Unlike women, men are viewed as a whole rather than for their parts. Their looks are considered as part of an overall package, one that includes not only the appearance they present, but their knowledge, intelligence, and status. Unlike women, who lack power, men are perceived as more serious, more confident, and more powerful than the women who anxiously labor to be beautiful in order to please them.

Going Further

Once you have gotten far enough to be comfortable with the writer's idea so that you can summarize it accurately, you are ready to return to the text to look for additional evidence to develop and expand your summary into a full-fledged essay. Earlier a process for accomplishing this revisionary reading was described. Now we will add some notes which, coupled with the summary, can prepare for the writing of a more elaborate essay about Sontag's perspective on women's beauty. The notes can help you expand your summary.

There are four basic steps in this process: observing details of the text, connecting or relating them, making inferences based on those connections, and drawing a conclusion about the text's meaning and significance. This four-stage process allows for the accumulation of the evidence needed to support a textual interpretation that could be formulated in an essay about it.

Observing Details

The kinds of observations you make about text depend on the kind of text you are reading. Here are some observations about Sontag's essay excerpt:

- Sontag focuses throughout on surface beauty—on appearance.
- She distinguishes between beauty in women and in men.
- She sees women's obsession with beauty as dangerous.
- She describes men as strong and competent.
- She italicizes certain key words.
- She places certain sentences in parentheses.
- She puts some words in quotation marks.
- She punctuates heavily with dashes.

Look back at the passage. Make your own observations about the ideas in Sontag's comments; select one sentence in each paragraph that crystallizes her thought. Make a few observations about Sontag's sentences: their type, length, and form. Notice how she begins and ends her paragraphs. Observe what evidence she provides to support her views.

Connecting Details

It is not enough, however, simply to observe details about a text. You must also connect them; relate them to one another. To make a connection is to see one thing in relation to another. You may notice that some details reinforce others, or that the writer repeats certain words or ideas. Perhaps she sets up a contrast, as Sontag does between men's and women's attitudes toward beauty.

While you are noticing aspects of a text, you can also begin making connections among its details. Your goal is to see how the connected details help you make sense of the text as a whole. One way to do this is to group information in lists or in outline form. This involves setting up categories or headings for related kinds of details. In the Sontag passage, for example, you could create heads for details about men and about women. Or you could group observations about style under one head and observations about ideas under another. Notice, for example, how the list of observations made earlier can be divided exactly in this manner, with the first four items concerning Sontag's ideas and the last four her style.

Making observations about a text and establishing connections among them form the basis of analysis. From that basis you begin to consider the significance of what you observe and proceed to develop an interpretation of the text overall. Breaking the interpretive process down in this manner enables you to understand what it involves and should prepare you to practice it on other occasions.

Making Inferences

An inference is a statement based on what has been observed. You infer a writer's idea or point of view, for instance, from the examples and evidence he or she provides. Inferences drive the interpretive process. They push readers beyond making observations and toward explaining their significance. Without inferences there can be no interpretation based on textual evidence.

There is nothing mysterious about the process of making inferences. We do it all the time in our everyday lives, from inferring what someone feels when they complain about something we have done (or failed to do) to inferring the significance of a situation based upon visual observation, as when we see someone with a large ring of keys opening rooms in an academic building early in the morning.

The same is true of making inferences about a text. The inferences we make in reading represent our way of "reading between the lines" by discovering what is implied rather than explicitly stated. The freewriting sample about the Sontag essay excerpt contains inferences. Here are a few additional inferences a reader could draw from the Sontag passage:

- Sontag thinks that the double standard by which women are judged for their beauty and men for other qualities is wrong (paragraph 1).
- She implies that few women can meet the high standards for beauty that society imposes (paragraph 2).
- She seems to approve of the way masculine beauty is considered as a sum of each feature of a man's overall appearance (paragraph 3).
- She implies that women would be better off regarded as whole beings as well.

Sontag does not say any of these things outright. But readers can infer them based on what she does say explicitly. Remember that an inference can be right or wrong, and thus different readers might debate the reliability of these or other inferences we might make about Sontag's essay excerpt. The important thing is not to be afraid to make inferences because of uncertainty about their accuracy. Critical reading and writing involve thinking, and thinking involves making inferences. It is this kind of inferential thinking, moreover, that is essential to good reading and good writing.

Arriving at an Interpretation

The step from making inferences to arriving at an interpretation is not an overly large one. An interpretation is a way of explaining the meaning of a text; it represents your way of understanding the text expressed as an idea. In formulating an interpretation of the Sontag essay, you might write something like the following:

> Sontag examines the meaning of beauty in the lives of women, seeing women's beauty, to echo her title, as more of a "put-down" than a source of power. Although she recognizes that beautiful women can use their attractive appearance to their advantage, she argues that the very beauty that gives beautiful women a social advantage, simultaneously detracts from the overall estimation and regard which others have of them.

This interpretation can be debated, and it can be, indeed needs to be, further elaborated and explained. But the interpretation is based on the inferences made while reading the text, and upon the observations and connections among them that provided the foundation for those inferences. In arriving at this or any interpretation, it is necessary to look back at the text's details to reconsider your initial observations, as well as to review the connections and inferences based upon them. Your inferences must be defensible, that is supportable, either by textual evidence or by logical reasoning.

In looking back at the Sontag passage, you might notice something you overlooked earlier. You might notice, for example, that Sontag mentions society's responsibility for foisting certain ideals of beauty upon women. In thinking about the implications of that observation, you might make other inferences, which may lead you to an interpretive emphasis that differs from your previous understanding of her text. You might decide that the central issue for Sontag is society's role and responsibility in forcing such an ideal of beauty upon women. In that case, you would probably select your evidence from the essay differently to support this new focus of your interpretation.

In writing a full-fledged interpretive essay based on Sontag's piece, or in writing your own essay on the subject of beauty—whether or not you restrict it to "women's beauty"—you would go through the same process described here. The only difference is that the essay you develop would be long enough to provide a full explanation of your ideas and sufficient evidence to make your ideas worthy of a reader's consideration, and that it be long and detailed enough either to fulfill the demands of an assignment to which it might be a response, or to satisfy you as its writer that you have said what you wanted to with enough evidence to make it convincing to others.

Francis Bacon (1561–1626) was born in London to parents who were members of the court of Queen Elizabeth I. He attended Trinity College, entered the practice of law in his late teens, and became a member of the House of Commons at the age of 23. His career flourished under King James I, but later scandals ended his life as a politician. A philosopher/scientist by nature and one of the most admired thinkers of his day, Bacon was a founder of the modern empirical tradition based on closely observing the physical world, conducting controlled experiments, and interpreting results rationally to discover the workings of the universe. Of his many published works, he is best remembered today for his Essays *(collected from 1597 until after his death), brief meditations noted for their wit and insight.*

Francis Bacon

Of Studies

In his classic essay, "Of Studies," Francis Bacon explains how and why study—knowledge—is important. Along with Michel de Montaigne, who published his first essays less than twenty years before Francis Bacon published his first collection in 1597, Bacon is concidered the father of the English essay (with Montaigne the father of the French essay). Bacon's essays differ from Montaigne's in being more compact and more formal. Where Montaigne conceived of the essay as an opportunity to explore a subject through mental association and a casual ramble of the mind, Bacon envisioned the essay as an opportunity to offer advice. The title of his essay collection: "Essays or Counsels: Civil and Moral," suggests that didactic intent.

In "Of Studies," Bacon lays out the value of knowledge in practical terms. Bacon considers to what use studies might be put. He is less interested in their theoretical promise than in their practical utility—a proclivity more English, perhaps, than French. Bacon's writing in "Of Studies" is direct and pointed. It avoids the meandering find-your-way free form of Montaigne's essays. From his opening sentence Bacon gets directly to the point: "Studies serve for delight, for ornament, and for ability." He then elaborates on how studies are useful in these three ways. And he wastes no words in detailing the uses of "studies" for a Renaissance gentleman.

One of the attractions of Bacon's essay is his skillful use of parallel sentence structure, as exemplified in the opening sentence and throughout "Of Studies." This stylistic technique lends clarity and order to the writing, as in "crafty men condemn studies, simple men admire them, and wise men use them," which in its straightforward assertiveness exhibits confidence and elegance in addition to clarity and emphasis.

Studies serve for delight, for ornament, and for ability. Their chief use for delight is in privateness and retiring; for ornament, is in discourse;

and for ability, is in the judgment and disposition of business. For expert men can execute, and perhaps judge of particulars, one by one; but the general counsels, and the plots and marshaling of affairs, come best from those that are learned. To spend too much time in studies is sloth; to use them too much for ornament is affectation; to make judgment wholly by their rules is the humor of a scholar. They perfect nature, and are perfected by experience; for natural abilities are like natural plants, that need pruning by study; and studies themselves do give forth directions too much at large, except they be bounded in by experience. Crafty men contemn studies, simple men admire them, and wise men use them, for they teach not their own use; but that is a wisdom without them, and above them, won by observation. Read not to contradict and confute, nor to believe and take for granted, nor to find talk and discourse, but to weigh and consider. Some books are to be tasted, others to be swallowed, and some few to be chewed and digested; that is, some books are to be read only in parts; others to be read, but not curiously and some few to be read wholly, and with diligence and attention. Some books also may be read by deputy and extracts made of them by others, but that would be only in the less important arguments and the meaner sort of books; else distilled books are like common distilled waters, flashy things. Reading maketh a full man, conference a ready man, and writing an exact man. And therefore, if a man write little, he had need have a great memory; if he confer little, he had need have a present wit and if he read little, he had need have much cunning, to seem to know that he doth not. Histories make men wise; poets, witty, the mathematics, subtle; natural philosophy, deep; moral, grave; logic and rhetoric, able to contend. *Abeunt studia in mores*, Nay, there is no stond or impediment in the wit but may be wrought out by fit studies, like as diseases of the body may have appropriate exercises. Bowling is good for the stone and reins, shooting for the lungs and breast, gentle walking for the stomach, riding for the head, and the like. So if a man's wit be wandering, let him study the mathematics; for in demonstrations, if his wit be called away never so little, he must begin again. If his wit be not apt to distinguish or find differences, let him study the schoolmen, for they are *cumini sectores*. If he be not apt to beat over matters and to call up one thing to prove and illustrate another, let him study the lawyer's cases. So every defect of the mind may have a special receipt.

Possibilities for Writing

1. Bacon's essay was composed some four hundred years ago in a society that was in many ways very different from ours today. Write an analysis of "Of Studies" in which you summarize the main points Bacon makes and then go on to explore the extent to which his remarks continue to seem relevant. As you reread "Of Studies" and make preliminary notes, you will need to find ways to "translate" much of his vocabulary into its modern equivalent.

2. Bacon's brief essay contains many aphorisms, concise statements of a general principle or truth—for example, "Read not to contradict and confute, nor to believe and take for granted, nor to find talk and discourse, but to weigh and consider." Take one of these, put it into your own words, and use it as the starting point for an essay of your own. Elaborate on the statement with examples and further details that come from your own experience or imagination.

3. Changing Bacon's focus a bit, write an essay for modern audiences titled "On Reading." In it consider different types of reading, purposes for reading, benefits of reading, difficulties involved in reading, and so forth. Your essay may be quite personal, focusing on your own experiences as a reader, or, like Bacon's, more formal.

Roland Barthes (1915–1980) was born in France and studied French literature and classics at the University of Paris. After teaching in universities in Bucharest, Romania, and Alexandria, Egypt, he joined the National Center for Scientific Research, where he pursued research studies in sociology and language. As a leader of France's new critics, Barthes drew on the insights of Karl Marx and Sigmund Freud as well as on the work of the influential linguist Ferdinand de Saussure to expand the science of semiology, the study of signs and symbols underlying all aspects of human culture. His many works include Elements of Semiology, Empire of Signs, A Lover's Discourse, The Pleasure of the Text, *and* Mythologies, *from which "Toys" has been taken.*

Roland Barthes

Toys

In "Toys," Barthes meditates on the cultural significance of French toys, seeing them as a "microcosm" of the adult world. Barthes analyzes the social implications of French toys, arguing that it is no accident that toys reflect the "myths and techniques" of modern life. Toys, according to Barthes, epitomize what is socially important and culturally validated by the country in which they are produced and purchased.

A second area Barthes investigates concerns the forms and materials from which French toys are made. He considers the extent to which certain kinds of toys are imitative of actual life—girl's dolls that take in and eliminate water being one example. He contrasts such imitative toys with simple toys such as wooden blocks, which allow children to be more creative in their play.

French toys: one could not find a better illustration of the fact that the adult Frenchman sees the child as another self. All the toys one commonly sees are essentially a microcosm of the adult world; they are all reduced copies of human objects, as if in the eyes of the public the child was, all told, nothing but a smaller man, a homunculus to whom must be supplied objects of his own size.

Invented forms are very rare: a few sets of blocks, which appeal to the spirit of do-it-yourself, are the only ones which offer dynamic forms. As for the others, French toys *always mean something*, and this something is always entirely socialized, constituted by the myths or the techniques of modern adult life: the Army, Broadcasting, the Post Office, Medicine (miniature instrument-cases, operating theatres for dolls), School, Hair-Styling (driers for permanent-waving), the Air

Force (Parachutists), Transport (trains, Citroëns, Vedettes, Vespas, petrol-stations), Science (Martian toys).

The fact that French toys *literally* prefigure the world of adult functions obviously cannot but prepare the child to accept them all, by constituting for him, even before he can think about it, the alibi of a Nature which has at all times created soldiers, postmen and Vespas. Toys here reveal the list of all the things the adult does not find unusual: war, bureaucracy, ugliness, Martians, etc. It is not so much, in fact, the imitation which is the sign of an abdication, as its literalness: French toys are like a Jivaro head, in which one recognizes, shrunken to the size of an apple, the wrinkles and hair of an adult. There exist, for instance, dolls which urinate; they have an oesophagus, one gives them a bottle, they wet their nappies; soon, no doubt, milk will turn to water in their stomachs. This is meant to prepare the little girl for the causality of house-keeping, to 'condition' her to her future role as mother. However, faced with this world of faithful and complicated objects, the child can only identify himself as owner, as user, never as creator; he does not invent the world, he uses it: there are, prepared for him, actions without adventure, without wonder, without joy. He is turned into a little stay-at-home householder who does not even have to invent the mainsprings of adult causality; they are supplied to him ready-made: he has only to help himself, he is never allowed to discover anything from start to finish. The merest set of blocks, provided it is not too refined, implies a very different learning of the world: then, the child does not in any way create meaningful objects, it matters little to him whether they have an adult name; the actions he performs are not those of a user but those of a demiurge. He creates forms which walk, which roll, he creates life, not property: objects now act by themselves, they are no longer an inert and complicated material in the palm of his hand. But such toys are rather rare: French toys are usually based on imitation, they are meant to produce children who are users, not creators.

The bourgeois status of toys can be recognized not only in their forms, which are all functional, but also in their substances. Current toys are made of a graceless material, the product of chemistry, not of nature. Many are now moulded from complicated mixtures; the plastic material of which they are made has an appearance at once gross and hygienic, it destroys all the pleasure, the sweetness, the humanity of touch. A sign which fills one with consternation is the gradual disappearance of wood,

in spite of its being an ideal material because of its firmness and its softness, and the natural warmth of its touch. Wood removes, from all the
forms which it supports, the wounding quality of angles which are too
sharp, the chemical coldness of metal. When the child handles it and
knocks it, it neither vibrates nor grates, it has a sound at once muffled
and sharp. It is a familiar and poetic substance, which does not sever the
child from close contact with the tree, the table, the floor. Wood does not
wound or break down; it does not shatter, it wears out, it can last a long
time, live with the child, alter little by little the relations between the
object and the hand. If it dies, it is in dwindling, not in swelling out like
those mechanical toys which disappear behind the hernia of a broken
spring. Wood makes essential objects, objects for all time. Yet there
hardly remain any of these wooden toys from the Vosges, these fretwork
farms with their animals, which were only possible, it is true, in the days
of the craftsman. Henceforth, toys are chemical in substance and colour;
their very material introduces one to a coenaesthesis of use, not pleasure.
These toys die in fact very quickly, and once dead, they have no posthu-
mous life for the child.

Possibilities for Writing

1. Barthes suggests that French toys "always mean something."
   Consider the examples he provides and identify just how and
   what they signify about French society and culture at the time
   the essay was written.
2. To what extent do you agree with Barthes that toys can stifle as
   well as stimulate creativity? What sorts of toys limit the imagination of children, and what kinds of toys help them develop their
   imaginative capacity? Why?
3. Write an essay in which you explore and analyze contemporary
   American toys and the extent to which they convey implications
   about American cultural and social life today. Or write an essay
   in which you analyze another aspect of American popular culture, such as fast food, wrestling, casino gambling, or video
   games, to explain how and what they reveal about American
   social and cultural life.

Judith Ortiz Cofer *(b. 1952) spent her childhood in the small Puerto Rican town where she was born and in Paterson, New Jersey, where her family lived for most of each year, from the time she was three. She attended Catholic schools in Paterson and holds degrees from the University of Georgia and Florida Atlantic University. She has published several volumes of poetry, including* Reaching for the Mainland *(1996), and her 1989 novel* The Line of the Sun *was nominated for a Pulitzer Prize. Cofer has also published two autobiographical works:* Silent Dancing: A Partial Remembrance of a Puerto Rican Childhood *(1990) and* The Latin Deli: Prose and Poetry *(1993). Her most recent books are* Woman in Front of the Sun: On Becoming a Writer *(2000) and* The Meaning of Consuelo *(2003). She currently teaches creative writing at the University of Georgia.*

Judith Ortiz Cofer

Casa: A Partial Remembrance of a Puerto Rican Childhood

In "Casa: A Partial Remembrance of a Puerto Rican Childhood," Judith Ortiz Cofer describes the bonds that obtain among a community of women—three generations of a family headed by the matriarch, Mamá, the author's grandmother. In celebrating the intertwined lives of these women of her family, Cofer simultaneously celebrates the power of storytelling. Weaving these two strands of her essay together—family and stories—Cofer conveys some important ideas about women and their relations with men along with important ideas about culture and its significance for identity.

Cofer's "Casa" is about living in and moving between two worlds—the warm world of her Puerto Rican tropical home and the cold new world of New York and Paterson, New Jersey. Cofer alludes to this dual existence early on and explains its significance later in her essay, referring to herself as an outsider who spoke English with a Spanish accent and Spanish with an English accent. And although this dual linguistic identity made her stand out in both groups, Cofer benefits from her double linguistic and cultural heritage. It allows her to shift back and forth readily between two very different worlds, with their different sets of cultural values.

At three or four o'clock in the afternoon, the hour of *café con leche*, the women of my family gathered in Mamá's living room to speak of important things and retell familiar stories meant to be overheard by us young girls, their daughters. In Mamá's house (everyone called my grandmother

Mamá) was a large parlor built by my grandfather to his wife's exact specifications so that it was always cool, facing away from the sun. The doorway was on the side of the house so no one could walk directly into her living room. First they had to take a little stroll through and around her beautiful garden where prize-winning orchids grew in the trunk of an ancient tree she had hollowed out for that purpose. This room was furnished with several mahogany rocking chairs, acquired at the births of her children, and one intricately carved rocker that had passed down to Mamá at the death of her own mother.

It was on these rockers that my mother, her sisters, and my grandmother sat on these afternoons of my childhood to tell their stories, teaching each other, and my cousin and me, what it was like to be a woman, more specifically, a Puerto Rican woman. They talked about life on the island, and life in *Los Nueva Yores*, their way of referring to the United States from New York City to California: the other place, not home, all the same. They told real-life stories though, as I later learned, always embellishing them with a little or a lot of dramatic detail. And they told *cuentos*, the morality and cautionary tales told by the women in our family for generations: stories that became a part of my subconscious as I grew up in two worlds, the tropical island and the cold city, and that would later surface in my dreams and in my poetry.

One of these tales was about the woman who was left at the altar. Mamá liked to tell that one with histrionic intensity. I remember the rise and fall of her voice, the sighs, and her constantly gesturing hands, like two birds swooping through her words. This particular story usually would come up in a conversation as a result of someone mentioning a forthcoming engagement or wedding. The first time I remember hearing it, I was sitting on the floor at Mamá's feet, pretending to read a comic book. I may have been eleven or twelve years old, at that difficult age when a girl was no longer a child who could be ordered to leave the room if the women wanted freedom to take their talk into forbidden zones, nor really old enough to be considered a part of their conclave. I could only sit quietly, pretending to be in another world, while absorbing it all in a sort of unspoken agreement of my status as silent auditor. On this day, Mamá had taken my long, tangled mane of hair into her ever-busy hands. Without looking down at me and with no interruption of her flow of words, she began braiding my hair, working at it with the quickness and determination that characterized all her actions. My mother was watching us impassively from her rocker across the room. On her lips played a little ironic smile. I would never sit still for *her* ministrations, but even then, I instinctively knew that she did not possess Mamá's matriarchal power to command and keep everyone's attention. This was never more evident than in the spell she cast when telling a story.

"It is not like it used to be when I was a girl," Mamá announced. "Then, a man could leave a girl standing at the church altar with a bouquet of fresh flowers in her hands and disappear off the face of the earth. No way to track him down if he was from another town. He could be a married man, with maybe even two or three families all over the island. There was no way to know. And there were men who did this. Hombres with the devil in their flesh who would come to a pueblo, like this one, take a job at one of the haciendas, never meaning to stay, only to have a good time and to seduce the women."

The whole time she was speaking, Mamá would be weaving my hair into a flat plait that required pulling apart the two sections of hair with little jerks that made my eyes water; but knowing how grandmother detested whining and *boba* (sissy) tears, as she called them, I just sat up as straight and stiff as I did at La Escuela San Jose, where the nuns enforced good posture with a flexible plastic ruler they bounced off of slumped shoulders and heads. As Mamá's story progressed, I noticed how my young Aunt Laura lowered her eyes, refusing to meet Mamá's meaningful gaze. Laura was seventeen, in her last year of high school, and already engaged to a boy from another town who had staked his claim with a tiny diamond ring, then left for Los Nueva Yores to make his fortune. They were planning to get married in a year. Mamá had expressed serious doubts that the wedding would ever take place. In Mamá's eyes, a man set free without a legal contract was a man lost. She believed that marriage was not something men desired, but simply the price they had to pay for the privilege of children and, of course, for what no decent (synonymous with "smart") woman would give away for free.

"María La Loca was only seventeen when *it* happened to her." I listened closely at the mention of this name. María was a town character, a fat middle-aged woman who lived with her old mother on the outskirts of town. She was to be seen around the pueblo delivering the meat pies the two women made for a living. The most peculiar thing about María, in my eyes, was that she walked and moved like a little girl though she had the thick body and wrinkled face of an old woman. She would swing her hips in an exaggerated, clownish way, and sometimes even hop and skip up to someone's house. She spoke to no one. Even if you asked her a question, she would just look at you and smile, showing her yellow teeth. But I had heard that if you got close enough, you could hear her humming a tune without words. The kids yelled out nasty things at her calling her *La Loca*, and the men who hang out at the bodega playing dominoes sometimes whistled mockingly as she passed by with her funny, outlandish walk. But María seemed impervious to it all, carrying her basket of *pasteles* like a grotesque Little Red Riding Hood through the forest.

María La Loca interested me, as did all the eccentrics and crazies of our pueblo. Their weirdness was a measuring stick I used in my serious quest for a definition of normal. As a Navy brat shuttling between New Jersey and the pueblo, I was constantly made to feel like an oddball by my peers, who made fun of my two-way accent: a Spanish accent when I spoke English, and when I spoke Spanish I was told that I sounded like a *Gringa*. Being the outsider had already turned my brother and me into cultural chameleons. We developed early on the ability to blend into a crowd, to sit and read quietly in a fifth story apartment building for days and days when it was too bitterly cold to play outside, or, set free, to run wild in Mamá's realm, where she took charge of our lives, releasing Mother for a while from the intense fear for our safety that our father's absences instilled in her. In order to keep us from harm when Father was away, Mother kept us under strict surveillance. She even walked us to and from Public School No. 11, which we attended during the months we lived in Paterson, New Jersey, our home base in the states. Mamá freed all three of us like pigeons from a cage. I saw her as my liberator and my model. Her stories were parables from which to glean the *Truth*.

"María La Loca was once a beautiful girl. Everyone thought she would marry the Méndez boy." As everyone knew, Rogelio Méndez was the richest man in town. "But," Mamá continued, knitting my hair with the same intensity she was putting into her story, "this *macho* made a fool out of her and ruined her life." She paused for the effect of her use of the word "Macho," which at that time had not yet become a popular epithet for an unliberated man. This word had for us the crude and comical connotation of "male of the species," stud; a *macho* was what you put in a pen to increase your stock.

I peeked over my comic book at my mother. She too was under Mamá's spell, smiling conspiratorially at this little swipe at men. She was safe from Mamá's contempt in this area. Married at an early age, an unspotted lamb, she had been accepted by a good family of strict Spaniards whose name was old and respected, though their fortune had been lost long before my birth. In a rocker Papá had painted sky blue sat Mamá's oldest child, Aunt Nena. Mother of three children, stepmother of two more, she was a quiet woman who liked books but had married an ignorant and abusive widower whose main interest in life was accumulating wealth. He too was in the mainland working on his dream of returning home rich and triumphant to buy the *finca* of his dreams. She was waiting for him to send for her. She would leave her children with Mamá for several years while the two of them slaved away in factories. He would one day be a rich man, and she a sadder woman. Even now her life-light was dimming. She spoke little, an aberration in Mamá's house, and she read avidly, as if storing up spiritual food for the long winters that awaited her in Los Nueva Yores without her family. But even Aunt Nena came alive to Mamá's words, rocking gently, her hands over a thick book in her lap.

Her daughter, my cousin Sara, played jacks by herself on the tile porch outside the room where we sat. She was a year older than I. We shared a bed and all our family's secrets. Collaborators in search of answers, Sara and I discussed everything we heard the women say, trying to fit it all together like a puzzle that, once assembled, would reveal life's mysteries to us. Though she and I still enjoyed taking part in boys' games—chase, volleyball, and even *vaqueros*, the island version of cowboys and Indians involving cap-gun battles and violent shoot-outs under the mango tree in Mamá's backyard—we loved best the quiet hours in the afternoon when the men were still at work, and the boys had gone to play serious baseball at the park. Then Mamá's house belonged only to us women. The aroma of coffee perking in the kitchen, the mesmerizing creaks and groans of the rockers, and the women telling their lives in *cuentos* are forever woven into the fabric of my imagination, braided like my hair that day I felt my grandmother's hands teaching me about strength, her voice convincing me of the power of storytelling.

That day Mamá told how the beautiful María had fallen prey to a man whose name was never the same in subsequent versions of the story;

it was Juan one time, José, Rafael, Diego, another. We understood that neither the name nor any of the *facts* were important, only that a woman had allowed love to defeat her. Mamá put each of us in María's place by describing her wedding dress in loving detail: how she looked like a princess in her lace as she waited at the altar. Then, as Mamá approached the tragic denouement of her story, I was distracted by the sound of my aunt Laura's violent rocking. She seemed on the verge of tears. She knew the fable was intended for her. That week she was going to have her wedding gown fitted, though no firm date had been set for the marriage. Mamá ignored Laura's obvious discomfort, digging out a ribbon from the sewing basket she kept by her rocker while describing María's long illness, "a fever that would not break for days." She spoke of a mother's despair: "that woman climbed the church steps on her knees every morning, wore only black as a *promesa* to the Holy Virgin in exchange for her daughter's health." By the time María returned from her honeymoon with death, she was ravished, no longer young or sane. "As you can see, she is almost as old as her mother already," Mamá lamented while tying the ribbon to the ends of my hair, pulling it back with such force that I just knew I would never be able to close my eyes completely again.

"That María's getting crazier every day." Mamá's voice would take a lighter tone now, expressing satisfaction, either for the perfection of my braid, or for a story well told—it was hard to tell. "You know that tune María is always humming?" Carried away by her enthusiasm, I tried to nod, but Mamá still had me pinned between her knees.

"Well, that's the wedding march." Surprising us all, Mamá sang out, "Da, da, dara ... da, da, dara." Then lifting me off the floor by my skinny shoulders, she would lead me around the room in an impromptu waltz—another session ending with the laughter of women, all of us caught up in the infectious joke of our lives.

Possibilities for Writing

1. The longest and most elaborate example Cofer uses is that of María La Loca. Explain the significance of this example, and identify and explain the significance of another example that Cofer includes.

2. Cofer uses a number of Spanish words and phrases in "Casa," some of which she translates and others of which she leaves

untranslated. What is the effect of these Spanish words and phrases? What would be gained or lost if they had been omitted?

3. Use the following quotation as a springboard to write about identity as a theme in "Casa": "It was on these rockers that my mother, her sisters, and my grandmother sat on these afternoons of my childhood to tell their stories, teaching each other, and my cousin and me, what it was like to be a woman, more specifically, a Puerto Rican woman."

Charles Darwin (1809–1882) was born in Shrewsbury, England, and studied both medicine and religion before turning his attention full-time to his first love, natural history. From 1831 to 1836, he served as official naturalist on an ocean voyage exploring the coast of South America, and his studies there, along with the many specimens he shipped back to England, led him to develop the theory of organic evolution based on natural selection that still predominates in scientific thinking today. His seminal Origin of Species *(1859) outlined his theory with abundant supporting detail and was followed by subsequent works in which he refined and elaborated on the theory, including* The Descent of Man *(1871). He is considered one of the most original thinkers in history.*

Charles Darwin
Natural Selection

In the following excerpt from "Natural Selection," a chapter from *The Origin of Species*, Charles Darwin explains the concept of natural selection and provides scientific evidence for its existence and its ramifications. According to Darwin, natural selection is the process by which the evolution of species occurs. He lays out his theory of evolution by natural selection in great detail, postulating a world governed not by the providential design of an almighty creator, but by the irrevocable laws of species' adaptation to their environment.

Darwin's emphasis on the mechanism of natural selection undermined conventional theological and philosophical assumptions about the special place of human beings in the divine order of creation. According to this view, human beings are simply a species of animal that has adapted successfully to changing conditions, thus ensuring its capacity for survival.

How will the struggle for existence, discussed too briefly in the last chapter, act in regard to variation? Can the principle of selection, which we have seen is so potent in the hands of man, apply in nature? I think we shall see that it can act most effectually. Let it be borne in mind in what an endless number of strange peculiarities our domestic productions, and, in a lesser degree, those under nature, vary; and how strong the hereditary tendency is. Under domestication, it may be truly said that the whole organisation becomes in some degree plastic. Let it be borne in mind how infinitely complex and close-fitting are the mutual relations of all organic beings to each other and to their physical conditions of life. Can it, then, be thought improbable, seeing that variations useful to man have undoubtedly occurred, that other variations useful in some way to each being in the great and complex battle of life, should sometimes occur in the course of thousands of generations? If such do occur, can we doubt (remembering that many more individuals are born than can possibly survive) that individuals having any advantage, however slight, over others, would have the best chance of surviving and of procreating their kind? On the other hand, we may feel sure that any variation in the least degree injurious would be rigidly destroyed. This preservation of favourable variations and the rejection of injurious variations, I call Natural Selection. Variations neither useful nor injurious would not be affected by natural selection, and would be left a fluctuating element, as perhaps we see in the species called polymorphic.

We shall best understand the probable course of natural selection by taking the case of a country undergoing some physical change, for instance, of climate. The proportional numbers of its inhabitants would almost immediately undergo a change, and some species might become extinct. We may conclude, from what we have seen of the intimate and complex manner in which the inhabitants of each country are bound together, that any change in the numerical proportions of some of the inhabitants, independently of the change of climate itself, would most seriously affect many of the others. If the country were open on its borders, new forms would certainly immigrate, and this also would seriously disturb the relations of some of the former inhabitants. Let it be remembered how powerful the influence of a single introduced tree or mammal has been shown to be. But in the case of an island, or of a country partly surrounded by barriers, into which new and better adapted forms could not freely enter, we should then have places in the economy of nature which would assuredly be better filled up, if some of the original inhabitants were in some manner modified; for, had the area been open to immigration, these same places would have been seized on by intruders. In such case, every slight modification, which in the course of ages chanced to arise, and which in any way favoured the individuals of any of the species, by better adapting them to their altered conditions, would tend to be preserved; and natural selection would thus have free scope for the work of improvement.

We have reason to believe, as stated in the first chapter, that a change in the conditions of life, by specially acting on the reproductive system, causes or increases variability; and in the foregoing case the conditions of life are supposed to have undergone a change, and this would manifestly be favourable to natural selection, by giving a better

chance of profitable variations occurring; and unless profitable variations do occur, natural selection can do nothing. Not that, as I believe,
any extreme amount of variability is necessary; as man can certainly
produce great results by adding up in any given direction mere individual differences, so could Nature, but far more easily, from having
incomparably longer time at her disposal. Nor do I believe that any
great physical change, as of climate, or any unusual degree of isolation
to check immigration, is actually necessary to produce new and unoccu-
pied places for natural selection to fill up by modifying and improving
some of the varying inhabitants. For as all the inhabitants of each country are struggling together with nicely balanced forces, extremely slight
modifications in the structure or habits of one inhabitant would often
give it an advantage over others; and still further modifications of the
same kind would often still further increase the advantage. No country
can be named in which all the native inhabitants are now so perfectly
adapted to each other and to the physical conditions under which they
live, that none of them could anyhow be improved; for in all countries,
the natives have been so far conquered by naturalised productions, that
they have allowed foreigners to take firm possession of the land. And as
foreigners have thus everywhere beaten some of the natives, we may
safely conclude that the natives might have been modified with advantage, so as to have better resisted such intruders.

As man can produce and certainly has produced a great result by his
methodical and unconscious means of selection, what may not nature
effect? Man can act only on external and visible characters: nature
cares nothing for appearances, except in so far as they may be useful to
any being. She can act on every internal organ, on every shade of constitutional difference, on the whole machinery of life. Man selects only
for his own good; Nature only for that of the being which she tends.
Every selected character is fully exercised by her; and the being is
placed under well-suited conditions of life. Man keeps the natives of
many climates in the same country; he seldom exercises each selected
character in some peculiar and fitting manner; he feeds a long and a
short beaked pigeon on the same food; he does not exercise a long-
backed or long-legged quadruped in any peculiar manner; he exposes
sheep with long and short wool to the same climate. He does not allow
the most vigorous males to struggle for the females. He does not rigidly
destroy all inferior animals, but protects during each varying season, as

far as lies in his power, all his productions. He often begins his selection by some half-monstrous form; or at least by some modification prominent enough to catch his eye, or to be plainly useful to him. Under nature, the slightest difference of structure or constitution may well turn the nicely-balanced scale in the struggle for life, and to be preserved. How fleeting are the wishes and efforts of man! How short his time! and consequently how poor will his products be, compared with those accumulated by nature during whole geological periods. Can we wonder, then, that nature's productions should be far 'truer' in character than man's productions; that they should be infinitely better adapted to the most complex conditions of life, and should plainly bear the stamp of far higher workmanship?

It may be said that natural selection is daily and hourly scrutinising, throughout the world, every variation, even the slightest; rejecting that which is bad, preserving and adding up all that is good; silently and insensibly working, whenever and wherever opportunity offers, at the improvement of each organic being in relation to its organic and inorganic conditions of life. We see nothing of these slow changes in progress, until the hand of time has marked the long lapses of ages, and then so imperfect is our view into long past geological ages, that we only see that the forms of life are now different from what they formerly were.

Although natural selection can act only through and for the good of each being, yet characters and structures, which we are apt to consider as of very trifling importance, may thus be acted on. When we see leaf-eating insects green, and bark-feeders mottled-grey; the alpine ptarmigan white in winter, the red-grouse the colour of heather, and the black-grouse that of peaty earth, we must believe that these tints are of service to these birds and insects in preserving them from danger. Grouse, if not destroyed at some period of their lives, would increase in countless numbers; they are known to suffer largely from birds of prey; and hawks are guided by eyesight to their prey,—so much so, that on parts of the Continent persons are warned not to keep white pigeons, as being the most liable to destruction. Hence I can see no reason to doubt that natural selection might be most effective in giving the proper colour to each kind of grouse, and in keeping that colour, when once acquired, true and constant. Nor ought we to think that the occasional destruction of an animal of any particular colour would produce little effect: we should remember how essential it is in a flock of white sheep to destroy every lamb with the faintest trace of black. In plants the down on the fruit and the colour of the flesh are considered by botanists as characters of the most trifling importance: yet we hear from an excellent horticulturist, Downing, that in the United States smooth-skinned fruits suffer far more from a beetle, a curculio, than those with down; that purple plums suffer far more from a certain disease than yellow plums; whereas another disease attacks yellow-fleshed peaches far more than those with other coloured flesh. If, with all the aids of art, these slight differences make a great difference in cultivating the several varieties, assuredly, in a state of nature, where the trees would have to struggle with other trees and with a host of enemies, such differences would effectually settle which variety, whether a smooth or downy, a yellow or purple fleshed fruit, should succeed.

In looking at many small points of difference between species, which, as far as our ignorance permits us to judge, seem to be quite unimportant, we must not forget that climate, food, &c., probably produce some slight and direct effect. It is, however far more necessary to bear in mind that there are many unknown laws of correlation of growth, which, when one part of the organisation is modified through variation, and the modifications are accumulated by natural selection for the good of the being, will cause other modifications, often of the most unexpected nature.

As we see that those variations which under domestication appear at any particular period of life, tend to reappear in the offspring at the same period; —for instance, in the seeds of the many varieties of our culinary and agricultural plants; in the caterpillar and cocoon stages of the varieties of the silkworm; in the eggs of poultry, and in the colour of the down of their chickens; in the horns of our sheep and cattle when nearly adult; —so in a state of nature, natural selection will be enabled to act on and modify organic beings at any age, by the accumulation of profitable variations at that age, and by their inheritance at a corresponding age. If it profit a plant to have its seeds more and more widely disseminated by the wind, I can see no greater difficulty in this being effected through natural selection, than in the cotton-planter increasing and improving by selection the down in the pods on his cotton-trees. Natural selection may modify and adapt the larva of an insect to a score of contingencies, wholly different from those which concern the mature insect. These modifications will no doubt affect, through the laws of correlation, the structure of the adult; and probably in the case of those insects which live only for a few hours, and which never feed, a large part of their structure is merely the correlated result of successive changes in the structure of their larvae. So, conversely, modifications in the adult will probably often affect the structure of the larva; but in all cases natural selection will ensure that modifications consequent on other modifications at a different period of life, shall not be in the least degree injurious: for if they became so, they would cause the extinction of the species.

Natural selection will modify the structure of the young in relation to the parent, and of the parent in relation to the young. In social animals it will adapt the structure of each individual for the benefit of the community; if each in consequence profits by the selected change. What natural selection cannot do, is to modify the structure of one species, without giving it any advantage, for the good of another species; and though statements to this effect may be found in works of natural history, I cannot find one case which will bear investigation. A structure used only once in an animal's whole life, if of high importance to it, might be modified to any extent by natural selection; for instance, the great jaws possessed by certain insects, and used exclusively for opening the cocoon—or the hard tip to the beak of nestling birds, used for breaking the egg. It has been asserted, that of the best short-beaked tumbler-pigeons more perish in the egg than are able to get out of it; so that fanciers assist in the act of hatching. Now, if nature had to make the beak of a full-grown pigeon very short for the bird's own advantage, the process of modification would be very slow, and there would be simultaneously the most rigorous selection of the young birds within the egg, which had the most powerful and hardest beaks, for all with weak beaks would inevitably perish: or, more delicate and more easily broken shells might be selected, the thickness of the shell being known to vary like every other structure. . . .

Illustrations of the Action of Natural Selection

In order to make it clear how, as I believe, natural selection acts, I must beg permission to give one or two imaginary illustrations. Let us take the case of a wolf, which preys on various animals, securing some by craft, some by strength, and some by fleetness; and let us suppose that the fleetest prey, a deer for instance, had from any change in the country increased in numbers, or that other prey had decreased in numbers, during that season of the year when the wolf is hardest pressed for food. I can under such circumstances see no reason to doubt that the swiftest and slimmest wolves would have the best chance of surviving, and so be preserved or selected, —provided always that they retained strength to master their prey at this or at some other period of the year, when they might be compelled to prey on other animals. I can see no more reason to doubt this, than that man can improve the fleetness of his greyhounds by careful and methodical selection, or by that unconscious selection which results from each man trying to keep the best dogs without any thought of modifying the breed.

Even without any change in the proportional numbers of the animals on which our wolf preyed, a cub might be born with an innate tendency to pursue certain kinds of prey. Nor can this be thought very improbable; for we often observe great differences in the natural tendencies of our domestic animals; one cat, for instance, taking to catch rats, another mice; one cat according to Mr. St. John, bringing home winged game, another hares or rabbits, and another hunting on marshy ground and almost nightly catching woodcocks or snipes. The tendency to catch rats rather than mice is known to be inherited. Now, if any slight innate change of habit or of structure benefited an individual wolf, it would have the best chance of surviving and of leaving offspring. Some of its young would probably inherit the same habits or structure, and by the repetition of this process, a new variety might be formed which would either supplant or coexist with the parent-form of wolf. Or, again, the wolves inhabiting a mountainous district, and those frequenting the lowlands, would naturally be forced to hunt different prey; and from the continued preservation of the individuals best fitted for the two sites, two varieties might slowly be formed. These varieties would cross and blend where they met; but to this subject of intercrossing we shall soon have to return. I may add, that, according to Mr. Pierce, there are two varieties of the wolf inhabiting the Catskill Mountains in the United States, one with a light greyhound-like form, which pursues deer, and the other more bulky, with shorter legs, which more frequently attacks the shepherd's flocks.

Let us now take a more complex case. Certain plants excrete a sweet juice, apparently for the sake of eliminating something injurious from their sap: this is effected by glands at the base of the stipules in some Leguminosae, and at the back of the leaf of the common laurel. This juice, though small in quantity, is greedily sought by insects. Let us now suppose a little sweet juice or nectar to be excreted by the inner bases of the petals of a flower. In this case insects in seeking the nectar would get dusted with pollen, and would certainly often transport the pollen from one flower to the stigma of another flower. The flowers of two distinct individuals of the same species would thus get crossed; and the act of crossing, we have good reason to believe (as will hereafter be more fully alluded to), would produce very vigorous seedlings, which consequently would have the best chance of flourishing and surviving. Some of these seedlings would probably inherit the nectar-excreting power. Those individual flowers which had the largest glands or nectaries, and which excreted most nectar, would be oftenest visited by insects and would be oftenest crossed; and so in the long-run would gain the upper hand. Those flowers, also, which had their stamens and pistils placed, in relation to the size and habits of the particular insects which visited them, so as to favour in any degree the transportal of their pollen from flower to flower, would likewise be favoured or selected. We might have taken the case of insects visiting flowers for the sake of collecting pollen instead of nectar; and as pollen is formed for the sole object of fertilisation, its destruction appears a simple loss to the plant; yet if a little pollen were carried, at first occasionally and then habitually, by the pollen-devouring insects from flower to flower, and a cross thus effected, although nine-tenths of the pollen were destroyed, it might still be a great gain to the plant; and those individuals which produced more and more pollen, and had larger and larger anthers, would be selected.

When our plant, by this process of the continued preservation or natural selection of more and more attractive flowers, had been rendered highly attractive to insects, they would, unintentionally on their part, regularly carry pollen from flower to flower; and that they can most effectually do this, I could easily show by many striking instances. I will give only one—not as a very striking case, but as likewise illustrating one step in the separation of the sexes of plants, presently to be alluded to. Some holly-trees bear only male flowers, which have four stamens producing rather a small quantity of pollen, and a rudimentary pistil; other holly-trees bear only female flowers; these have a full-sized pistil, and four stamens with shrivelled anthers, in which not a grain of pollen can be detected. Having found a female tree exactly sixty yards from a male tree, I put the stigmas of twenty flowers, taken from different branches, under the microscope, and on all, without exception, there were pollen-grains, and on some a profusion of pollen. As the wind had set for several days from the female to the male tree, the pollen could not thus have been carried. The weather had been cold and boisterous, and therefore not favourable to bees, nevertheless every female flower which I examined had been effectually fertilised by the bees, accidentally dusted with pollen, having flown from tree to tree in search of nectar. But to return to our imaginary case: as soon as the plant had been rendered so highly attractive to insects that pollen was regularly carried from flower to flower, another process might commence. No naturalist doubts the advantage of what has been called the physiological division of labour; hence we may believe that it would be advantageous to a plant to produce stamens alone in one flower or on one whole plant, and pistils alone in another flower or on another plant. In plants under culture and placed under new conditions of life, sometimes the male organs and sometimes the female organs become more or less impotent; now if we suppose this to occur in ever so slight a degree under nature, then as pollen is already carried regularly from flower to flower, and as a more complete separation of the sexes of our plant would be advantageous on the principle of the division of labour, individuals with this tendency more and more increased, would be continually favoured or selected, until at last a complete separation of the sexes would be effected.

Let us now turn to the nectar-feeding insects in our imaginary case: we may suppose the plant of which we have been slowly increasing the nectar by continued selection, to be a common plant; and that certain insects depended in main part on its nectar for food. I could give many facts, showing how anxious bees are to save time; for instance, their habit of cutting holes and sucking the nectar at the bases of certain flowers, which they can, with a very little more trouble, enter by the mouth. Bearing such facts in mind, I can see no reason to doubt that an accidental deviation in the size and form of the body, or in the curvature and length of the proboscis, &c., far too slight to be appreciated by us, might profit a bee or other insect, so that an individual so characterised would be able to obtain its food more quickly, and so have a better chance of living and leaving descendants. Its descendants would probably inherit a tendency to a similar slight deviation of structure.

The tubes of the corollas of the common red and incarnate clovers (Trifolium pratense and incarnatum) do not on a hasty glance appear to differ in length; yet the hive-bee can easily suck the nectar out of the incarnate clover, but not out of the common red clover, which is visited by humble-bees alone; so that whole fields of the red clover offer in vain an abundant supply of precious nectar to the hive-bee. Thus it might be a great advantage to the hive-bee to have a slightly longer or differently constructed proboscis. On the other hand, I have found by experiment that the fertility of clover greatly depends on bees visiting and moving parts of the corolla, so as to push the pollen on to the stigmatic surface. Hence, again, if humble-bees were to become rare in any country, it might be a great advantage to the red clover to have a shorter or more deeply divided tube to its corolla, so that the hive-bee could visit its flowers. Thus I can understand how a flower and a bee might slowly become, either simultaneously or one after the other, modified and adapted in the most perfect manner to each other, by the continued preservation of individuals presenting mutual and slightly favourable deviations of structure.

I am well aware that this doctrine of natural selection, exemplified in the above imaginary instances, is open to the same objections which were at first urged against Sir Charles Lyell's noble views on 'the modern changes of the earth, as illustrative of geology;' but we now very seldom hear the action, for instance, of the coast-waves, called a trifling and insignificant cause, when applied to the excavation of gigantic valleys or to the formation of the longest lines of inland cliffs. Natural selection can act only by the preservation and accumulation of infinitesimally small inherited modifications, each profitable to the preserved being; and as modern geology has almost banished such views as the excavation of a great valley by a single diluvial wave, so will natural selection, if it be a true principle, banish the belief of the continued creation of new organic beings, or of any great and sudden modification in their structure.

Summary of Chapter

If during the long course of ages and under varying conditions of life, organic beings vary at all in the several parts of their organisation, and I think this cannot be disputed; if there be, owing to the high geometrical powers of increase of each species, at some age, season, or year, a severe struggle for life, and this certainly cannot be disputed; then, considering the infinite complexity of the relations of all organic beings to each other and to their conditions of existence, causing an infinite diversity in structure, constitution, and habits, to be advantageous to them, I think it would be a most extraordinary fact if no variation ever had occurred useful to each being's own welfare, in the same way as so many variations have occurred useful to man. But if variations useful to any organic being do occur, assuredly individuals thus characterised will have the best chance of being preserved in the struggle for life; and from the strong principle of inheritance they will tend to produce offspring similarly characterised. This principle of preservation, I have called, for the sake of brevity, Natural Selection. Natural selection, on the principle of qualities being inherited at corresponding ages, can modify the egg, seed, or young, as easily as the adult. Amongst many animals, sexual selection will give its aid to ordinary selection, by assuring to the most vigorous and best adapted males the greatest number of offspring. Sexual selection will also give characters useful to the males alone, in their struggles with other males.

Whether natural selection has really thus acted in nature, in modifying and adapting the various forms of life to their several conditions and stations, must be judged of by the general tenour and balance of evidence given in the following chapters. But we already see how it entails extinction; and how largely extinction has acted in the world's history, geology plainly declares. Natural selection, also, leads to divergence of character; for more living beings can be supported on the same area the more they diverge in structure, habits, and constitution, of which we see proof by looking at the inhabitants of any small spot or at naturalised productions. Therefore during the modification of the descendants of any one species, and during the incessant struggle of all species to increase in numbers, the more diversified these descendants become, the better will be their chance of succeeding in the battle of life. Thus the small differences distinguishing varieties of the same species, will steadily tend to increase till they come to equal the greater differences between species of the same genus, or even of distinct genera.

We have seen that it is the common, the widely-diffused, and widely-ranging species, belonging to the larger genera, which vary most; and these will tend to transmit to their modified offspring that superiority which now makes them dominant in their own countries. Natural selection, as has just been remarked, leads to divergence of character and to much extinction of the less improved and intermediate forms of life. On these principles, I believe, the nature of the affinities of all organic beings may be explained. It is a truly wonderful fact—the wonder of which we are apt to overlook from familiarity—that all animals and all plants throughout all time and space should be related to each other in group subordinate to group, in the manner which we everywhere behold—namely, varieties of the same species most closely related together, species of the same genus less closely and unequally related together, forming sections and sub-genera, species of distinct genera much less closely related, and genera related in different degrees, forming subfamilies, families, orders, sub-classes, and classes. The several subordinate groups in any class cannot be ranked in a single file, but seem rather to be clustered round points, and these round other points, and so on in almost endless cycles. On the view that each species has been independently created, I can see no explanation of this great fact in the classification of all organic beings; but, to the best of my judgment, it is explained through inheritance and the complex action of natural selection, entailing extinction and divergence of character, as we have seen illustrated in the diagram.

The affinities of all the beings of the same class have sometimes been represented by a great tree. I believe this simile largely speaks the truth. The green and budding twigs may represent existing species; and those produced during each former year may represent the long succession of extinct species. At each period of growth all the growing twigs have tried to branch out on all sides, and to overtop and kill the surrounding twigs and branches, in the same manner as species and groups of species have tried to overmaster other species in the great battle for life. The limbs divided into great branches, and these into lesser and lesser branches, were themselves once, when the tree was small, budding twigs; and this connexion of the former and present buds by ramifying branches may well represent the classification of all extinct and living species in groups subordinate to groups. Of the many twigs which flourished when the tree was a mere bush, only two or three, now grown into great branches, yet survive and bear all the other branches; so with the species which lived during long-past geological periods, very few now have living and modified descendants. From the first growth of the tree, many a limb and branch has decayed and dropped off; and these lost branches of various sizes may represent those whole orders, families, and genera which have now no living representatives, and which are known to us only from having been found in a fossil state. As we here and there see a thin straggling branch springing from a fork low down in a tree, and which by some chance has been favoured and is still alive on its summit, so we occasionally see an animal like the Ornithorhynchus or Lepidosiren, which in some small degree connects by its affinities two large branches of life, and which has apparently been saved from fatal competition by having inhabited a protected station. As buds give rise by growth to fresh buds, and these, if vigorous, branch out and overtop on all sides many a feebler branch, so by generation I believe it has been with the great Tree of Life, which fills with its dead and broken branches the crust of the earth, and covers the surface with its ever branching and beautiful ramifications.

Possibilities for Writing

1. Based on Darwin's explanations here, define "natural selection." You may quote from the text, but cast your definition primarily in your own words.
2. Focusing on the "Summary of Chapter" at the conclusion of the essay, analyze Darwin's logic. How does Darwin lay out his case and distill his primary ideas?
3. Do some research to write an essay focusing on current controversies surrounding teaching evolution in public schools. Why do Darwin's discoveries continue to trouble some, and where does the scientific community stand on the question of evolution?

Joan Didion (b. 1934) grew up in central California, where her family had lived for many generations. After graduating from the University of California at Berkeley in 1956, she joined the staff of Vogue *magazine, where she worked until the publication of her first novel,* Run River, *in 1963. Other novels followed—including* Play It As It Lays *(1970),* A Book of Common Prayer *(1977), and* The Last Thing He Wanted *(1996)—but it is her essays, particularly those collected in* Slouching Towards Bethlehem *(1968) and* The White Album *(1979), that established Didion as one of the most admired voices of her generation. A meticulous stylist who combines sharply observed detail with wry—even bracing—irony, she has examined subjects that range from life in Southern California to the Washington political scene to the war in El Salvador to marriage Las Vegas–style.*

Joan Didion
Marrying Absurd

In "Marrying Absurd," Joan Didion takes a critical look at the Las Vegas wedding industry. In keeping with the portraits of people and places throughout her work, Didion uses carefully selected details to convey her impression of Las Vegas and to render her judgment of its values. She uses a number of ironic techniques to establish and sustain her satiric tone, most significantly, perhaps, including details that mean one thing to the Las Vegas wedding people and something quite different to the reader. Examples include the signs advertising weddings posted throughout the city, as well as comments made by participants, in which they condemn themselves, unwittingly. Some of the most damning examples of this ironic use of dialogue occur in the essay's concluding paragraph.

"Marrying Absurd," however, conveys more than Joan Didion's acerbic criticism of Las Vegas marriages. It also suggests something of Didion's attitude toward the larger national problem of what she describes as "venality" and a "devotion to immediate gratification."

To be married in Las Vegas, Clark County, Nevada, a bride must swear that she is eighteen or has parental permission and a bridegroom that he is twenty-one or has parental permission. Someone must put up five dollars for the license. (On Sundays and holidays, fifteen dollars. The Clark County Courthouse issues marriage licenses at any time of the day or night except between noon and one in the afternoon, between eight and nine in the evening, and between four and five in the morning.) Nothing else is required. The State of Nevada, alone among these United States, demands neither a premarital blood test nor a waiting period before or after the issuance of a marriage license. Driving in across the Mojave from Los Angeles, one sees the signs way out on the desert, looming up from that moonscape of rattlesnakes and mesquite, even before the Las Vegas lights appear like a mirage on the horizon: "GETTING MARRIED? Free License Information First Strip Exit." Perhaps the Las Vegas wedding industry achieved its peak operational efficiency between 9:00 p.m. and midnight of August 26, 1965, an otherwise unremarkable Thursday which happened to be, by Presidential order, the last day on which anyone could improve his draft status merely by getting married. One hundred and seventy-one couples were pronounced man and wife in the name of Clark County and the State of Nevada that night, sixty-seven of them by a single justice of the peace, Mr. James A. Brennan. Mr. Brennan did one wedding at the Dunes and the other sixty-six in his office, and charged each couple eight dollars. One bride lent her veil to six others. "I got it down from five to three minutes," Mr. Brennan said later of his feat. "I could've married them *en masse*, but they're people, not cattle. People expect more when they get married."

What people who get married in Las Vegas actually do expect—what, in the largest sense, their "expectations" are—strikes one as a curious and self-contradictory business. Las Vegas is the most extreme and allegorical of American settlements, bizarre and beautiful in its venality and in its devotion to immediate gratification, a place the tone of which is set by mobsters and call girls and ladies' room attendants with amyl nitrite poppers in their uniform pockets. Almost everyone notes that there is no "time" in Las Vegas, no night and no day and no past and no future (no Las Vegas casino, however, has taken the obliteration of the ordinary time sense quite so far as Harold's Club in Reno, which for a while issued, at odd intervals in the day and night, mimeographed "bulletins" carrying news from the world outside); neither is there any logical sense of where one is. One is standing on a highway in the middle of a vast hostile desert looking at an eighty-foot sign which blinks "Stardust" or "Caesar's Palace." Yes, but what does that explain? This geographical implausibility reinforces the sense that what happens there has no connection with "real" life; Nevada cities like Reno and Carson are ranch towns, Western towns, places behind which there is some historical imperative. But Las Vegas seems to exist only in the eye of the beholder. All of which makes it an extraordinarily stimulating and interesting place, but an odd one in which to want to wear a candlelight satin Priscilla of Boston wedding dress with Chantilly lace insets, tapered sleeves and a detachable modified train.

And yet the Las Vegas wedding business seems to appeal to precisely that impulse. "Sincere and Dignified Since 1954," one wedding chapel advertises. There are nineteen such wedding chapels in Las Vegas, intensely competitive, each offering better, faster, and, by implication, more sincere services than the next: Our Photos Best Anywhere, Your Wedding on A Phonograph Record, Candlelight with Your Ceremony, Honeymoon Accommodations, Free Transportation from Your Motel to Courthouse to Chapel and Return to Motel, Religious or Civil Ceremonies, Dressing Rooms, Flowers, Rings, Announcements, Witnesses Available, and Ample Parking. All of these services, like most others in Las Vegas (sauna baths, payroll-check cashing, chinchilla coats for sale or rent), are offered twenty-four hours a day, seven days a week, presumably on the premise that marriage, like craps, is a game to be played when the table seems hot.

But what strikes one most about the Strip chapels, with their wishing wells and stained-glass paper windows and their artificial bouvardia, is that so much of their business is by no means a matter of simple convenience, of late-night liaisons between show girls and baby Crosbys. Of course there is some of that. (One night about eleven o'clock in Las Vegas I watched a bride in an orange minidress and masses of flame-colored hair stumble from a Strip chapel on the arm of her bridegroom, who looked the part of the expendable nephew in movies like *Miami Syndicate*. "I gotta get the kids," the bride whimpered. "I gotta pick up the sitter, I gotta get to the midnight show." "What you gotta get," the bridegroom said, opening the door of a Cadillac Coupe de Ville and watching her crumple on the seat, "is sober.") But Las Vegas seems to offer something other than "convenience"; it is merchandising "niceness," the facsimile of proper ritual, to children who do not know how else to find it, how to make the arrangements, how to do it "right." All day and evening long on the Strip, one sees actual wedding parties, waiting under the harsh lights at a crosswalk, standing uneasily in the parking lot of the Frontier while the photographer hired by The Little Church of the West ("Wedding Place of the Stars") certifies the occasion, takes the picture: the bride in a veil and white satin pumps, the bridegroom usually in a white dinner jacket, and even an attendant or two, a sister or a best friend in hot-pink *peau de soie*, a flirtation veil, a carnation nosegay. "When I Fall in Love It Will Be Forever," the organist plays, and then a few bars of Lohengrin. The mother cries; the stepfather, awkward in his role, invites the chapel hostess to join them for a drink at the Sands. The hostess declines with a professional smile; she has already transferred her interest to the group waiting outside. One bride out, another in, and again the sign goes up on the chapel door: "One Moment please—Wedding."

I sat next to one such wedding party in a Strip restaurant the last time I was in Las Vegas. The marriage had just taken place; the bride still wore her dress, the mother her corsage. A bored waiter poured out a few swallows of pink champagne ("on the house") for everyone but the bride, who was too young to be served. "You'll need something with more kick than that," the bride's father said with heavy jocularity to his new son-in-law; the ritual jokes about the wedding night had a certain Pangiossian character, since the bride was clearly several months pregnant. Another round of pink champagne, this time not on the house, and the bride began to cry. "It was just as nice," she sobbed, "as I hoped and dreamed it would be."

Possibilities for Writing

1. Didion inevitably conveys an air of superiority in this essay—her purpose, after all, is to point out what she sees as the absurdity of the marriage business in Las Vegas. In an essay, analyze how you respond to this tone and this attitude towards her subjects. Use specific quotations to elaborate on the reasons for your response.

2. One of Didion's main points is that many of those who marry in Las Vegas chapels do so in order to have "the facsimile of proper ritual"; they are "children who do not know how else to find it, how to make the arrangements, how to do it 'right.' " Didion was writing in 1967. What is most people's notion of "proper ritual" today? In considering this question, think not only of weddings but of anything that is traditionally considered a "solemn occasion": graduations, church services, funerals, and the like. What do you think is the proper level of formality for such occasions?

3. Pick a setting where you think people engage in "absurd" behavior. Either spend some time observing what happens there, or re-create these activities in detail from memory. Then write an essay, as Didion does, in which you describe this setting and these activities in an ironic light. Be as specific as possible.

Annie Dillard *(b. 1945) developed an interest in nature at the age of ten, after discovering* The Field Book of Ponds and Streams *in a branch of the Pittsburgh library system. While studying creative writing and theology at Hollins College in rural Virginia, she began a journal of observations of natural phenomena that would eventually become the Pulitzer Prize–winning* Pilgrim at Tinker Creek *(1974), her first published work of nonfiction. This was followed by* Holy the Firm *(1977), a mystical meditation on the natural world, and* Teaching a Stone to Talk *(1982), a collection of philosophical essays. A professor at Wesleyan College, Dillard has also published several volumes of poetry, a novel, and a memoir of her youth,* An America Childhood *(1987). Her most recent book is* For the Time Being *(1999), which questions the concept of a merciful God.*

Annie Dillard
Living Like Weasels

In "Living Like Weasels," Annie Dillard describes an encounter with a weasel she had one day while resting on a log in a patch of woods near a housing development in Virginia. Dillard begins in the expository mode, detailing facts about weasels, especially their tenacity and wildness. But she shifts, before long, into a meditation on the value and necessity of instinct and tenacity in human life. Dillard's tone changes from the factual declaration of the opening into speculative wonder at the weasel's virtues and, finally, into urgent admonition. By the end of the essay Dillard has made the weasel a symbol of how human beings might live.

As a "nature writer," Dillard is compelling. She digs deep beneath the surface of her subjects, always looking for connections between the natural and human worlds. In "Living Like Weasels," these connections take the form of speculating about the connections and disjunctions between the wildness and ferocity of a little brown-bodied, furry creature, and the human need to find our necessity, lock onto it, and never let go. Dillard privileges wildness over civilization, mystical communion over separateness, instinct over intellect. She clearly values the weasel's tenacity.

I

A weasel is wild. Who knows what he thinks? He sleeps in his underground den, his tail draped over his nose. Sometimes he lives in his den for two days without leaving. Outside, he stalks rabbits, mice, muskrats, and birds, killing more bodies than he can eat warm, and often dragging the carcasses home. Obedient to instinct, he bites his prey at the neck, either splitting the jugular vein at the throat or crunching the brain at the base of the skull, and he does not let go. One naturalist refused to kill a weasel who was socketed into his hand deeply as a rattlesnake. The man could in no way pry the tiny weasel off, and he had to walk half a mile to water, the weasel dangling from his palm, and soak him off like a stubborn label.

And once, says Ernest Thompson Seton—once, a man shot an eagle out of the sky. He examined the eagle and found the dry skull of a weasel fixed by the jaws to his throat. The supposition is that the eagle had pounced on the weasel and the weasel swiveled and bit as instinct taught him, tooth to neck, and nearly won. I would like to have seen that eagle from the air a few weeks or months before he was shot: was the whole weasel still attached to his feathered throat, a fur pendant? Or did the eagle eat what he could reach, gutting the living weasel with his talons before his breast, bending his beak, cleaning the beautiful airborne bones?

II

I have been reading about weasels because I saw one last week. I startled a weasel who startled me, and we exchanged a long glance.

Twenty minutes from my house, through the woods by the quarry and across the highway, is Hollins Pond, a remarkable piece of shallowness, where I like to go at sunset and sit on a tree trunk. Hollins Pond is also called Murray's Pond; it covers two acres of bottomland near Tinker Creek with six inches of water and six thousand lily pads. In winter, brown-and-white steers stand in the middle of it, merely dampening their hooves; from the distant shore they look like miracle itself, complete with miracle's nonchalance. Now, in summer, the steers are gone. The water lilies have blossomed and spread to a green horizontal plane that is terra firma to plodding blackbirds, and tremulous ceiling to black leeches, cray fish, and carp.

This is, mind you, suburbia. It is a five-minute walk in three directions to rows of houses, though none is visible here. There's a 55 mph highway at one end of the pond, and a nesting pair of wood ducks at the other. Under every bush is a muskrat hole or a beer can. The far end is an alternating series of fields and woods, fields and woods, threaded everywhere with motorcycle tracks—in whose bare clay wild turtles lay eggs.

So, I had crossed the highway, stepped over two low barbed-wire fences, and traced the motorcycle path in all gratitude through the wild rose and poison ivy of the pond's shoreline up into high grassy fields. Then I cut down through the woods to the mossy fallen tree where I sit. This tree is excellent. It makes a dry, upholstered bench at the upper, marshy end of the pond, a plush jetty raised from the thorn shore between a shallow blue body of water and a deep blue body of sky.

The sun had just set. I was relaxed on the tree trunk, ensconced in the lap of lichen, watching the lily pads at my feet tremble and part dreamily over the thrusting path of a carp. A yellow bird appeared to my right and flew behind me. It caught my eye; I swiveled around—and the next instant, inexplicably, I was looking down at a weasel, who was looking up at me.

III

Weasel! I'd never seen one wild before. He was ten inches long, thin as a curve, a muscled ribbon, brown as fruitwood, soft-furred, alert. His face was fierce, small and pointed as a lizard's; he would have made a good arrowhead. There was just a dot of chin, maybe two brown hairs' worth, and then the pure white fur began that spread down his underside. He had two black eyes I didn't see, any more than you see a window.

The weasel was stunned into stillness as he was emerging from beneath an enormous shaggy wild rose bush four feet away. I was stunned into stillness twisted backward on the tree trunk. Our eyes locked, and someone threw away the key.

Our look was as if two lovers, or deadly enemies, met unexpectedly on an overgrown path when each had been thinking of something else: a clearing blow to the gut. It was also a bright blow to the brain, or a sudden beating of brains with all the charge and intimate grate of rubbed balloons. It emptied our lungs. It felled the forest, moved the fields, and drained the pond; the world dismantled and tumbled into that black hole of eyes. If you and I looked at each other that way, our skulls would split and drop to our shoulders. But we don't. We keep our skulls. So.

He disappeared. This was only last week, and already I don't remember what shattered the enchantment. I think I blinked, I think I retrieved my brain from the weasel's brain, and tried to memorize what

I was seeing, and the weasel felt the yank of separation, the careening splashdown into real life and the urgent current of instinct. He vanished under the wild rose. I waited motionless, my mind suddenly full of data and my spirit with pleadings, but he didn't return.

Please do not tell me about "approach-avoidance conflicts." I tell you I've been in that weasel's brain for sixty seconds, and he was in mine. Brains are private places, muttering through unique and secret tapes—but the weasel and I both plugged into another tape simultaneously, for a sweet and shocking time. Can I help it if it was a blank?

What goes on in his brain the rest of the time? What does a weasel think about? He won't say. His journal is tracks in clay, a spray of feathers, mouse blood and bone: uncollected, unconnected, loose-leaf, and blown.

IV

I would like to learn, or remember, how to live. I come to Hollins Pond not so much to learn how to live as, frankly, to forget about it. That is, I don't think I can learn from a wild animal how to live in particular—shall I suck warm blood, hold my tail high, walk with my footprints precisely over the prints of my hands?—but I might learn something of mindlessness, something of the purity of living in the physical senses and the dignity of living without bias or motive. The weasel lives in necessity and we live in choice, hating necessity and dying at the last ignobly in its talons. I would like to live as I should, as the weasel lives as he should. And I suspect that for me the way is like the weasel's: open to time and death painlessly, noticing everything, remembering nothing, choosing the given with a fierce and pointed will.

V

I missed my chance. I should have gone for the throat. I should have lunged for that streak of white under the weasel's chin and held on, held on through mud and into the wild rose, held on for a dearer life. We could live under the wild rose wild as weasels, mute and uncomprehending. I could very calmly go wild. I could live two days in the den, curled, leaning on mouse fur, sniffing bird bones, blinking, licking, breathing musk, my hair tangled in the roots of grasses. Down is a good place to go, where the mind is single. Down is out, out of your ever-loving mind and back to your careless senses. I remember muteness as a prolonged and giddy fast, where every moment is a feast of utterance received. Time and events are merely poured, unre- marked, and ingested directly, like blood pulsed into my gut through a jugular vein. Could two live that way? Could two live under the wild rose, and explore by the pond, so that the smooth mind of each is as everywhere present to the other, and as received and as unchallenged, as falling snow?

We could, you know. We can live any way we want. People take vows of poverty, chastity, and obedience—even of silence—by choice. The thing is to stalk your calling in a certain skilled and supple way, to locate the most tender and live spot and plug into that pulse. This is yielding, not fighting. A weasel doesn't "attack" anything; a weasel lives as he's meant to, yielding at every moment to the perfect freedom of single necessity.

VI

I think it would be well, and proper, and obedient, and pure, to grasp your one necessity and not let it go, to dangle from it limp wherever it takes you. Then even death, where you're going no matter how you live, cannot you part. Seize it and let it seize you up aloft even, till your eyes burn out and drop; let your musky flesh fall off in shreds, and let your very bones unhinge and scatter, loosened over fields, over fields and woods, lightly, thoughtless, from any height at all, from as high as eagles.

Possibilities for Writing

1. Central to Dillard's point here are the concepts of "mindlessness" and "necessity" as opposed to consciousness and choice. In an essay, explore what Dillard means by these terms and what value she apparently finds in giving oneself over to mindlessness and necessity.
2. Dillard's essay is divided into six parts, all linked by repeated images and words. Analyze the essay to note as many of these

linkages as you can. Then explore how several of these threads function meaningfully in the essay.

3. Dillard's encounter with the weasel provides her with a profound insight about humans and the natural world. Recall a time when an encounter or experience led you to see some aspect of life in a new light. In an essay explore the circumstances of this sudden insight.

> **Frederick Douglass** *(1817–1895) was born a slave in rural Maryland and as a boy worked as a house servant in Baltimore, where his mistress taught him the rudiments of reading until her husband objected. Continuing his education surreptitiously on his own, Douglass escaped to New York when he was twenty. Within three years, he had become an ardent campaigner against slavery and for the rights of free blacks. In 1846 his freedom was officially purchased by British supporters, and in 1847 he began publishing a weekly newspaper,* North Star. *During the Civil War, he promoted the use of black troops to fight the Confederacy, and following the war he held several government posts, including U. S. Minister to Haiti. Today he is best known for his autobiographical works, most notably his first publication,* Narrative of the Life of Frederick Douglass *(1845).*

Frederick Douglass
Learning to Read and Write

In this excerpt from his autobiography, Frederick Douglass, an American slave, describes how he learned to read and write, and the consequences that his literacy brought him. Douglass entwines the story of his entry into literacy with that of his enslavement. He makes clear how, by keeping black slaves ignorant through denying them literacy, white slaveowners kept them under control. In telling this part of his life story, Douglass conveys a sense of the power of literacy. Learning to read and write transformed Douglass from a passive person to an active one, from an obedient slave who accepted his lot to a thoughtful critic of the institution of slavery and a spirited rebel against it.

Douglass links the stories of how he learned to read and to write with a bridge anecdote about his resolve to run away from his master. In this section, Douglass reveals his mistrust of white people, some of whom were actually eager to help him, and he reveals as well his gradual understanding of the abolitionist movement, in which he himself would later become a prominent figure. Douglass exercised the same ingenuity and determination in learning to write as he did in learning to read. Ingenuity and determination, in fact, are central themes of Douglass's story.

I lived in Master Hugh's family about seven years. During this time, I succeeded in learning to read and write. In accomplishing this, I was compelled to resort to various stratagems. I had no regular teacher.

My mistress, who had kindly commenced to instruct me, had, in compliance with the advice and direction of her husband, not only ceased to instruct, but had set her face against my being instructed by any one else. It is due, however, to my mistress to say of her, that she did not adopt this course of treatment immediately. She at first lacked the depravity indispensable to shutting me up in mental darkness. It was at least necessary for her to have some training in the exercise of irresponsible power, to make her equal to the task of treating me as though I were a brute.

My mistress was, as I have said, a kind and tender-hearted woman; and in the simplicity of her soul she commenced, when I first went to live with her, to treat me as she supposed one human being ought to treat another. In entering upon the duties of a slaveholder, she did not seem to perceive that I sustained to her the relation of a mere chattel, and that for her to treat me as a human being was not only wrong, but dangerously so. Slavery proved as injurious to her as it did to me. When I went there, she was a pious, warm, and tender-hearted woman. There was no sorrow or suffering for which she had not a tear. She had bread for the hungry, clothes for the naked, and comfort for every mourner that came within her reach. Slavery soon proved its ability to divest her of these heavenly qualities. Under its influence, the tender heart became stone, and the lamb-like disposition gave way to one of tiger-like fierceness. The first step in her downward course was in her ceasing to instruct me. She now commenced to practise her husband's precepts. She finally became even more violent in her opposition than her husband himself. She was not satisfied with simply doing as well as he had commanded; she seemed anxious to do better. Nothing seemed to make her more angry than to see me with a newspaper. She seemed to think that here lay the danger. I have had her rush at me with a face made all up of fury, and snatch from me a newspaper, in a manner that fully revealed her apprehension. She was an apt woman; and a little experience soon demonstrated, to her satisfaction, that education and slavery were incompatible with each other.

From this time I was most narrowly watched. If I was in a separate room any considerable length of time, I was sure to be suspected of having a book, and was at once called to give an account of myself. All this, however, was too late. The first step had been taken. Mistress, in teaching me the alphabet, had given me the *inch*, and no precaution could prevent me from taking the *ell*.

The plan which I adopted, and the one by which I was most success-ful, was that of making friends of all the little white boys whom I met in the street. As many of these as I could, I converted into teachers. With their kindly aid, obtained at different times and in different places, I finally succeeded in learning to read. When I was sent of errands, I always took my book with me, and by going one part of my errand quickly, I found time to get a lesson before my return. I used also to carry bread with me, enough of which was always in the house, and to which I was always welcome; for I was much better off in this regard than many of the poor white children in our neighborhood. This bread I used to bestow upon the hungry little urchins, who, in return, would give me that more valuable bread of knowledge. I am strongly tempted to give the names of two or three of those little boys, as a testimonial of the grat-itude and affection I bear them; but prudence forbids:—not that it would injure me, but it might embarrass them; for it is almost an unpardonable offence to teach slaves to read in this Christian country. It is enough to say of the dear little fellows, that they lived on Philpot Street, very near Durgin and Bailey's ship-yard. I used to talk this matter of slavery over with them. I would sometimes say to them, I wished I could be as free as they would be when they got to be men. "You will be free as soon as you are twenty-one, *but I am a slave for life!* Have not I as good a right to be free as you have?" These words used to trouble them; they would express for me the liveliest sympathy, and console me with the hope that some-thing would occur by which I might be free.

I was now about twelve years old, and the thought of being *a slave for life* began to bear heavily upon my heart. Just about this time, I got hold of a book entitled "The Columbian Orator." Every opportu-nity I got, I used to read this book. Among much of other interesting matter, I found in it a dialogue between a master and his slave. The slave was represented as having run away from his master three times. The dialogue represented the conversation which took place between them, when the slave was retaken the third time. In this dia-logue, the whole argument in behalf of slavery was brought forward by the master, all of which was disposed of by the slave. The slave was made to say some very smart as well as impressive things in reply to his master—things which had the desired though unexpected effect; for the conversation resulted in the voluntary emancipation of the slave on the part of the master.

In the same book, I met with one of Sheridan's mighty speeches on and in behalf of Catholic emancipation. These were choice documents to me. I read them over and over again with unabated interest. They gave tongue to interesting thoughts of my own soul, which had frequently flashed through my mind, and died away for want of utterance. The moral which I gained from the dialogue was the power of truth over the conscience of even a slaveholder. What I got from Sheridan was a bold denunciation of slavery, and a powerful vindication of human rights. The reading of these documents enabled me to utter my thoughts, and to meet the arguments brought forward to sustain slavery; but while they relieved me of one difficulty, they brought on another even more painful than the one of which I was relieved. The more I read, the more I was led to abhor and detest my enslavers. I could regard them in no other light than a band of successful robbers, who had left their homes, and gone to Africa, and stolen us from our homes, and in a strange land reduced us to slavery. I loathed them as being the meanest as well as the most wicked of men. As I read and contemplated the subject, behold! that very discontentment which Master Hugh had predicted would follow my learning to read had already come, to torment and sting my soul to unutterable anguish. As I writhed under it, I would at times feel that learning to read had been a curse rather than a blessing. It had given me a view of my wretched condition, without the remedy. It opened my eyes to the horrible pit, but to no ladder upon which to get out. In moments of agony, I envied my fellow-slaves for their stupidity. I have often wished myself a beast. I preferred the condition of the meanest reptile to my own. Any thing, no matter what, to get rid of thinking! It was this everlasting thinking of my condition that tormented me. There was no getting rid of it. It was pressed upon me by every object within sight or hearing, animate or inanimate. The silver trump of freedom had roused my soul to eternal wakefulness. Freedom now appeared, to disappear no more forever. It was heard in every sound, and seen in every thing. It was ever present to torment me with a sense of my wretched condition. I saw nothing without seeing it, I heard nothing without hearing it, and felt nothing without feeling it. It looked from every star, it smiled in every calm, breathed in every wind, and moved in every storm.

I often found myself regretting my own existence, and wishing myself dead; and but for the hope of being free, I have no doubt but that I should have killed myself, or done something for which I should have been killed. While in this state of mind, I was eager to hear any one speak of slavery. I was a ready listener. Every little while, I could hear something about the abolitionists. It was some time before I found what the word meant. It was always used in such connections as to make it an interesting word to me. If a slave ran away and succeeded in getting clear, or if a slave killed his master, set fire to a barn, or did any thing very wrong in the mind of a slaveholder, it was spoken of as the fruit of *abolition.* Hearing the word in this connection very often, I set about learning what it meant. The dictionary afforded me little or no help. I found it was "the act of abolishing;" but then I did not know what was to be abolished. Here I was perplexed. I did not dare to ask any one about its meaning, for I was satisfied that it was something they wanted me to know very little about. After a patient waiting, I got one of our city papers, containing an account of the number of petitions from the north, praying for the abolition of slavery in the District of Columbia, and of the slave trade between the States. From this time I understood the words *abolition* and *abolition-ist*, and always drew near when that word was spoken, expecting to hear something of importance to myself and fellow-slaves. The light broke in upon me by degrees. I went one day down on the wharf of Mr. Waters; and seeing two Irishmen unloading a scow of stone, I went, unasked, and helped them. When we had finished, one of them came to me and asked me if I were a slave. I told him I was. He asked, "Are ye a slave for life?" I told him that I was. The good Irishman seemed to be deeply affected by the statement. He said to the other that it was a pity so fine a little fellow as myself should be a slave for life. He said it was a shame to hold me. They both advised me to run away to the north; that I should find friends there, and that I should be free. I pretended not to be interested in what they said, and treated them as if I did not understand them; for I feared they might be treacherous. White men have been known to encourage slaves to escape, and then, to get the reward, catch them and return them to their masters. I was afraid that these seemingly good men might use me so; but I nevertheless remembered their advice, and from that time I resolved to run away. I looked forward to a time at which it would be safe for me to escape. I was too young to think of doing so immediately; besides, I wished to learn how to write, as I might have occasion to write my own pass. I consoled myself with the hope that I should one day find a good chance. Meanwhile, I would learn to write.

The idea as to how I might learn to write was suggested to me by being in Durgin and Bailey's ship-yard, and frequently seeing the ship carpenters, after hewing, and getting a piece of timber ready for use, write on the timber the name of that part of the ship for which it was intended. When a piece of timber was intended for the larboard side, it would be marked thus—"L." When a piece was for the starboard side, it would be marked thus—"S." A piece for the larboard side forward, would be marked thus—"L. F." When a piece was for starboard side forward, it would be marked thus—"S. F." For larboard aft, it would be marked thus—"L. A." For starboard aft, it would be marked thus—"S. A." I soon learned the names of these letters, and for what they were intended when placed upon a piece of timber in the ship-yard. I immediately commenced copying them, and in a short time was able to make the four letters named. After that, when I met with any boy who I knew could write, I would tell him I could write as well as he. The next word would be, "I don't believe you. Let me see you try it." I would then make the letters which I had been so fortunate as to learn, and ask him to beat that. In this way I got a good many lessons in writing, which it is quite possible I should never have gotten in any other way. During this time, my copy-book was the board fence, brick wall, and pavement; my pen and ink was a lump of chalk. With these, I learned mainly how to write. I then commenced and continued copying the Italics in Webster's Spelling Book, until I could make them all without looking on the book. By this time, my little Master Thomas had gone to school, and learned how to write, and had written over a number of copy-books. These had been brought home, and shown to some of our near neighbors, and then laid aside. My mistress used to go to class meeting at the Wilk Street meetinghouse every Monday afternoon, and leave me to take care of the house. When left thus, I used to spend the time in writing in the spaces left in Master Thomas's copy-book, copying what he had written. I continued to do this until I could write a hand very similar to that of Master Thomas. Thus, after a long, tedious effort for years, I finally succeeded in learning how to write.

Possibilities for Writing

1. In various ways throughout this essay, Douglass makes the point that education—learning to read and write—and slavery are "incompatible with each other," for both slaves and those who own them. Using evidence from the text, as well as your own conclusions, explore why this would be so.

2. Douglass's autobiography was written before slavery was fully abolished in the United States. In what ways can his narrative be read as an argument against slavery? Consider this issue from the perspective of readers who might be slaveholders, those who were already abolitionists, and those who did not own slaves but were undecided on the question.

3. How do you respond to Douglass's situation and to the portrait he presents of himself as you read it today, more than a hundred and fifty years after it was written? Do you find that you can apply any of what he says to the world you live in today? Explain why you feel as you do.

W(illiam) E(dward) B(urghardt) DuBois (1868–1963) was born in Great Barrington, Massachusetts, and received his B.A., M.A., and Ph.D from Harvard University, an unusual achievement for a black man of his day. A tireless advocate of full civil rights for African Americans, he was a founder of the organization that would later become the National Association for the Advancement of Colored People (NAACP) and for several years edited its official magazine, Crisis. *He organized a number of international conferences on the condition of black people worldwide, and he also advised U.S. government representatives on policy issues with regard to civil rights. His writings include* The Souls of Black Folk *(1903),* The Negro *(1915), and* Color and Democracy *(1945).*

W.E.B. DuBois

Of Our Spiritual Striving

In this excerpt from *The Souls of Black Folk*, W. E. B. DuBois describes the American Negro's desire to be able "to husband and use his best powers and his latent genius," after having been freed from slavery in the 1860s and given the right to vote in 1870, by the fifteenth amendment to the Constitution. DuBois makes clear his belief in the dignity of Black people, who possess two cultures—their adopted American culture and their African ancestral culture. DuBois sees the value of not so much mingling these two cultures as of preserving each of them intact.

DuBois describes the problem of the "veil" that separates American Blacks from their African past and from their American present. He sees that to a large extent American Blacks in 1900 had yet to be integrated and accepted on their own terms into American society and culture. DuBois's ideas were revolutionary when advocated a century ago, as he urged African Americans not to deny their African heritage and roots and become culturally indistinguishable from white society. Instead, he encouraged them to preserve their distinctiveness while claiming political and social equality.

> O water, voice of my heart, crying in the sand,
>   All night long crying with a mournful cry,
> As I lie and listen, and cannot understand
>   The voice of my heart in my side or the voice of the sea,
>   O water, crying for rest, is it I, is it I?
>   All night long the water is crying to me.
>
> Unresting water, there shall never be rest
>   Till the last moon droop and the last tide fail,

And the fire of the end begin to burn in the west;
  And the heart shall be weary and wonder and cry like the sea,
All life long crying without avail,
  As the water all night long is crying to me.

—*Arthur Symons*

Between me and the other world there is ever an unasked question: unasked by some through feelings of delicacy; by others through the difficulty of rightly framing it. All, nevertheless, flutter round it. They approach me in a half-hesitant sort of way, eye me curiously or compassionately, and then, instead of saying directly, How does it feel to be a problem? they say, I know an excellent colored man in my town; or, I fought at Mechanicsville; or, Do not these Southern outrages make your blood boil? At these I smile, or am interested, or reduce the boiling to a simmer, as the occasion may require. To the real question, How does it feel to be a problem? I answer seldom a word.

And yet, being a problem is a strange experience,—peculiar even for one who has never been anything else, save perhaps in babyhood and in Europe. It is the early days of rollicking boyhood that the revelation first bursts upon one, all in a day, as it were. I remember well when the shadow swept across me. I was a little thing, away up in the hills of New England, where the dark Housatonic winds between Hoosac and Taghkanic to the sea. In a wee wooden schoolhouse, something put it into the boys' and girls' heads to buy gorgeous visiting-cards—ten cents a package—and exchange. The exchange was merry, till one girl, a tall newcomer, refused my card,—refused it peremptorily, with a glance. Then it dawned upon me with a certain suddenness that I was different from the others; or like, mayhap, in heart and life and longing, but shut out from their world by a vast veil. I had thereafter no desire to tear down that veil, to creep through; I held all beyond it in common contempt, and lived above it in a region of blue sky and great wandering shadows. That sky was bluest when I could beat my mates at examination-time, or beat them at a foot-race, or even beat their stringy heads. Alas, with the years all this fine contempt began to fade; for the worlds I longed for, and all their dazzling opportunities, were theirs, not mine. But they should not keep these prizes, I said; some, all, I would wrest from them. Just how I would do it I could never decide: by reading law, by healing the sick, by telling the wonderful tales that swam in my head,—some way. With other black boys the strife was not so fiercely sunny: their youth shrunk into tasteless sycophancy, or into silent hatred of the pale world about them and mocking distrust of everything white; or wasted itself in a bitter cry, Why did God make me an outcast and a stranger in mine own house? The shades of the prison-house closed round about us all: walls strait and stubborn to the whitest, but relentlessly narrow, tall, and unscalable to sons of night who must plod darkly on in resignation, or beat unavailing palms against the stone, or steadily, half hopelessly, watch the streak of blue above.

After the Egyptian and Indian, the Greek and Roman, the Teuton and Mongolian, the Negro is a sort of seventh son, born with a veil, and gifted with second-sight in this American world,—a world which yields him no true self-consciousness, but only lets him see himself through the revelation of the other world. It is a peculiar sensation, this double-consciousness, this sense of always looking at one's self through the eyes of others, of measuring one's soul by the tape of a world that looks on in amused contempt and pity. One ever feels his two-ness,—an American, a Negro; two souls, two thoughts, two unreconciled strivings; two warring ideals in one dark body, whose dogged strength alone keeps it from being torn asunder.

The history of the American Negro is the history of this strife,—this longing to attain self-conscious manhood, to merge his double self into a better and truer self. In this merging he wishes neither of the older selves to be lost. He would not Africanize America, for America has too much to teach the world and Africa. He would not bleach his Negro soul in a flood of white Americanism, for he knows that Negro blood has a message for the world. He simply wishes to make it possible for a man to be both a Negro and an American, without being cursed and spit upon by his fellows, without having the doors of Opportunity closed roughly in his face.

This, then, is the end of his striving: to be a co-worker in the kingdom of culture, to escape both death and isolation, to husband and use his best powers and his latent genius. These powers of body and mind have in the past been strangely wasted, dispersed, or forgotten. The shadow of a mighty Negro past flits through the tale of Ethiopia the Shadowy and of Egypt the Sphinx. Throughout history, the powers of single black men flash here and there like falling stars, and die sometimes before the world has rightly gauged their brightness. Here in America, in the few days since Emancipation, the black man's turning hither and thither in hesitant and doubtful striving has often made his very strength to lose effectiveness, to seem like absence of power, like weakness. And yet it is not weakness,—it is the contradiction of double aims. The double-aimed struggle of the black artisan—on the one hand to escape white contempt for a nation of mere hewers of wood and drawers of water, and on the other hand to plough and nail and dig for a poverty-stricken horde—could only result in making him a poor craftsman, for he had but half a heart in either cause. By the poverty and ignorance of his people, the Negro minister or doctor was tempted toward quackery and demagogy; and by the criticism of the other world, toward ideals that made him ashamed of his lowly tasks. The would-be black *savant* was confronted by the paradox that the knowledge his people needed was a twice-told tale to his white neighbors, while the knowledge which would teach the white world was Greek to his own flesh and blood. The innate love of harmony and beauty that set the rude souls of his people a-dancing and a-singing raised but confusion and doubt in the soul of the black artist; for the beauty revealed to him was the soul-beauty of a race which his larger audience despised, and he could not articulate the message of another people. This waste of double aims, this seeking to satisfy two unreconciled ideals, has wrought sad havoc with the courage and faith and deeds of ten thousand thousand people,—has sent them often wooing false gods and invoking false means of salvation, and at times has even seemed about to make them ashamed of themselves.

Away back in the days of bondage they thought to see in one divine event the end of all doubt and disappointment; few men ever worshipped Freedom with half such unquestioning faith as did the American Negro for two centuries. To him, so far as he thought and dreamed, slavery was indeed the sum of all villainies, the cause of all sorrow, the root of all prejudice; Emancipation was the key to a promised land of sweeter beauty than ever stretched before the eyes of wearied Israelites. In song and exhortation swelled one refrain—Liberty; in his tears and curses the God he implored had Freedom in his right hand. At last it came,—suddenly, fearfully, like a dream. With one wild carnival of blood and passion came the message in his own plaintive cadences:—

> "Shout, O children!
> Shout, you're free!
> For God has bought your liberty!"

Years have passed away since then,—ten, twenty, forty; forty years of national life, forty years of renewal and development, and yet the swarthy spectre sits in its accustomed seat at the Nation's feast. In vain do we cry to this our vastest social problem:—

> "Take any shape but that, and my firm nerves
> Shall never tremble!"

The Nation has not yet found peace from its sins; the freedman has not yet found in freedom his promised land. Whatever of good may have come in these years of change, the shadow of a deep disappointment rests upon the Negro people,—a disappointment all the more bitter because the unattained ideal was unbounded save by the simple ignorance of a lowly people.

The first decade was merely a prolongation of the vain search for freedom, the boon that seemed ever barely to elude their grasp,—like a tantalizing will-o'-the-wisp, maddening and misleading the headless host. The holocaust of war, the terrors of the Ku-Klux Klan, the lies of carpet-baggers, the disorganization of industry, and the contradictory advice of friends and foes, left the bewildered serf with no new watch-word beyond the old cry for freedom. As the time flew, however, he began to grasp a new idea. The ideal of liberty demanded for its attainment powerful means, and these the Fifteenth Amendment gave him. The ballot, which before he had looked upon as a visible sign of freedom, he now regarded as the chief means of gaining and perfecting the liberty with which war had partially endowed him. And why not? Had not votes made war and emancipated millions? Had not votes enfranchised the freedmen? Was anything impossible to a power that had done all this? A million black men started with renewed zeal to vote themselves into the kingdom. So the decade flew away, the revolution of 1876 came, and left the half-free serf weary, wondering, but still inspired. Slowly but steadily, in the following years, a new vision began gradually to replace the dream of political power,—a powerful movement, the rise of another ideal to guide the unguided, another pillar of fire by night after a clouded day. It was the ideal of "book-learning"; the curiosity, born of compulsory ignorance, to know and test the power of the cabalistic letters of the white man, the longing to know. Here at last seemed to have been discovered the mountain path to Canaan; longer than the highway of

Emancipation and law, steep and rugged, but straight, leading to heights high enough to overlook life.

Up the new path the advance guard toiled, slowly, heavily, doggedly; only those who have watched and guided the faltering feet, the misty minds, the dull understandings, of the dark pupils of these schools know how faithfully, how piteously, this people strove to learn. It was weary work. The cold statistician wrote down the inches of progress here and there, noted also where here and there a foot had slipped or some one had fallen. To the tired climbers, the horizon was ever dark, the mists were often cold, the Canaan was always dim and far away. If, however, the vistas disclosed as yet no goal, no resting-place, little but flattery and criticism, the journey at least gave leisure for reflection and self-examination; it changed the child of Emancipation to the youth with dawning self-consciousness, self-realization, self-respect. In those sombre forests of his striving his own soul rose before him, and he saw himself,—darkly as through a veil; and yet he saw in himself some faint revelation of his power, of his mission. He began to have a dim feeling that, to attain his place in the world, he must be himself, and not another. For the first time he sought to analyze the burden he bore upon his back, that dead-weight of social degradation partially masked behind a half-named Negro problem. He felt his poverty; without a cent, without a home, without land, tools, or savings, he had entered into competition with rich, landed, skilled neighbors. To be a poor man is hard, but to be a poor race in a land of dollars is the very bottom of hardships. He felt the weight of his ignorance,—not simply of letters, but of life, of business, of the humanities; the accumulated sloth and shirking and awkwardness of decades and centuries shackled his hands and feet. Nor was his burden all poverty and ignorance. The red stain of bastardy, which two centuries of systematic legal defilement of Negro women had stamped upon his race, meant not only the loss of ancient African chastity, but also the hereditary weight of a mass of corruption from white adulterers, threatening almost the obliteration of the Negro home.

A people thus handicapped ought not to be asked to race with the world, but rather allowed to give all its time and thought to its own social problems. But alas! while sociologists gleefully count his bastards and his prostitutes, the very soul of the toiling, sweating black man is darkened by the shadow of a vast despair. Men call the shadow prejudice, and learnedly explain it as the natural defence of culture against barbarism, learning against ignorance, purity against crime, the "higher" against the "lower" races. To which the Negro cries Amen! and swears that to so much of this strange prejudice as is founded on just homage to civilization, culture, righteousness, and progress, he humbly bows and meekly does obeisance. But before that nameless prejudice that leaps beyond all this he stands helpless, dismayed, and well-nigh speechless; before that personal disrespect and mockery, the ridicule and systematic humiliation, the distortion of fact and wanton license of fancy, the cynical ignoring of the better and the boisterous welcoming of the worse, the all-pervading desire to inculcate disdain for everything black, from Toussaint to the devil,—before this there rises a sickening despair that would disarm and discourage any nation save that black host to whom "discouragement" is an unwritten word.

But the facing of so vast a prejudice could not but bring the inevitable self-questioning, self-disparagement, and lowering of ideals which ever accompany repression and breed in an atmosphere of contempt and hate. Whisperings and portents came borne upon the four winds: Lo! we are diseased and dying, cried the dark hosts; we cannot write, our voting is vain; what need of education, since we must always cook and serve? And the Nation echoed and enforced this self-criticism, saying: Be content to be servants, and nothing more; what need of higher culture for half-men? Away with the black man's ballot, by force or fraud,—and behold the suicide of a race! Nevertheless, out of the evil came something of good,—the more careful adjustment of education to real life, the clearer perception of the Negroes' social responsibilities, and the sobering realization of the meaning of progress.

So dawned the time of *Sturm und Drang:* storm and stress to-day rocks our little boat on the mad waters of the world-sea; there is within and without the sound of conflict, the burning of body and rending of soul; inspiration strives with doubt, and faith with vain questionings. The bright ideals of the past,—physical freedom, political power, the training of brains and the training of hands,—all these in turn have waxed and waned, until even the last grows dim and overcast. Are they all wrong,—all false? No, not that, but each alone was over-simple and incomplete,—the dreams of a credulous race-childhood, or the fond

imaginings of the other world which does not know and does not want
to know our power. To be really true, all these ideals must be melted
and welded into one. The training of the schools we need to-day more
than ever,—the training of deft hands, quick eyes and ears, and above
all the broader, deeper, higher culture of gifted minds and pure hearts.
The power of the ballot we need in sheer self-defence,—else what shall
save us from a second slavery? Freedom, too, the long-sought, we still
seek,—the freedom of life and limb, the freedom to work and think,
the freedom to love and aspire. Work, culture, liberty,—all these we
need, not singly but together, not successively but together, each growing and aiding each, and all striving toward that vaster ideal that
swims before the Negro people, the ideal of human brotherhood,
gained through the unifying ideal of Race; the ideal of fostering and
developing the traits and talents of the Negro, not in opposition to or
contempt for other races, but rather in large conformity to the greater
ideals of the American Republic, in order that some day on American
soil two world-races may give each to each those characteristics both so
sadly lack. We the darker ones come even now not altogether empty-
handed: there are to-day no truer exponents of the pure human spirit
of the Declaration of Independence than the American Negroes; there is
no true American music but the wild sweet melodies of the Negro slave;
the American fairy tales and folklore are Indian and African; and, all
in all, we black men seem the sole oasis of simple faith and reverence
in a dusty desert of dollars and smartness. Will America be poorer
if she replace her brutal dyspeptic blundering with light-hearted but
determined Negro humility? or her coarse and cruel wit with loving
jovial good-humor? or her vulgar music with the soul of the Sorrow
Songs?

Merely a concrete test of the underlying principles of the great
republic is the Negro Problem, and the spiritual striving of the freedmen's sons is the travail of souls whose burden is almost beyond the
measure of their strength, but who bear it in the name of an historic
race, in the name of this the land of their fathers' fathers, and in the
name of human opportunity.

And now what I have briefly sketched in large outline let me on coming
pages tell again in many ways, with loving emphasis and deeper detail,
that men may listen to the striving in the souls of black folk.

Possibilities for Writing

1. What are DuBois's main themes here, and how does he relate them to the past, to his present day, and to a possible future?
2. DuBois's later paragraphs focus on "the shadow prejudice." What does he see as the causes and results of prejudice? How, in his view, can prejudice be overcome?
3. DuBois was one of the first defenders of full social and civil equality for African Americans. How are the ideas he puts forth here reflected in contemporary cultural reality and societal attitudes?

Gretel Ehrlich (b. 1946), a native Californian, attended Bennington College and later the film school at New York University. Her work as a documentary filmmaker took her to Wyoming in 1979, and she found herself drawn to the state's sweeping open countryside and to the people who inhabit it. During her seventeen years working as a rancher there, she produced several books of reflections on her experiences, including The Solace of Open Spaces *(1985) and* A Match to the Heart *(1994), as well a novel and other works. Currently dividing her time between California and Wyoming, she has most recently published* Questions from Heaven *(1997), an account of her pilgrimage as a Buddhist to shrines in China, and* John Muir: Nature's Visionary *(2000), a biography of the great American naturalist and conservationist.*

Gretel Ehrlich

About Men

Ehrlich's brief essay, "About Men," originally appeared in *Time* magazine, and was included in her first essay collection, *The Solace of Open Spaces*. Ehrlich's primary purpose in the essay is to reconsider some basic stereotypes about men—particularly western men, including, of course, "cowboys." Through a series of carefully chosen examples graced by vivid description, revealing dialogue, and sharply etched details, Ehrlich reveals the complex nature of the American cowboy. She suggests that cowboys, usually thought of as rugged and tough, are kind and tender hearted. In debunking stereotypes about cowboys, Ehrlich encourages readers to consider how manliness is a quality which, for cowboys, also requires a balancing of more conventionally typical feminine qualities, such as caring and compassion. The cowboys Ehrlich knows and describes are, as she writes, "androgynous at the core."

While describing what cowboys are really like, Ehrlich also conveys a powerful impression of the natural world, which so dramatically and inescapably affects their lives. She describes the sheer beauty of nature, while not ignoring the darker dangers it poses for beasts and men alike. But it's clear from her tone of respectful admiration, she wouldn't trade her western world and the western men she describes for anything, regardless of the challenges both nature and cowboys present.

When I'm in New York but feeling lonely for Wyoming I look for the Marlboro ads in the subway. What I'm aching to see is horseflesh, the glint of a spur, a line of distant mountains, brimming creeks, and a reminder of the ranchers and cowboys I've ridden with for the last eight years. But the men I see in those posters with their stern, humorless looks remind me of no one I know here. In our hellbent earnestness to romanticize the cowboy we've ironically disesteemed his true character.

If he's "strong and silent" it's because there's probably no one to talk to. If he "rides away into the sunset" it's because he's been on horseback since four in the morning moving cattle and he's trying, fifteen hours later, to get home to his family. If he's "a rugged individualist" he's also part of a team: ranch work is teamwork and even the glorified open-range cowboys of the 1880s rode up and down the Chisholm Trail in the company of twenty or thirty other riders. Instead of the macho, trigger-happy man our culture has perversely wanted him to be, the cowboy is more apt to be convivial, quirky, and softhearted. To be "tough" on a ranch has nothing to do with conquests and displays of power. More often than not, circumstances—like the colt he's riding or an unexpected blizzard—are overpowering him. It's not toughness but "toughing it out" that counts. In other words, this macho, cultural arti-fact the cowboy has become is simply a man who possesses resilience, patience, and an instinct for survival. "Cowboys are just like a pile of rocks—everything happens to them. They get climbed on, kicked, rained and snowed on, scuffed up by wind. Their job is 'just to take it,' " one old-timer told me.

A cowboy is someone who loves his work. Since the hours are long—ten to fifteen hours a day—and the pay is $30 he has to. What's required of him is an odd mixture of physical vigor and maternalism. His part of the beef-raising industry is to birth and nurture calves and take care of their mothers. For the most part his work is done on horse-back and in a lifetime he sees and comes to know more animals than people. The iconic myth surrounding him is built on American notions of heroism: the index of a man's value as measured in physical courage. Such ideas have perverted manliness into a self-absorbed race for cheap thrills. In a rancher's world, courage has less to do with facing danger than with acting spontaneously—usually on behalf of an animal or another rider. If a cow is stuck in a boghole he throws a loop around her neck, takes his dally (a half hitch around the saddle horn), and pulls her out with horsepower. If a calf is born sick, he may take her home, warm her in front of the kitchen fire, and massage her legs until dawn. One friend, whose favorite horse was trying to swim a lake with hobbles on, dove under water and cut her legs loose with a knife, then swam her to shore, his arm around her neck lifeguard-style, and saved her from drowning. Because these incidents are usually linked to someone or something outside himself, the westerner's courage is selfless, a form of compassion.

The physical punishment that goes with cowboying is greatly under-played. Once fear is dispensed with, the threshold of pain rises to meet the demands of the job. When Jane Fonda asked Robert Redford (in the film *Electric Horseman*) if he was sick as he struggled to his feet one morning, he replied, "No, just bent." For once the movies had it right. The cowboys I was sitting with laughed in agreement. Cowboys are rarely complainers; they show their stoicism by laughing at themselves.

If a rancher or cowboy has been thought of as a "man's man"—laconic, hard-drinking, inscrutable—there's almost no place in which the balancing act between male and female, manliness and femininity, can be more natural. If he's gruff, handsome, and physically fit on the outside, he's androgynous at the core. Ranchers are midwives, hunters, nurturers, providers, and conservationists all at once. What we've interpreted as toughness—weathered skin, calloused hands, a squint in the eye and a growl in the voice—only masks the tenderness inside. "Now don't go telling me these lambs are cute," one rancher warned me the first day I walked into the football-field-sized lambing sheds. The next thing I knew he was holding a black lamb. "Ain't this little rat good-lookin'?"

So many of the men who came to the West were southerners—men looking for work and a new life after the Civil War—that chivalrousness and strict codes of honor were soon thought of as western traits. There were very few women in Wyoming during territorial days, so when they did arrive (some as mail-order brides from places like Philadelphia) there was a stand-offishness between the sexes and a formality that per-sists now. Ranchers still tip their hats and say, "Howdy, ma'am" instead of shaking hands with me.

Even young cowboys are often evasive with women. It's not that they're Jekyll and Hyde creatures—gentle with animals and rough on women—but rather, that they don't know how to bring their tenderness into the house and lack the vocabulary to express the complexity of what they feel. Dancing wildly all night becomes a metaphor for the explosive emotions pent up inside, and when these are, on occasion, released, they're so battery-charged and potent that one caress of the face or one "I love you" will peal for a long while.

The geographical vastness and the social isolation here make emo-tional evolution seem impossible. Those contradictions of the heart between respectability, logic, and convention on the one hand, and impulse, passion, and intuition on the other, played out wordlessly against the paradisical beauty of the West, give cowboys a wide-eyed but drawn look. Their lips pucker up, not with kisses but with immutability. They may want to break out, staying up all night with a lover just to talk, but they don't know how and can't imagine what the consequences will be. Those rare occasions when they do bare themselves result in confusion. "I feel as if I'd sprained my heart," one friend told me a month after such a meeting.

My friend Ted Hoagland wrote, "No one is as fragile as a woman but no one is as fragile as a man." For all the women here who use "fragileness" to avoid work or as a sexual ploy, there are men who try to hide theirs, all the while clinging to an adolescent dependency on women to cook their meals, wash their clothes, and keep the ranch house warm in winter. But there is true vulnerability in evidence here. Because these men work with animals, not machines or numbers, because they live outside in landscapes of torrential beauty, because they are confined to a place and a routine embellished with awesome variables, because calves die in the arms that pulled others into life, because they go to the mountains as if on a pilgrimage to find out what makes a herd of elk tick, their strength is also a softness, their toughness, a rare delicacy.

Possibilities for Writing

1. What does Ehrlich find so admirable and so sympathetic about the cowboys and ranchers she encounters in Wyoming? What does this suggest about her view of male roles more generally in our culture? Using specific examples from her essay, explore her central themes.

2. Cowboys, as Ehrlich describes them, seem to have trouble communicating with and relating to women, yet cling to an "adolescent dependency" on women to take care of them. How does Ehrlich square this with her positive image of cowboys? Do you think she does so effectively, or does this point diminish her image of cowboys in your eyes?

3. The media depict many different stereotypes in terms of gender, ethnicity, and so on. Choose a particular stereotype you have encountered, describe it and how it is exemplified in the media, then, as Ehrlich does, question the stereotype based on your own experiences.

Benjamin Franklin (1706–1790), one of the most versatile and widely admired figures in American history, was born in Boston and apprenticed at an early age to a printer and newpaper publisher. As a young man, he moved to Philadelphia to make his fortune, eventually acquiring his own printing and newspaper house where he produced the popular Poor Richard's Almanack *from 1732 to 1757. Essentially self-taught, Franklin helped to establish what became the American Philosophical Society and the University of Pennsylvania, and his experiments with electricity were noted worldwide. A leading figure in the American Revolution and the establishment of the United States as a democracy, Franklin has been referred to as the "wisest American." His autobiography of his early years is considered a classic of American literature.*

Benjamin Franklin
Arriving at Perfection

In "Arriving at Perfection," an excerpt from his *Autobiography*, Benjamin Franklin lays out a plan for his own self-improvement. Franklin was a conscious and a conscientious perfectionist. His little essay on self-improvement reflects the enlightenment ideals of his time with their emphasis on reason and progress. But it also reflects an older tendency in American culture: the tendency toward self-examination and self-correction, a meditative cast of mind Franklin inherited from his Puritan ancestors. Franklin weds these two tendencies toward self-examination and toward self-improvement, toward the moral and the practical.

Franklin's goal for what he calls this "bold and arduous Project" is to live each day without committing any faults. As a rationalist, he sees no reason why he shouldn't be able to live according to a standard of moral propriety. He comes to realize, however, that there are many ways he can lapse from his high standard—through habit, carelessness, inclination, and bad example.

It was about this time that I conceiv'd the bold and arduous Project of arriving at moral Perfection. I wish'd to live without committing any Fault at any time; I would conquer all that either Natural Inclination, Custom, or Company might lead me into. As I knew, or thought I knew, what was right and wrong, I did not see why I might not *always* do the one and avoid the other. But I soon found I had undertaken a Task of more Difficulty than I had imagined: While my Care was employ'd in guarding against one Fault, I was often surpriz'd by another. Habit took the Advantage of Inattention. Inclination was sometimes too strong for

Reason. I concluded at length, that the mere speculative Conviction that it was our Interest to be compleatly virtuous, was not sufficient to prevent our Slipping, and that the contrary Habits must be broken and good Ones acquired and established, before we can have any Dependance on a steady uniform Rectitude of Conduct. For this purpose I therefore contriv'd the following Method.

In the various Enumerations of the moral Virtues I had met with in my Reading, I found the Catalogue more or less numerous, as different Writers included more or fewer Ideas under the same Name. Temperance, for Example, was by some confin'd to Eating and Drinking, while by others it was extended to mean the moderating every other Pleasure, Appetite, Inclination or Passion, bodily or mental, even to our Avarice and Ambition. I propos'd to myself, for the sake of Clearness, to use rather more Names with fewer Ideas annex'd to each, than a few Names with more Ideas; and I included after Thirteen Names of Virtues all that at that time occurr'd to me as necessary or desirable, and annex'd to each a short Precept, which fully express'd the Extent I gave to its Meaning.

These Names of Virtues with their Precepts were

1. *Temperance.* Eat not to Dulness. Drink not to Elevation.
2. *Silence.* Speak not but what may benefit others or your self. Avoid trifling conversation.
3. *Order.* Let all your Things have their Places. Let each Part of your Business have its Time.
4. *Resolution.* Resolve to perform what you ought. Perform without fail what you resolve.
5. *Frugality.* Make no Expence but to do good to others or yourself: i.e. Waste nothing.
6. *Industry.* Lose no Time. Be always employ'd in something useful. Cut off all unnecessary Actions.
7. *Sincerity.* Use no hurtful Deceit. Think innocently and justly; and, if you speak; speak accordingly.
8. *Justice.* Wrong none, by doing Injuries or omitting the Benefits that are your Duty.
9. *Moderation.* Avoid Extreams. Forbear resenting Injuries so much as you think they deserve.
10. *Cleanliness.* Tolerate no Uncleanness in Body, Cloaths or Habitation.
11. *Tranquility.* Be not disturbed at Trifles, or at Accidents common or unavoidable.

12. *Chastity*. Rarely use Venery but for Health or Offspring; Never to Dulness, Weakness, or the Injury of your own or another's Peace or Reputation.

13. *Humility*. Imitate Jesus and Socrates.

My intention being to acquire the *Habitude* of all these Virtues, I judg'd it would be well not to distract my Attention by attempting the whole at once, but to fix it on one of them at a time, and when I should be Master of that, then to proceed to another, and so on till I should have gone thro' the thirteen. And as the previous Acquisition of some might facilitate the Acquisition of certain others, I arrang'd them with that View as they stand above. *Temperance* first, as it tends to procure that Coolness and Clearness of Head, which is so necessary where constant Vigilance was to be kept up, and Guard maintained, against the unremitting Attraction of ancient Habits, and the Force of perpetual Temptations. This being acquir'd and establish'd, *Silence* would be more easy, and my Desire being to gain Knowledge at the same time that I improv'd in Virtue, and considering that in Conversation it was obtain'd rather by the Use of the Ears than of the Tongue, and therefore wishing to break a Habit I was getting into of Prattling, Punning and Joking, which only made me acceptable to trifling Company, I gave *Silence* the second Place. This, and the next, *Order*, I expected would allow me more Time for attending to my Project and my Studies; RESOLUTION once become habitual, would keep me firm in my Endeavors to obtain all the subsequent Virtues; *Frugality* and *Industry*, by freeing me from my remaining Debt, and producing Affluence and Independance would make more easy the Practice of *Sincerity* and *Justice*, etc. etc. Conceiving then that agreable to the Advice of Pythagoras in his Golden Verses, daily examination would be necessary, I contriv'd the following Method for conducting that Examination.

I made a little Book in which I allotted a Page for each of the Virtues. I rul'd each Page with red Ink so as to have seven Columns, one for each Day of the Week, marking each Column with a Letter for the Day. I cross'd these Columns with thirteen red Lines, marking the Beginning of each Line with the first Letter of one of the Virtues, on which Line and in its proper Column I might mark by a little black Spot every Fault I found upon Examination, to have been committed respecting that Virtue upon that Day.

TEMPERANCE						
Eat not to Dulness. Drink not to Elevation.						
	S	M	T	W	T	F	S

	S	M	T	W	T	F	S
T							
S	••	•		•		•	
O	•	•	•		•	•	•
R			•			•	
F		•			•		
I			•				
S							
J							
M							
Cl.							
T							
Ch.							
H							

I determined to give a Week's strict Attention to each of the Virtues successively. Thus in the first Week my great Guard was to avoid every the least Offence against Temperance, leaving the other Virtues to their ordinary Chance, only marking every Evening the faults of the Day. Thus if in the first Week I could keep my first Line marked T clear of Spots, I suppos'd the Habit of that Virtue so much strengthen'd and its opposite weaken'd, that I might venture extending my Attention to include the next, and for the following Week keep both Lines clear of Spots. Proceeding thus to the last, I could go thro' a Course compleat in Thirteen Weeks, and four Courses in a Year. And like him who having a Garden to weed, does not attempt to eradicate all the bad Herbs at once, which would exceed his Reach and his Strength, but works on one of the Beds at a time, and having accomplish'd the first proceeds to a second; so I should have, (I hoped) the encouraging Pleasure of seeing on my Pages the Progress I made in Virtue, by clearing successively my Lines of their Spots, till in the End by a Number of Courses.

I should be happy in viewing a clean Book after a thirteen Weeks daily Examination. . . .

Possibilities for Writing

1. Revise, reorder, and supplement Franklin's list of practical virtues as a guide for contemporary college students. Why do you make any changes that you do?

2. Compare Franklin's program for self-improvement with contemporary self-improvement books found in the advice section of a bookstore. To what extent are the values expressed similiar and different?

3. Franklin's goal here is not just moral behavior but moral "perfection." Why do you think so few people today believe in such perfection?

William Hazlitt *(1778–1830), one of the most popular writers of his day,
worked during his early years as a journalist and theatrical critic for a variety
of London publications. Later in life, he was particularly noted for his writings
on the history of English literature in such collections as* Characters of
Shakespeare's Plays *(1817),* Lectures on the English Comic Writers *(1819),
and* Dramatic Literature of the Age of Elizabeth *(1820). But Hazlitt is best
remembered today for his many and varied personal essays: witty,
sophisticated, and highly graceful meditations on a variety of subjects ranging
from the grand to the homely.*

William Hazlitt
On the Pleasure of Hating

In "On the Pleasure of Hating," William Hazlitt catalogues the many ways
human beings express and act out their anger and antipathy toward other
creatures and toward one another. Hazlitt explores the reasons why hatred and
its associated feelings fascinate and excite us. In the process Hazlitt shows
people to be nasty, mean-spirited, and vengeful, enjoying the suffering of others
as idle amusement.

Hazlitt's long paragraphs are replete with instances of humanity's splenetic
nature and habits. He piles on example upon example, from our fear of and
disgust with insects and spiders to our fascination with disasters such as fires,
our cruelty toward those different from ourselves, and our eagerness to
maintain old animosities and hostilities whose original causes are long buried in
history. According to Hazlitt, we even enjoy hating our old friends, amusing
ourselves with their weaknesses and eccentricities. He writes, "We grow tired of
every thing but turning others into ridicule, and congratulating ourselves on
their defects."

There is a spider crawling along the matted floor of the room where I sit
(not the one which has been so well allegorised in the admirable *Lines
to a Spider*, but another of the same edifying breed); he runs with heedless, hurried haste, he hobbles awkwardly towards me, he stops—he
sees the giant shadow before him, and, at a loss whether to retreat or
proceed, meditates his huge foe—but as I do not start up and seize upon
the straggling caitiff, as he would upon a hapless fly within his toils, he
takes heart, and ventures on with mingled cunning, impudence, and
fear. As he passes me, I lift up the matting to assist his escape, am glad
to get rid of the unwelcome intruder, and shudder at the recollection
after he is gone. A child, a woman, a clown, or a moralist a century ago,

would have crushed the little reptile to death—my philosophy has got beyond that—I bear the creature no ill-will, but still I hate the very sight of it. The spirit of malevolence survives the practical exertion of it. We learn to curb our will and keep our overt actions within the bounds of humanity, long before we can subdue our sentiments and imaginations to the same mild tone. We give up the external demonstration, the *brute* violence, but cannot part with the essence or principle of hostility. We do not tread upon the poor little animal in question (that seems barbarous and pitiful!) but we regard it with a sort of mystic horror and superstitious loathing. It will ask another hundred years of fine writing and hard thinking to cure us of the prejudice, and make us feel towards this ill-omened tribe with something of "the milk of human kindness," instead of their own shyness and venom.

Nature seems (the more we look into it) made up of antipathies: without something to hate, we should lose the very spring of thought and action. Life would turn to a stagnant pool, were it not ruffled by the jarring interests, the unruly passions, of men. The white streak in our own fortunes is brightened (or just rendered visible) by making all around it as dark as possible; so the rainbow paints its form upon the cloud. Is it pride? Is it envy? Is it the force of contrast? Is it weakness or malice? But so it is, that there is a secret affinity [with], a *hankering* after, evil in the human mind, and that it takes a perverse, but a fortunate delight in mischief, since it is a never-failing source of satisfaction. Pure good soon grows insipid, wants variety and spirit. Pain is a bittersweet, which never surfeits. Love turns, with a little indulgence, to indifference or disgust: hatred alone is immortal. Do we not see this principle at work everywhere? Animals torment and worry one another without mercy: children kill flies for sport: every one reads the accidents and offences in a newspaper as the cream of the jest: a whole town runs to be present at a fire, and the spectator by no means exults to see it extinguished. It is better to have it so, but it diminishes the interest; and our feelings take part with our passions rather than with our understandings. Men assemble in crowds, with eager enthusiasm, to witness a tragedy: but if there were an execution going forward in the next street, as Mr. Burke observes, the theatre would be left empty. A strange cur in a village, an idiot, a crazy woman, are set upon and baited by the whole community. Public nuisances are in the nature of public benefits. How long did the Pope, the Bourbons, and the Inquisition keep the people of

England in breath, and supply them with nicknames to vent their spleen upon! Had they done us any harm of late? No: but we have always a quantity of superfluous bile upon the stomach, and we wanted an object to let it out upon. How loth were we to give up our pious belief in ghosts and witches, because we liked to persecute the one, and frighten ourselves to death with the other! It is not the quality so much as the quantity of excitement that we are anxious about: we cannot bear a state of indifference and *ennui:* the mind seems to abhor a *vacuum* as much as ever nature was supposed to do. Even when the spirit of the age (that is, the progress of intellectual refinement, warring with our natural infirmities) no longer allows us to carry our vindictive and headstrong humours into effect, we try to revive them in description, and keep up the old bugbears, the phantoms of our terror and our hate, in imagination. We burn Guy Fawx in effigy, and the hooting and buffeting and maltreating that poor tattered figure of rags and straw makes a festival in every village in England once a year. Protestants and Papists do not now burn one another at the stake: but we subscribe to new editions of Fox's *Book of Martyrs;* and the secret of the success of the *Scotch Novels* is much the same—they carry us back to the feuds, the heart-burnings, the havoc, the dismay, the wrongs, and the revenge of a barbarous age and people—to the rooted prejudices and deadly animosities of sects and parties in politics and religion, and of contending chiefs and clans in war and intrigue. We feel the full force of the spirit of hatred with all of them in turn. As we read, we throw aside the trammels of civilization, the flimsy veil of humanity. "Off, you lendings!" The wild beast resumes its sway within us, we feel like hunting-animals, and as the hound starts in his sleep and rushes on the chase in fancy, the heart rouses itself in its native lair, and utters a wild cry of joy, at being restored once more to freedom and lawless, unrestrained impulses. Every one has his full swing, or goes to the Devil his own way. Here are no Jeremy Bentham Panopticons, none of Mr. Owen's impassable Parallelograms (Rob Roy would have spurned and poured a thousand curses on them), no long calculations of self-interest—the will takes its instant way to its object, as the mountain-torrent flings itself over the precipice: the greatest possible good of each individual consists in doing all the mischief he can to his neighbour: that is charming, and finds a sure and sympathetic chord in every breast! So Mr. Irving, the celebrated preacher, has rekindled the old, original, almost exploded hell-fire in the aisles of the Caledonian Chapel, as they introduce the real water of the New River at Sadler's Wells, to the delight and astonishment of his fair audience. *'Tis pretty, though a plague,* to sit and peep into the pit of Tophet, to play at *snap-dragon* with flames and brimstone (it gives a smart electrical shock, a lively filip to delicate constitutions), and to see Mr. Irving, like a huge Titan, looking as grim and swarthy as if he had to forge tortures for all the damned! What a strange being man is! Not content with doing all he can to vex and hurt his fellows here, "upon this bank and shoal of time," where one would think there were heartaches, pain, disappointment, anguish, tears, sighs, and groans enough, the bigoted maniac takes him to the top of the high peak of school divinity to hurl him down the yawning gulf of penal fire; his speculative malice asks eternity to wreak its infinite spite in, and calls on the Almighty to execute its relentless doom! The cannibals burn their enemies and eat them in good-fellowship with one another: meek Christian divines cast those who differ from them but a hair's-breadth, body and soul into hell-fire for the glory of God and the good of His creatures! It is well that the power of such persons is not co-ordinate with their wills: indeed, it is from the sense of their weakness and inability to control the opinions of others, that they thus "outdo termagant," and endeavour to frighten them into conformity by big words and monstrous denunciations.

The pleasure of hating, like a poisonous mineral, eats into the heart of religion, and turns it to rankling spleen and bigotry; it makes patriotism an excuse for carrying fire, pestilence, and famine into other lands: it leaves to virtue nothing but the spirit of censoriousness, and a narrow, jealous, inquisitorial watchfulness over the actions and motives of others. What have the different sects, creeds, doctrines in religion been but so many pretexts set up for men to wrangle, to quarrel, to tear one another in pieces about, like a target as a mark to shoot at? Does any one suppose that the love of country in an Englishman implies any friendly feeling or disposition to serve another bearing the same name? No, it means only hatred to the French or the inhabitants of any other country that we happen to be at war with for the time. Does the love of virtue denote any wish to discover or amend our own faults? No, but it atones for an obstinate adherence to our own vices by the most virulent intolerance to human frailties. This principle is of a most universal application. It extends to good as well as evil: if it makes us hate folly, it makes us no less dissatisfied with distinguished merit. If it inclines us to resent the wrongs of others, it impels us to be as impatient of their prosperity. We revenge injuries: we repay benefits with ingratitude. Even our strongest partialities and likings soon take this turn. "That which was luscious as locusts, anon becomes bitter as coloquintida;" and love and friendship melt in their own fires. We hate old friends: we hate old books: we hate old opinions; and at last we come to hate ourselves.

I have observed that few of those whom I have formerly known most intimate, continue on the same friendly footing, or combine the steadiness with the warmth of attachment. I have been acquainted with two or three knots of inseparable companions, who saw each other "six days in the week," that have broken up and dispersed. I have quarrelled with almost all my old friends, (they might say this is owing to my bad temper, but) they have also quarrelled with one another. What is become of "that set of whist-players," celebrated by ELIA in his notable *Epistle to Robert Southey, Esq.* (and now I think of it—that I myself have celebrated in this very volume) "that for so many years called Admiral Burney friend? They are scattered, like last year's snow. Some of them are dead, or gone to live at a distance, or pass one another in the street like strangers, or if they stop to speak, do it as coolly and try to *cut* one another as soon as possible." Some of us have grown rich, others poor. Some have got places under Government, others a *niche* in the *Quarterly Review.* Some of us have dearly earned a name in the world; whilst others remain in their original privacy. We despise the one, and envy and are glad to mortify the other. Times are changed; we cannot revive our old feelings; and we avoid the sight, and are uneasy in the presence of, those who remind us of our infirmity, and put us upon an effort at seeming cordiality which embarrasses ourselves, and does not impose upon our *quondam* associates. Old friendships are like meats served up repeatedly, cold, comfortless, and distasteful, The stomach turns against them. Either constant intercourse and familiarity breed weariness and contempt; or, if we meet again after an interval of absence, we appear no longer the same. One is too wise, another too foolish, for us; and we wonder we did not find this out before. We are disconcerted and kept in a state of continual alarm by the wit of one, or tired to death of the dullness of another. The *good things* of the first (besides leaving stings behind them) by repetition grow stale, and lose their startling effect; and the insipidity of the last becomes intolerable. The most amusing or

instructive companion is at best like a favourite volume, that we wish
after a time to *lay upon the shelf*; but as our friends are not willing to be
laid there, this produces a misunderstanding and ill-blood between us.
Or if the zeal and integrity of friendship is not abated, [n]or its career
interrupted by any obstacle arising out of its own nature, we look out
for other subjects of complaint and sources of dissatisfaction. We begin
to criticize each other's dress, looks, and general character. "Such a one
is a pleasant fellow, but it is a pity he sits so late!" Another fails to keep
his appointments, and that is a sore that never heals. We get acquainted
with some fashionable young men or with a mistress, and wish to introduce our friend; but he is awkward and a sloven, the interview does not
answer, and this throws cold water on our intercourse. Or he makes
himself obnoxious to opinion; and we shrink from our own convictions
on the subject as an excuse for not defending him. All or any of these
causes mount up in time to a ground of coolness or irritation; and at last
they break out into open violence as the only amends we can make ourselves for suppressing them so long, or the readiest means of banishing
recollections of former kindness so little compatible with our present
feelings. We may try to tamper with the wounds or patch up the carcase
of departed friendship; but the one will hardly bear the handling, and
the other is not worth the trouble of embalming! The only way to be
reconciled to old friends is to part with them for good: at a distance we
may chance to be thrown back (in a waking dream) upon old times and
old feelings: or at any rate we should not think of renewing our intimacy, till we have fairly *spit our spite*, or said, thought, and felt all the
ill we can of each other. Or if we can pick a quarrel with some one else,
and make him the scape-goat, this is an excellent contrivance to heal a
broken bone. I think I must be friends with Lamb again, since he has
written that magnanimous Letter to Southey, and told him a piece of his
mind! I don't know what it is that attaches me to H——— so much,
except that he and I, whenever we meet, sit in judgment on another set
of old friends, and "carve them as a dish fit for the Gods." There was
L[eigh] [Hunt], John Scott, Mrs. [Montagu], whose dark raven locks
make a picturesque background to our discourse, B———, who is
grown fat, and is, they say, married, R[ickman]; these had all separated
long ago, and their foibles are the common link that holds us together.
We do not affect to condole or whine over their follies; we enjoy, we
laugh at them, till we are ready to burst our sides, "*sans* intermission,

for hours by the dial." We serve up a course of anecdotes, *traits*, master-strokes of character, and cut and hack at them till we are weary. Perhaps some of them are even with us. For my own part, as I once said, I like a friend the better for having faults that one can talk about. "Then," said Mrs. [Montagu], "you will never cease to be a philanthro-pist!" Those in question were some of the choice-spirits of the age, not "fellows of no mark or likelihood"; and we so far did them justice: but it is well they did not hear what we sometimes said of them. I care little what any one says of me, particularly behind my back, and in the way of critical and analytical discussion: it is looks of dislike and scorn that I answer with the worst venom of my pen. The expression of the face wounds me more than the expressions of the tongue. If I have in one instance mistaken this expression, or resorted to this remedy where I ought not, I am sorry for it. But the face was too fine over which it man-tled, and I am too old to have misunderstood it! . . . I sometimes go up to ———'s; and as often as I do, resolve never to go again. I do not find the old homely welcome. The ghost of friendship meets me at the door, and sits with me all dinner-time. They have got a set of fine notions and new acquaintance. Allusions to past occurrences are thought trivial, nor is it always safe to touch upon more general subjects. M. does not begin as he formerly did every five minutes, "Fawcett used to say," &c. That topic is something worn. The girls are grown up, and have a thousand accomplishments. I perceive there is a jealousy on both sides. They think I give myself airs, and I fancy the same of them. Every time I am asked, "If I do not think Mr. Washington Irving a very fine writer?" I shall not go again till I receive an invitation for Christmas Day in com-pany with Mr. Liston. The only intimacy I never found to flinch or fade was a purely intellectual one. There was none of the cant of candour in it, none of the whine of mawkish sensibility. Our mutual acquaintance were considered merely as subjects of conversation and knowledge, not at all of affection. We regarded them no more in our experiments than "mice in an air-pump:" or like malefactors, they were regularly cut down and given over to the dissecting-knife. We spared neither friend nor foe. We sacrificed human infirmities at the shrine of truth. The skeletons of character might be seen, after the juice was extracted, dangling in the air like flies in cobwebs: or they were kept for future inspection in some refined acid. The demonstration was as beautiful as it was new. There is no surfeiting on gall: nothing keeps so well as a decoction of spleen. We grow tired of every thing but turning others into ridicule, and congratulating ourselves on their defects.

We take a dislike to our favourite books, after a time, for the same reason. We cannot read the same works for ever. Our honey-moon, even though we wed the Muse, must come to an end; and is followed by indifference, if not by disgust. There are some works, those indeed that produce the most striking effect at first by novelty and boldness of outline, that will not bear reading twice: others of a less extravagant character, and that excite and repay attention by a greater nicety of details, have hardly interest enough to keep alive our continued enthusiasm. The popularity of the most successful writers operates to wean us from them, by the cant and fuss that is made about them, by hearing their names everlastingly repeated, and by the number of ignorant and indiscriminate admirers they draw after them:—we as little like to have to drag others from their unmerited obscurity, lest we should be exposed to the charge of affectation and singularity of taste. There is nothing to be said respecting an author that all the world have made up their minds about: it is a thankless as well as hopeless task to recommend one that nobody has ever heard of. To cry up Shakespear as the god of our idolatry, seems like a vulgar national prejudice: to take down a volume of Chaucer, or Spenser, or Beaumont and Fletcher, or Ford, or Marlowe, has very much the look of pedantry and egotism. I confess it makes me hate the very name of Fame and Genius, when works like these are "gone into the wastes of time," while each successive generation of fools is busily employed in reading the trash of the day, and women of fashion gravely join with their waiting-maids in discussing the preference between the *Paradise Lost* and Mr. Moore's *Loves of the Angels.* I was pleased the other day on going into a shop to ask, "If they had any of the *Scotch Novels?*" to be told—"That they had just sent out the last, *Sir Andrew Wylie!*"—Mr. Galt will also be pleased with this answer! The reputation of some books is raw and *unaired:* that of others is worm-eaten and mouldy. Why fix our affections on that which we cannot bring ourselves to have faith in, or which others have long ceased to trouble themselves about? I am half afraid to look into *Tom Jones,* lest it should not answer my expectations at this time of day; and if it did not, I should certainly be disposed to fling it into the fire, and never look into another novel while I lived. But surely, it may be said, there are some works that, like nature, can never grow

old; and that must always touch the imagination and passions alike! Or
there are passages that seem as if we might brood over them all our
lives, and not exhaust the sentiments of love and admiration they
excite: they become favourites, and we are fond of them to a sort of
dotage. Here is one:

> —"Sitting in my window
> Printing my thoughts in lawn, I saw a god,
> I thought (but it was you), enter our gates;
> My blood flew out and back again, as fast
> As I had puffed it forth and sucked it in
> Like breath; then was I called away in haste
> To entertain you: never was a man
> Thrust from a sheepcote to a sceptre, raised
> So high in thoughts as I; you left a kiss
> Upon these lips then, which I mean to keep
> From you for ever. I did hear you talk
> Far above singing!"

A passage like this, indeed, leaves a taste on the palate like nectar,
and we seem in reading it to sit with the Gods at their golden tables: but
if we repeat it often in ordinary moods, it loses its flavour, becomes
vapid, "the wine of *poetry* is drank, and but the lees remain." Or, on the
other hand, if we call in the aid of extraordinary circumstances to set it
off to advantage, as the reciting it to a friend, or after having our feelings excited by a long walk in some romantic situation, or while we

> —"play with Amaryllis in the shade,
> Or with the tangles of Neaera's hair"—

we afterwards miss the accompanying circumstances, and instead of
transferring the recollection of them to the favourable side, regret what
we have lost, and strive in vain to bring back "the irrevocable hour"—
wondering in some instances how we survive it, and at the melancholy
blank that is left behind! The pleasure rises to its height in some moment
of calm solitude or intoxicating sympathy, declines ever after, and from
the comparison and a conscious falling-off, leaves rather a sense of sati-
ety and irksomeness behind it. . . . "Is it the same in pictures?" I confess
it is, with all but those from Titian's hand. I don't know why, but an
air breathes from his landscapes, pure, refreshing, as if it came from
other years; there is a look in his faces that never passes away. I saw
one the other day. Amidst the heartless desolation and glittering finery

of Fonthill, there is a portfolio of the Dresden Gallery. It opens, and a young female head looks from it; a child, yet woman grown; with an air of rustic innocence and the graces of a princess, her eyes like those of doves, the lips about to open, a smile of pleasure dimpling the whole face, the jewels sparkling in her crisped hair, her youthful shape compressed in a rich antique dress, as the bursting leaves contain the April buds! Why do I not call up this image of gentle sweetness, and place it as a perpetual barrier between mischance and me?—It is because pleasure asks a greater effort of the mind to support it than pain; and we turn after a little idle dalliance from what we love to what we hate!

As to my old opinions, I am heartily sick of them. I have reason, for they have deceived me sadly. I was taught to think, and I was willing to believe, that genius was not a bawd, that virtue was not a mask, that liberty was not a name, that love had its seat in the human heart. Now I would care little if these words were struck out of the dictionary, or if I had never heard them. They are become to my ears a mockery and a dream. Instead of patriots and friends of freedom, I see nothing but the tyrant and the slave, the people linked with kings to rivet on the chains of despotism and superstition. I see folly join with knavery, and together make up public spirit and public opinions. I see the insolent Tory, the blind Reformer, the coward Whig! If mankind had wished for what is right, they might have had it long ago. The theory is plain enough; but they are prone to mischief, "to every good work reprobate." I have seen all that had been done by the mighty yearnings of the spirit and intellect of men, "of whom the world was not worthy," and that promised a proud opening to truth and good through the vista of future years, undone by one man, with just glimmering of understanding enough to feel that he was a king, but not to comprehend how he could be king of a free people! I have seen this triumph celebrated by poets, the friends of my youth and the friends of man, but who were carried away by the infuriate tide that, setting in from a throne, bore down every distinction of right reason before it; and I have seen all those who did not join in applauding this insult and outrage on humanity proscribed, hunted down (they and their friends made a byword of), so that it has become an understood thing that no one can live by his talents or knowledge who is not ready to prostitute those talents and that knowledge to betray his species, and prey upon his fellowman. "This was some time a mystery: but the time gives evidence of it." The echoes of liberty had awakened once more in Spain, and the morning of human hope dawned again: but that dawn has been overcast by the foul breath of bigotry, and those reviving sounds stifled by fresh cries from the time-rent towers of the Inquisition—man yielding (as it is fit he should) first to brute force, but more to the innate perversity and dastard spirit of his own nature which leaves no room for farther hope or disappointment. And England, that arch-reformer, that heroic deliverer, that mouther about liberty, and tool of power, stands gaping by, not feeling the blight and mildew coming over it, nor its very bones crack and turn to a paste under the grasp and circling folds of this new monster, Legitimacy! In private life do we not see hypocrisy, servility, selfishness, folly, and impudence succeed, while modesty shrinks from the encounter, and merit is trodden under foot? How often is "the rose plucked from the forehead of a virtuous love to plant a blister there!" What chance is there of the success of real passion? What certainty of its continuance? Seeing all this as I do, and unravelling the web of human life into its various threads of meanness, spite, cowardice, want of feeling, and want of understanding, of indifference towards others, and ignorance of ourselves—seeing custom prevail over all excellence, itself giving way to infamy—mistaken as I have been in my public and private hopes, calculating others from myself, and calculating wrong; always disappointed where I placed most reliance; the dupe of friendship, and the fool of love;—have I not reason to hate and to despise myself? Indeed I do; and chiefly for not having hated and despised the world enough.

Possibilities for Writing

1. As expressed here, are Hazlitt's views those of a pessimist, a realist, or something in between? How do you respond to the writer's views of hating?
2. "Hating" takes on a variety of meanings here, some more intense than others. Explore these various meanings, using examples from the text to explain your reasoning.
3. Pick a passage or two from Hazlitt's essay that you find relevant to contemporary life and write an essay exploring its implications for the world today.

Michael Hogan (b. 1943) was born in Newport, Rhode Island. He is the author of fourteen books of fiction, poetry, and nonficion, including Teaching from the Heart, *a collection of his essays and speeches, and the seminal work on the Irish Soldiers in the Mexican War of 1846–1848. His poetry and prose have been published in such literary magazines as* The Paris Review, *the* Harvard Review, *the* Iowa Review, *and the* American Poetry Review. *He is the recipient of numerous awards, including the NEA Creative Writing Fellowship and two Puschcart Prizes. He lives in Guadalajara, Mexico, with the well-known textile artist Lucinda Mayo.*

Michael Hogan
The Colonel

In "The Colonel," Michael Hogan describes his experiences in watching, learning, and playing tennis from his boyhood years into late middle age. Hogan's essay focuses on an army colonel, whose war stories induced the twelve-year-old Hogan to give up the pleasures of baseball, football, and basketball for the rigors of tennis. Colonel Flack taught the young Hogan not only the rudiments of the game, but also important lessons about sportsmanship, competitiveness, courage, and grace.

Hogan conveys these and other lessons about the discipline of the game in a clear, direct, and graceful style, which echoes the way he plays the game. And he suggests that played over a lifetime with diligence, passion, and attentive devotion, tennis can make a difference in a person's quality of life, a difference for which Hogan expresses "a sure sense of gratitude."

Tennis is so popular these days and so much a part of the average teenager's sports experience, that it is difficult for most of them to imagine a time when it was not. Yet, in the post–war period and the Fifties of my childhood, tennis was considered more a rich man's sport played at country clubs and exclusive resorts. Competitive singles was largely a sport of the male sex and, although women had been competing for years at Wimbledon and other international venues, most were amateurs and the few professionals who did compete got paid so little it was laughable. It wasn't until Billie Jean King's assertiveness in 1967 and the Virginia Slim tournaments of the 1970s that the sport opened up for generations of Chris Everts and Steffi Grafs, and finally grew to include million-dollar players like Venus Williams who changed the sport forever making it the dream of every athletic boy and girl.

The courts in my hometown of Newport, RI, were mostly off-limits to working class kids like me. The excellent grass center courts and the red clay courts of the private Newport Casino where the National Doubles Championships were held, were open only to wealthy members who paid a hefty annual fee. The courts at the Newport Country Club were restricted to those few rich families who were members, as were those at the even more exclusive Bailey's Beach. At the Brenton Village navy facility inside Fort Adams there were courts for officers and their dependents but these were not accessible to locals. Both composition and clay courts were available at Salve Regina College but only for registered students and faculty. So that left two casually-maintained asphalt courts at the city park on Carroll Avenue where during the summer, students home from college would bang away in lusty volleys and dominate the courts in rugged comradery.

A twelve-year-old working at a summer job, I had little interest in tennis. To me, pickup games of basketball and football were more fun and interesting. I played both at the Carroll Street Park and at the YMCA, and in the prolonged light of New England summer evenings practicing shots alone in the backyard with a hoop hung from the front of the garage. As fall approached and football season began, I'd play touch games with my friends and rougher tackle games with boys from uptown in the same park that abutted the tennis area. On occasion we might glance over at the courts if a particular cute coed was playing doubles. Sometimes we would head over to the water fountains close by to get a drink and watch a game or two. "Love-fifteen. Love-thirty. Deuce." We had no idea what this absurd scoring method could signify. It was remote from our experience, as were the crisp white shorts, the spotless tennis shoes, and the white sports shirts which were *de rigueur* in those days. We were ragamuffins, I suppose; heady youth, and tennis seemed effete, subtle, complex and sophisticated—more like an elaborate dance than a sport, a dance to which we would never be invited.

So, it came as a surprise to me when an Army colonel who lived up the street from us began talking about tennis one day with my Dad. "Does the boy play?" I heard him ask. "No," my Dad said, "but he loves sports and plays basketball, baseball, football." "Well," replied the Colonel, "if he ever wants a lesson tell him to stop by. I was an Army champion in my day."

Later my Dad would mention it, and when I replied that I thought it was a sissy game, he would begin to tell me of some of the great players of the day: Poncho Gonzalez, Jack Kramer, Ken Rosewell, but the names meant little to me. But I did like the old Colonel who had great stories to tell about the War which was not too distant in memory. My father's brother Harry had died in the forests of Belgium in 1944 during the last German push. A Little League baseball field in our neighborhood carried his name. War games in the local hills were still very much a part of our youthful pastimes. So, on a Saturday afternoon, home from a half day's labor at my summer job with a landscape company, I stopped by to talk to the Colonel. When the subject turned to tennis, his eyes lit up as he described the competition he faced in college and in the service. He regaled me with stories of tournaments, matches with famous players, games played at officer clubs in remote parts of the world. He said, "Tennis is the one game that, once you learn it, you will be able to play for the rest of your life. When your knees go out and you can't play football, when there is no gang of boys around for the pickup game of basketball or baseball, you can always find someone to play tennis with." So he convinced me. Or, perhaps it was his enthusiasm, my love for his stories and respect for his retired rank, his war experiences, or his genial personality and his enthusiasm, that I just felt I didn't want to disappoint. However it was, we agreed.

He loaned me one of his wooden rackets in its complicated screw-down press and the following day, right after early mass on a Sunday morning, he began teaching me the basics. In between suggestions about how to hold the racket and how to volley, he lectured me on the history of the sport, taught me how to score, how to adjust the net, how to anticipate the ball, how to refrain from cussing or displaying untoward emotional behavior. I think he probably bought me my first set of tennis whites that summer as well, although the first few games I'm sure I played in T-shirt and Levi cutoffs much to his distaste. That July was my thirteenth birthday and my father bought me my own racket, a Bancroft wood—expensive, highly polished and tightly strung with catgut and protected in a standard wooden press with butterfly screw-downs. The racket would be re-strung many times over the four years that I owned it. I would play with it in local matches, city tournaments, and even one memorable morning at the Newport Casino, where I got to volley with Poncho Gonzalez on the grass center court, courtesy of my father who owned a business next door and had persuaded the famous champion to trade a few strokes with his son.

The Colonel was, I suppose, in his mid-sixties which seemed ancient to me then. I could not imagine, as I improved in my tennis skills, and learned to volley deep, hit cross-court passing shots and top-spin lobs, that he would be able to keep up with me. Surely, the student would outplay the master any day now. But it never happened. Colonel Flack had a whole repertoire of moves; drop shots, slices, topspin backhands, corkscrew serves, and high-bouncing serves which just cut the end of the line. He knew the angles and limits of the court and, comfortable with these absorbed geometries, kept his young opponent racing from the net to the baseline, ragged and breathless.

As the summer passed, I improved, the muscles on my right forearm grew oversized, my lung capacity deepened, and my strokes improved from the gradual anticipation of the slides and twists that the ball would take as it came off the Colonel's racket. My service improved as well, so that I sometimes caught him wrong-footed and could come to the net quickly and put the ball away. I still didn't win a set but the games were closer and I noticed the Colonel was flushed and winded more and more often.

We played less the following year as I found new and younger competition among military dependants, boys from De La Salle Academy, and returning college players. I was often on the courts for hours each evening and on the weekends. With only two courts to play on, you had to win to keep the court and I was often a winner. Sometimes I would generously concede to play mixed doubles with couples who were waiting patiently on the sidelines.

Then one afternoon, shortly after my fourteenth birthday, all of that changed. A new boy appeared on the block; redheaded, cocky, with an easy confidence and grace and a powerful serve that could knock a poorly-gripped racket clear out of your hand. Tommy Gallagher was a compact, good-looking Irish boy who appeared from nowhere and had all the natural moves of a champion. I was blown off the court again and again in swift, blurred games of intense ferocity. I began to learn the difference between a "club player" as opposed to a "show player" or competitive athlete. Tommy played like he was born to it. There was nothing you could hit to him that he could not return. When I tried to play his game he beat me ruthlessly, contemptuously, as if I were wasting his time.

On one of those occasions, the semifinals of a citywide tournament, Colonel Flack was in the audience. Shamed by the 6–1, 6–0 defeat, I did not look him in the eye as I retreated back to the bench. "I'm not going to try and console you, Mike," he said. "You got sent to hell and back by that lad. And if you play him again, he'll beat you again. He's one of these kids who's a natural. But don't let him take away your pleasure in the game; don't let him do that to you. You're a club player and a decent one. Play your own game, take the shots you can, don't get caught up in his game. And don't be intimidated."

I was to play Tommy Gallagher several times over the next two years. He beat me, as he beat most of his competitors, but he won less easily as time went by, and never with the contemptuous indifference I had felt in that one semifinal. More importantly, losing to him did not take away from me the love of the game or my sense of myself as a player. Partly this was true because Colonel Flack and I returned to our early morning volleys interspersed with lessons. But now the lessons had more to do with eliminating distractions, watching the ball, and feeling the sun, the sweat on my skin, the slight breeze from the ocean, hearing the thwock of the perfectly hit ball coming off the strings. He taught me to be totally present in the moment, totally aware, totally focused.

He also trained me to go after every ball regardless of whether it seemed returnable or not. He taught me to play according to my skill level, placing shots carefully, not overhitting because of a desire to put it away like a pro, but stroking with the steady grace and pressure of a good club player who often tires out his more ambitious, more aggressive opponent.

Finally, he taught me that graciousness is what saves the game from savagery and ugliness. He instructed me not to give in to the temptation to call a ball out when it was in, to always give the opponent the benefit of the doubt, and that it was better to lose than to win unfairly. He reminded me to hold my temper in check, to always be polite, to return the balls in a single bounce to the server when there was no one to fetch balls.

But what he couldn't teach me and what I learned for myself over the years was that all of this was a gift. Tennis would change with the Australian 100 mph serves of Rod Laver, the aluminum and then titanium rackets, the oversized head rackets, with Wilson and Adidas logos covering every piece of equipment and raiment. Bad boys like John McEnroe would cuss out line judges and umpires, as aggressiveness had its day and then subsided ... though never completely. Competitive tennis would be enshrined in every high school and university; tennis camps would groom a new generation of players like Pete Sampras and Andre Agassi intent on making millions as they made their mark in the sport. Still, I would go right on playing my 3.5 club-level game. I would play tennis in the dry heat of the Sonoran deserts of Tucson and on the mile-high courts of Denver. I would play in Argentina and Panama. I would play after clearing the debris off a hurricane-littered court in Florida; I would hit the low-bounce ball while bundled in a jacket in up-state New York after sweeping off the snow-covered court, and—year after year—I would sweat through grueling sets in the tropical heat of May in Guadalajara. I would play through days of political unrest and assassination in my twenties, through the bitter, rancorous divorce in my thirties, through the crushing death of a beloved child in my forties, then through uncertain days of financial disasters and overseas currency devaluations in my fifties.

Now here I am in my sixties, approaching inexorably the age of my mentor, Colonel Flack, who on a summer morning took a skinny twelve-year old out to the concrete courts of a seaside town to give him the gift of lifelong victory. It is a way of maintaining both physical and psychological fitness, but also a way of moving through life with a focus, with grace and a sure sense of gratitude. One of those ineffable spiritual gifts which continue to give again and again when I walk on to a sun-speckled court, go over to measure the net with my "stick" (a Wilson H-26 titanium racket), and all the world narrows down to the clear geometries of the white lines, to the sound of the thwock as the ball hits the strings, as my muscles respond again in their dependable way to the known rhythms of the game, and everything is suddenly whole and perfect, and the world completely intelligible.

Possibilities for Writing

1. Write a brief character sketch of Colonel Flack. Try to convey a sense of the colonel as a man and as a teacher.
2. Summarize the lessons Hogan learned from the colonel. To what extent do you think that these lessons are valuable for life as well as for tennis? Explain.
3. Write an essay about a sport, game, hobby, or other leisure pursuit for which you have a passion. Explain how you became involved in it and what values it holds for you.

Langston Hughes (1902–1967) was born in Joplin, Missouri, to a prominent African-American family. Interested in poetry from childhood, he attended Columbia University as an engineering major but dropped out after his first year to pursue his literary aspirations (he later graduated from Lincoln University). Spurred by the flourishing of black artists known as the Harlem Renaissance, he quickly found a distinctive voice that reflected the culture of everyday life, and he had published his first works before he was out of his teens. Hughes is best known for his poetry, which often employs vernacular language and jazz-like rhythms, but he also wrote popular works of fiction, essays, plays, books for children, and several volumes of autobiography, including The Big Sea *(1940), focusing on his childhood and teenage years.*

Langston Hughes

Salvation

In "Salvation," Hughes describes a memorable incident from his youth, one that had a decisive impact on his view of the world. In the span of just a few pages, Hughes tells a story of faith and doubt, of belief and disbelief, of how he was "saved from sin" when he was going on thirteen. "But not really saved." This paradoxical opening to "Salvation" establishes a tension that characterizes the essay, which culminates in an ironic reversal of expectations for the reader, and a life-altering realization for Hughes.

The power of Hughes's "Salvation" derives not only from its language, but also from the irony of its action, as well as its blend of humor and sadness, the humor of the child's literal understanding of what his aunt tells him to expect, and the sadness of his disappointed belief, which ironically, turns against itself. In restricting the point-of-view to that of a twelve-year-old child, Hughes enhances the credibility of his narrative and increases its dramatic power. His concluding paragraph is a quietly resounding tour-de-force of irony and epiphany.

I was saved from sin when I was going on thirteen. But not really saved. It happened like this. There was a big revival at my Auntie Reed's church. Every night for weeks there had been much preaching, singing, praying, and shouting, and some very hardened sinners had been brought to Christ, and the membership of the church had grown by leaps and bounds. Then just before the revival ended, they held a special meeting for children, "to bring the young lambs to the fold." My aunt spoke of it for days ahead. That night I was escorted to the front row and placed on the mourners' bench with all the other young sinners, who had not yet been brought to Jesus.

My aunt told me that when you were saved you saw a light, and something happened to you inside! And Jesus came into your life! And God was with you from then on! She said you could see and hear and feel Jesus in your soul. I believed her. I had heard a great many old people say the same thing and it seemed to me they ought to know. So I sat there calmly in the hot, crowded church, waiting for Jesus to come to me.

The preacher preached a wonderful rhythmical sermon, all moans and shouts and lonely cries and dire pictures of hell, and then he sang a song about the ninety and nine safe in the fold, but one little lamb was left out in the cold. Then he said: "Won't you come? Won't you come to Jesus? Young lambs, won't you come?" And he held out his arms to all us young sinners there on the mourners' bench. And the little girls cried. And some of them jumped up and went to Jesus right away. But most of us just sat there.

A great many old people came and knelt around us and prayed, old women with jet-black faces and braided hair, old men with work-gnarled hands. And the church sang a song about the lower lights are burning, some poor sinners to be saved. And the whole building rocked with prayer and song.

Still I kept waiting to *see* Jesus.

Finally all the young people had gone to the altar and were saved, but one boy and me. He was a rounder's son named Westley. Westley and I were surrounded by sisters and deacons praying. It was very hot in the church, and getting late now. Finally Westley said to me in a whisper: "God damn! I'm tired o' sitting here. Let's get up and be saved." So he got up and was saved.

Then I was left all alone on the mourners' bench. My aunt came and knelt at my knees and cried, while prayers and songs swirled all around me in the little church. The whole congregation prayed for me alone, in a mightly wail of moans and voices. And I kept waiting serenely for Jesus, waiting, waiting—but he didn't come. I wanted to see him, but nothing happened to me. Nothing! I wanted something to happen to me, but nothing happened.

I heard the songs and the minister saying: "Why don't you come? My dear child, why don't you come to Jesus? Jesus is waiting for you. He wants you. Why don't you come? Sister Reed, what is this child's name?"

"Langston," my aunt sobbed.

"Langston, why don't you come? Why don't you come and be saved? Oh, Lamb of God! Why don't you come?"

Now it was really getting late. I began to be ashamed of myself, holding everything up so long. I began to wonder what God thought about Westley, who certainly hadn't seen Jesus either, but who was now sitting proudly on the platform, swinging his knickerbockered legs and grinning down at me, surrounded by deacons and old women on their knees praying. God had not struck Westley dead for taking his name in vain or for lying in the temple. So I decided that maybe to save further trouble, I'd better lie, too, and say that Jesus had come, and get up and be saved.

So I got up.

Suddenly the whole room broke into a sea of shouting, as they saw me rise. Waves of rejoicing swept the place. Women leaped in the air. My aunt threw her arms around me. The minister took me by the hand and led me to the platform.

When things quieted down, in a hushed silence, punctuated by a few ecstatic "Amens," all the new young lambs were blessed in the name of God. Then joyous singing filled the room.

That night, for the last time in my life but one—for I was a big boy twelve years old—I cried. I cried, in bed alone, and couldn't stop. I buried my head under the quilts, but my aunt heard me. She woke up and told my uncle I was crying because the Holy Ghost had come into my life, and because I had seen Jesus. But I was really crying because I couldn't bear to tell her that I had lied, that I had deceived everybody in the church, and I hadn't seen Jesus, and that now I didn't believe there was a Jesus any more, since he didn't come to help me.

Possibilities for Writing

1. Recall a time when, like Hughes, you did something you didn't really believe in because you found it easier to go along with the crowd. In an essay, narrate the experience, focusing on the situation, the other people involved, your feelings at the time, and the aftermath of the incident.

2. In this brief narration, Hughes does a great deal to re-create his experience vividly and concretely. Analyze Hughes's use of language—specific nouns, verbs, and adjectives—as well as his use of dialogue and repetition to add punch to his story.

3. Hughes ends his narration on a note of disillusionment: "now I didn't believe there was a Jesus any more, since he didn't come to help me." Have you ever been disillusioned about a deeply held and cherished belief? In an essay, explore that experience and its consequences in detail. How did you eventually cope with your disappointment?

Martin Luther King, Jr. (1929–1968), the most revered leader of the civil rights movement, was born in Atlanta, the son of a Baptist clergyman. A graduate of Morehouse College and Boston University, King was himself ordained in 1947 and became the minister at a church in Montgomery, Alabama, in 1954. There he spearheaded a year-long boycott of segregated city buses, which eventually resulted in the system's integration, and as head of the Southern Christian Leadership Conference, he took his crusade against segregation to other Southern cities. Noted for his commitment to peaceful demonstration and nonviolent resistance, King and those who protested with him often ended up in jail. An international figure by the 1960s, he was awarded a Nobel Peace Prize in 1964. King was assassinated in 1968 in Memphis, Tennessee.

Martin Luther King, Jr.
Letter from Birmingham Jail

King's "Letter" is a response to criticism made against his effort to use peaceful, nonviolent demonstrations as forms of public disruption to advance the cause of racial integration. King addresses his letter to an audience of clergymen, whom he assures from the start that he respects their sincerity and good will in presenting their criticism. But he quickly seizes the moral ground by explaining why he came to Birmingham, linking himself with the biblical prophets, who preached against social injustice. Developing his argument carefully, King answers their actual questions and anticipates their additional potential questions.

King takes up complex issues, including whether it is right to break a law to achieve a desired end, citing a roster of Christian and Jewish theologians and quoting the Roman Catholic theologian St. Augustine who wrote that "an unjust law is no law at all." He also cites examples of revolutionary thinkers whose ideas and example changed history—from Socrates and Martin Luther to Thoreau and Mahatma Gandhi, whose civil disobedience in the form of nonviolent protest was politically effective.

My Dear Fellow Clergymen:

While confined here in the Birmingham city jail, I came across your recent statement calling my present activities "unwise and untimely." Seldom do I pause to answer criticism of my work and ideas. If I sought to answer all the criticisms that cross my desk, my secretaries would have little time for anything other than such correspondence in the course of the day, and I would have no time for constructive work. But since I feel that you are men of genuine good will and that your criticisms are sincerely set forth, I want to try to answer your statement in what I hope will be patient and reasonable terms.

I think I should indicate why I am here in Birmingham, since you have been influenced by the view which argues against "outsiders coming in." I have the honor of serving as president of the Southern Christian Leadership Conference, an organization operating in every southern state, with headquarters in Atlanta, Georgia. We have some eighty-five affiliated organizations across the South, and one of them is the Alabama Christian Movement for Human Rights. Frequently we share staff, educational, and financial resources with our affiliates. Several months ago the affiliate here in Birmingham asked us to be on call to engage in a nonviolent direct-action program if such were deemed necessary. We readily consented, and when the hour came we lived up to our promise. So I, along with several members of my staff, am here because I was invited here. I am here because I have organizational ties here.

But more basically, I am in Birmingham because injustice is here. Just as the prophets of the eighth century B.C. left their villages and carried their "thus saith the Lord" far beyond the boundaries of their home towns, and just as the Apostle Paul left his village of Tarsus and carried the gospel of Jesus Christ to the far corners of the Greco-Roman world, so am I compelled to carry the gospel of freedom beyond my own home town. Like Paul, I must constantly respond to the Macedonian call for aid.

Moreover, I am cognizant of the interrelatedness of all communities and states. I cannot sit idly by in Atlanta and not be concerned about what happens in Birmingham. Injustice anywhere is a threat to justice everywhere. We are caught in an inescapable network of mutuality, tied in a single garment of destiny. Whatever affects one directly, affects all indirectly. Never again can we afford to live with the narrow, provincial "outside agitator" idea. Anyone who lives inside the United States can never be considered an outsider anywhere within its bounds.

You deplore the demonstrations taking place in Birmingham. But your statement, I am sorry to say, fails to express a similar concern for the conditions that brought about the demonstrations. I am sure that none of you would want to rest content with the superficial kind of social analysis that deals merely with effects and does not grapple with underlying causes. It is unfortunate that demonstrations are taking place in Birmingham, but it is even more unfortunate that the city's white power structure left the Negro community with no alternative.

In any nonviolent campaign there are four basic steps: collection of the facts to determine whether injustices exist; negotiation; self-purification; and direct action. We have gone through all these steps in Birmingham. There can be no gainsaying the fact that racial injustice engulfs this community. Birmingham is probably the most thoroughly segregated city in the United States. Its ugly record of brutality is widely known. Negroes have experienced grossly unjust treatment in the courts. There have been more unsolved bombings of Negro homes and churches in Birmingham than in any other city in the nation. These are the hard, brutal facts of the case. On the basis of these conditions, Negro leaders sought to negotiate with the city fathers. But the latter consistently refused to engage in good-faith negotiation.

Then, last September, came the opportunity to talk with leaders of Birmingham's economic community. In the course of the negotiations, certain promises were made by the merchants—for example, to remove the stores' humiliating racial signs. On the basis of these promises, the Reverend Fred Shuttlesworth and the leaders of the Alabama Christian Movement for Human Rights agreed to a moratorium on all demonstrations. As the weeks and months went by, we realized that we were the victims of a broken promise. A few signs, briefly removed, returned; the others remained.

As in so many past experiences, our hopes had been blasted, and the shadow of deep disappointment settled upon us. We had no alternative except to prepare for direct action, whereby we would present our very bodies as a means of laying our case before the conscience of the local and the national community. Mindful of the difficulties involved, we decided to undertake a process of self-purification. We began a series of workshops on nonviolence, and we repeatedly asked ourselves: "Are you able to accept blows without retaliating?" "Are you able to endure the ordeal of jail?" We decided to schedule our direct-action program for the Easter season, realizing that except for Christmas, this is the main shopping period of the year. Knowing that a strong economic-withdrawal program would be the by-product of direct action, we felt that this would be the best time to bring pressure to bear on the merchants for the needed change.

Then it occurred to us that Birmingham's mayoral election was coming up in March, and we speedily decided to postpone action until after election day. When we discovered that the Commissioner of Public

Safety, Eugene "Bull" Connor, had piled up enough votes to be in the run-off, we decided again to postpone action until the day after the run-off so that the demonstrations could not be used to cloud the issues. Like many others, we wanted to see Mr. Connor defeated, and to this end we endured postponement after postponement. Having aided in this community need, we felt that our direct-action program could be delayed no longer.

You may well ask, "Why direct action? Why sit-ins, marches, and so forth? Isn't negotiation a better path?" You are quite right in calling for negotiation. Indeed, this is the very purpose of direct action. Nonviolent direct action seeks to create such a crisis and foster such a tension that a community which has constantly refused to negotiate is forced to confront the issue. It seeks so to dramatize the issue that it can no longer be ignored. My citing the creation of tension as part of the work of the nonviolent-resister may sound rather shocking. But I must confess that I am not afraid of the word "tension." I have earnestly opposed violent tension, but there is a type of constructive, nonviolent tension which is necessary for growth. Just as Socrates felt that it was necessary to create a tension in the mind so that individuals could rise from the bondage of myths and half-truths to the unfettered realm of creative analysis and objective appraisal, so must we see the need for nonviolent gadflies to create the kind of tension in society that will help men rise from the dark depths of prejudice and racism to the majestic heights of understanding and brotherhood.

The purpose of our direct-action program is to create a situation so crisis-packed that it will inevitably open the door to negotiation. I therefore concur with you in your call for negotiation. Too long has our beloved Southland been bogged down in a tragic effort to live in monologue rather than dialogue.

One of the basic points in your statement is that the action that I and my associates have taken in Birmingham is untimely. Some have asked: "Why didn't you give the new city administration time to act?" The only answer that I can give to this query is that the new Birmingham administration must be prodded about as much as the outgoing one, before it will act. We are sadly mistaken if we feel that the election of Albert Boutwell as mayor will bring the millennium to Birmingham. While Mr. Boutwell is a much more gentle person than Mr. Connor, they are both segregationists, dedicated to maintenance of the status quo. I have hoped that Mr. Boutwell will be reasonable enough to see the futility of massive resistance to desegregation. But he will not see this without pressure from devotees of civil rights. My friends, I must say to you that we have not made a single gain in civil rights without determined legal and nonviolent pressure. Lamentably, it is an historical fact that privileged groups seldom give up their privileges voluntarily. Individuals may see the moral light and voluntarily give up their unjust posture, but, as Reinhold Niebuhr has reminded us, groups tend to be more immoral than individuals.

We know through painful experience that freedom is never voluntarily given by the oppressor; it must be demanded by the oppressed. Frankly, I have yet to engage in a direct-action campaign that was "well timed" in the view of those who have not suffered unduly from the disease of segregation. For years now I have heard the word "Wait!" It rings in the ear of every Negro with piercing familiarity. This "Wait" has almost always meant "Never." We must come to see, with one of our distinguished jurists, that "justice too long delayed is justice denied."

We have waited for more than 340 years for our constitutional and God-given rights. The nations of Asia and Africa are moving with jet-like speed toward gaining political independence, but we still creep at horse-and-buggy pace toward gaining a cup of coffee at a lunch counter. Perhaps it is easy for those who have never felt the stinging darts of segregation to say, "Wait." But when you have seen vicious mobs lynch your mothers and fathers at will and drown your sisters and brothers at whim; when you have seen hate-filled policemen curse, kick, and even kill your black brothers and sisters; when you see the vast majority of your twenty million Negro brothers smothering in an air-tight cage of poverty in the midst of an affluent society; when you suddenly find your tongue twisted and your speech stammering as you seek to explain to your six-year-old daughter why she can't go to the public amusement park that has just been advertised on television, and see tears welling up in her eyes when she is told that Funtown is closed to colored children, and see ominous clouds of inferiority beginning to form in her little mental sky, and see her beginning to distort her personality by developing an unconscious bitterness toward white people; when you have to concoct an answer for a five-year-old son who is asking, "Daddy, why do white people treat colored people so mean?"; when you take a cross-country drive and find it necessary to sleep night after night in the uncomfortable corners of your automobile because no motel will accept you; when you are humiliated day in and day out by nagging signs reading "white" and "colored"; when your first name becomes "nigger," your middle name becomes "boy" (however old you are) and your last name becomes "John," and your wife and mother are never given the respected title "Mrs."; when you are harried by day and haunted by night by the fact that you are a Negro, living constantly at tiptoe stance, never quite knowing what to expect next, and are plagued with inner fears and outer resentments; when you are forever fighting a degenerating sense of "nobodiness"—then you will understand why we find it difficult to wait. There comes a time when the cup of endurance runs over, and men are no longer willing to be plunged into the abyss of despair. I hope, sirs, you can understand our legitimate and unavoidable impatience.

You express a great deal of anxiety over our willingness to break laws. This is certainly a legitimate concern. Since we so diligently urge people to obey the Supreme Court's decision of 1954 outlawing segregation in the public schools, at first glance it may seem rather paradoxical for us consciously to break laws. One may well ask: "How can you advocate breaking some laws and obeying others?" The answer lies in the fact that there are two types of laws: just and unjust. I would be the first to advocate obeying just laws. One has not only a legal but a moral responsibility to obey just laws. Conversely, one has a moral responsibility to disobey unjust laws. I would agree with St. Augustine that "an unjust law is no law at all."

Now, what is the difference between the two? How does one determine whether a law is just or unjust? A just law is a man-made code that squares with the moral law or the law of God. An unjust law is a code that is out of harmony with the moral law. To put it in the terms of St. Thomas Aquinas: An unjust law is a human law that is not rooted in eternal law and natural law. Any law that uplifts human personality is just. Any law that degrades human personality is unjust. All segregation statutes are unjust because segregation distorts the soul and damages the personality. It gives the segregator a false sense of superiority and the segregated a false sense of inferiority. Segregation, to use the terminology of the Jewish philosopher Martin Buber, substitutes an "I-it" relationship for an "I-thou" relationship and ends up relegating persons to the status of things. Hence segregation is not only politically, economically, and sociologically unsound, it is morally wrong and sinful. Paul Tillich has said that sin is separation. Is not segregation an existential expression of man's tragic separation, his awful estrangement, his terrible sinfulness? Thus it is that I can urge men to obey the 1954 decision of the Supreme Court, for it is morally right; and I can urge them to disobey segregation ordinances, for they are morally wrong.

Let us consider a more concrete example of just and unjust laws. An unjust law is a code that a numerical or power majority group compels a minority group to obey but does not make binding on itself. This is *difference* made legal. By the same token, a just law is a code that a majority compels a minority to follow and that it is willing to follow itself. This is *sameness* made legal.

Let me give another explanation. A law is unjust if it is inflicted on a minority that, as a result of being denied the right to vote, had no part in enacting or devising the law. Who can say that the legislature of Alabama which set up that state's segregation laws was democratically elected? Throughout Alabama all sorts of devious methods are used to prevent Negroes from becoming registered voters, and there are some counties in which, even though Negroes constitute a majority of the population, not a single Negro is registered. Can any law enacted under such circumstances be considered democratically structured?

Sometimes a law is just on its face and unjust in its application. For instance, I have been arrested on a charge of parading without a permit. Now, there is nothing wrong in having an ordinance which requires a permit for a parade. But such an ordinance becomes unjust when it is used to maintain segregation and to deny citizens the First-Amendment privilege of peaceful assembly and protest.

I hope you are able to see the distinction I am trying to point out. In no sense do I advocate evading or defying the law, as would the rabid segregationist. That would lead to anarchy. One who breaks an unjust law must do so openly, lovingly, and with a willingness to accept the penalty. I submit that an individual who breaks a law that conscience tells him is unjust, and who willingly accepts the penalty of imprisonment in order to arouse the conscience of the community over its injustice, is in reality expressing the highest respect for law.

Of course, there is nothing new about this kind of civil disobedience. It was evidenced sublimely in the refusal of Shadrach, Meshach, and Abednego to obey the laws of Nebuchadnezzar, on the ground that a higher moral law was at stake. It was practiced superbly by the early Christians, who were willing to face hungry lions and the excruciating pain of chopping blocks rather than submit to certain unjust laws of the Roman Empire. To a degree, academic freedom is a reality today because Socrates practiced civil disobedience. In our own nation, the Boston Tea Party represented a massive act of civil disobedience.

We should never forget that everything Adolf Hitler did in Germany was "legal" and everything the Hungarian freedom fighters did in Hungary was "illegal." It was "illegal" to aid and comfort a Jew in Hitler's Germany. Even so, I am sure that, had I lived in Germany at the time, I would have aided and comforted my Jewish brothers. If today I lived in a Communist country where certain principles dear to the Christian faith are suppressed, I would openly advocate disobeying that country's anti-religious laws.

I must make two honest confessions to you, my Christian and Jewish brothers. First, I must confess that over the past few years I have been gravely disappointed with the white moderate. I have almost reached the regrettable conclusion that the Negro's great stumbling block in his stride toward freedom is not the White Citizen's Counciler or the Ku Klux Klanner, but the white moderate, who is more devoted to "order" than to justice; who prefers a negative peace which is the absence of tension to a positive peace which is the presence of justice; who constantly says, "I agree with you in the goal you seek, but I cannot agree with your methods of direct action"; who paternalistically believes he can set the timetable for another man's freedom; who lives by a mythical concept of time and who constantly advises the Negro to wait for a "more convenient season." Shallow understanding from people of good will is more frustrating than absolute misunderstanding from people of ill will. Lukewarm acceptance is much more bewildering than outright rejection.

I had hoped that the white moderate would understand that law and order exist for the purpose of establishing justice and that when they fail in this purpose they become the dangerously structured dams that block the flow of social progress. I had hoped that the white moderate would understand that the present tension in the South is a necessary phase of the transition from an obnoxious negative peace, in which the Negro passively accepted his unjust plight, to a substantive and positive peace, in which all men will respect the dignity and worth of human personality. Actually, we who engage in nonviolent direct action are not the creators of tension. We merely bring to the surface the hidden tension that is already alive. We bring it out in the open, where it can be seen and dealt with. Like a boil that can never be cured so long as it is covered up but must be opened with all its ugliness to the natural medicines of air and light, injustice must be exposed, with all the tension its exposure creates, to the light of human conscience and the air of national opinion, before it can be cured.

In your statement you assert that our actions, even though peaceful, must be condemned because they precipitate violence. But is this a logical assertion? Isn't this like condemning a robbed man because his possession of money precipitated the evil act of robbery? Isn't this like condemning Socrates because his unswerving commitment to truth and his philosophical inquiries precipitated the act by the misguided populace in which they made him drink hemlock? Isn't this like condemning Jesus because his unique God-consciousness and never-ceasing devotion to God's will precipitated the evil act of crucifixion? We must come to see that, as the federal courts have consistently affirmed, it is wrong to urge an individual to cease his efforts to gain his basic constitutional rights because the quest may precipitate violence. Society must protect the robbed and punish the robber.

I had also hoped that the white moderate would reject the myth concerning time in relation to the struggle for freedom. I have just received a letter from a white brother in Texas. He writes: "All Christians know that the colored people will receive equal rights eventually, but it is possible that you are in too great a religious hurry. It has taken Christianity almost two thousand years to accomplish what it has. The teachings of Christ take time to come to earth." Such an attitude stems from a tragic misconception of time, from the strangely irrational notion that there is something in the very flow of time that will inevitably cure all ills. Actually, time itself is neutral; it can be used either destructively or constructively. More and more I feel that the people of ill will have used time much more effectively than have the people of good will. We will have to repent in this generation not merely for the hateful words and actions of the bad people, but for the appalling silence of the good people. Human progress never rolls in on wheels of inevitability; it comes through the tireless efforts of men willing to be co-workers with God, and without this hard work, time itself becomes an ally of the forces of social stagnation. We must use time creatively, in the knowledge that the time is always ripe to do right. Now is the time to make real the promise of democracy and transform our pending national elegy into a creative psalm of brotherhood. Now is the time to lift our national policy from the quicksand of racial injustice to the solid rock of human dignity.

You speak of our activity in Birmingham as extreme. At first I was rather disappointed that fellow clergymen would see my nonviolent efforts as those of an extremist. I began thinking about the fact that I stand in the middle of two opposing forces in the Negro community. One is a force of complacency, made up in part of Negroes who, as a result of long years of oppression, are so drained of self-respect and a sense of "somebodiness" that they have adjusted to segregation; and in part of a few middle-class Negroes who, because of a degree of academic and economic security and because in some ways they profit by segregation, have become insensitive to the problems of the masses. The other force is one of bitterness and hatred, and it comes perilously close to advocating violence. It is expressed in the various black nationalist groups that are springing up across the nation, the largest and best-known being Elijah Muhammad's Muslim movement. Nourished by the Negro's frustration over the continued existence of racial discrimination, this movement is made up of people who have lost faith in America, who have absolutely repudiated Christianity, and who have concluded that the white man is an incorrigible "devil."

I have tried to stand between these two forces, saying that we need emulate neither the "do-nothingism" of the complacent nor the hatred and despair of the black nationalist. For there is the more excellent way of love and nonviolent protest. I am grateful to God that, through the influence of the Negro church, the way of nonviolence became an integral part of our struggle.

If this philosophy had not emerged, by now many streets of the South would, I am convinced, be flowing with blood. And I am further convinced that if our white brothers dismiss as "rabblerousers" and "outside agitators" those of us who employ nonviolent direct action, and if they refuse to support our nonviolent efforts, millions of Negroes will, out of frustration and despair, seek solace and security in black-nationalist ideologies—a development that would inevitably lead to a frightening racial nightmare.

Oppressed people cannot remain oppressed forever. The yearning for freedom eventually manifests itself, and that is what has happened to the American Negro. Something within has reminded him of his birthright of freedom, and something without has reminded him that it can be gained. Consciously or unconsciously, he has been caught up by the *Zeitgeist*, and with his black brothers of Africa and his brown and yellow brothers of Asia, South America, and the Caribbean, the United States Negro is moving with a sense of great urgency toward the promised land of racial justice. If one recognizes this vital urge that has engulfed the Negro community, one should readily understand why public demonstrations are taking place. The Negro has many pent-up resentments and latent frustrations, and he must release them. So let him march; let him make prayer pilgrimages to the city hall; let him go on freedom rides—and try to understand why he must do so. If his repressed emotions are not released in nonviolent ways, they will seek expression through violence; this is not a threat but a fact of history. So I have not said to my people, "Get rid of your discontent." Rather, I have tried to say that this normal and healthy discontent can be channeled into the creative outlet of nonviolent direct action. And now this approach is being termed extremist.

But though I was initially disappointed at being categorized as an extremist, as I continued to think about the matter I gradually gained a measure of satisfaction from the label. Was not Jesus an extremist for love: "Love your enemies, bless them that curse you, do good to them that hate you, and pray for them which despitefully use you, and persecute you." Was not Amos an extremist for justice: "Let justice roll down like waters and righteousness like an ever-flowing stream." Was not Paul an extremist for the Christian gospel: "I bear in my body the marks of the Lord Jesus." Was not Martin Luther an extremist: "Here I stand; I cannot do otherwise, so help me God." And John Bunyan: "I will stay in jail to the end of my days before I make a butchery of my conscience." And Abraham Lincoln: "This nation cannot survive half slave and half free." And Thomas Jefferson: "We hold these truths to be self-evident, that all men are created equal. . . ." So the question is not whether we will be extremists, but what kind of extremists we will be. Will we be extremists for hate or for love? Will we be extremists for the preservation of injustice or for the extension of justice? In that dramatic scene on Calvary's hill three men were crucified. We must never forget that all three were crucified for the same crime—the crime of extremism. Two were extremists for immorality, and thus fell below their environment. The other, Jesus Christ, was an extremist for love, truth, and goodness, and thereby rose above his environment. Perhaps the South, the nation, and the world are in dire need of creative extremists.

I had hoped that the white moderate would see this need. Perhaps I was too optimistic; perhaps I expected too much. I suppose I should have realized that few members of the oppressor race can understand the deep groans and passionate yearnings of the oppressed race, and still fewer have the vision to see that injustice must be rooted out by strong, persistent, and determined action. I am thankful, however, that some of our white brothers in the South have grasped the meaning of this social revolution and committed themselves to it. They are still all too few in quantity, but they are big in quality. Some—such as Ralph McGill, Lillian Smith, Harry Golden, James McBride Dabbs, Ann Braden, and Sarah Patton Boyle—have written about our struggle in eloquent and prophetic terms. Others have marched with us down nameless streets of the South. They have languished in filthy, roach-infested jails, suffering the abuse and brutality of policemen who view them as "dirty niggerlovers." Unlike so many of their moderate brothers and sisters, they have recognized the urgency of the moment and sensed the need for powerful "action" antidotes to combat the disease of segregation.

Let me take note of my other major disappointment. I have been so greatly disappointed with the white church and its leadership. Of course, there are some notable exceptions. I am not unmindful of the fact that each of you has taken some significant stands on this issue. I commend you, Reverend Stallings, for your Christian stand on this past Sunday, in welcoming Negroes to your worship service on a nonsegregated basis. I commend the Catholic leaders of this state for integrating Spring Hill College several years ago.

But despite these notable exceptions, I must honestly reiterate that I have been disappointed with the church. I do not say this as one of those negative critics who can always find something wrong with the church. I say this as a minister of the gospel, who loves the church; who was nurtured in its bosom; who has been sustained by its spiritual blessings and who will remain true to it as long as the cord of life shall lengthen.

When I was suddenly catapulted into the leadership of the bus protest in Montgomery, Alabama, a few years ago, I felt we would be supported by the white church. I felt that the white ministers, priests, and rabbis of the South would be among our strongest allies. Instead, some have been outright opponents, refusing to understand the freedom movement and misrepresenting its leaders; all too many others have been more cautious than courageous and have remained silent behind the anesthetizing security of stainedglass windows.

In spite of my shattered dreams, I came to Birmingham with the hope that the white religious leadership of this community would see the justice of our cause and, with deep moral concern, would serve as the channel through which our just grievances could reach the power structure. I had hoped that each of you would understand. But again I have been disappointed.

I have heard numerous southern religious leaders admonish their worshipers to comply with a desegregation decision because it is the law, but I have longed to hear white ministers declare: "Follow this decree because integration is morally right and because the Negro is your brother." In the midst of blatant injustices inflicted upon the Negro, I have watched white churchmen stand on the sideline and mouth pious irrelevancies and sanctimonious trivialities. In the midst of a mighty struggle to rid our nation of racial and economic injustice, I have heard many ministers say: "Those are social issues, with which the gospel has no real concern." And I have watched many churches commit themselves to a completely otherworldly religion which makes a strange, un-Biblical distinction between body and soul, between the sacred and the secular.

I have traveled the length and breadth of Alabama, Mississippi, and all the other southern states. On sweltering summer days and crisp autumn mornings I have looked at the South's beautiful churches with their lofty spires pointing heavenward. I have beheld the impressive outlines of her massive religious-education buildings. Over and over I have found myself asking: "What kind of people worship here? Who is their God? Where were their voices when the lips of Governor Barnett dripped with words of interposition and nullification? Where were they when Governor Wallace gave a clarion call for defiance and hatred? Where were their voices of support when bruised and weary Negro men and women decided to rise from the dark dungeons of complacency to the bright hills of creative protest?"

Yes, these questions are still in my mind. In deep disappointment I have wept over the laxity of the church. But be assured that my tears have been tears of love. There can be no deep disappointment where there is not deep love. Yes, I love the church. How could I do otherwise? I am in the rather unique position of being the son, the grandson, and the great-grandson of preachers. Yes, I see the church as the body of Christ. But, oh! How we have blemished and scarred that body through social neglect and through fear of being nonconformists.

There was a time when the church was very powerful—in the time when the early Christians rejoiced at being deemed worthy to suffer for what they believed. In those days the church was not merely a thermometer that recorded the ideas and principles of popular opinion; it was a thermostat that transformed the mores of society. Whenever the early Christians entered a town, the people in power became disturbed and immediately sought to convict the Christians for being "disturbers of the peace" and "outside agitators." But the Christians pressed on, in the conviction that they were "a colony of heaven," called to obey God rather than man. Small in number, they were big in commitment. They were too God-intoxicated to be "astronomically intimidated." By their effort and example they brought an end to such ancient evils as infanticide and gladiatorial contests.

Things are different now. So often the contemporary church is a weak, ineffectual voice with an uncertain sound. So often it is an archdefender of the status quo. Far from being disturbed by the presence of the church, the power structure of the average community is consoled by the church's silent—and often even vocal—sanction of things as they are.

But the judgment of God is upon the church as never before. If today's church does not recapture the sacrificial spirit of the early church, it will lose its authenticity, forfeit the loyalty of millions, and be dismissed as an irrelevant social club with no meaning for the twentieth century. Every day I meet young people whose disappointment with the church has turned into outright disgust.

Perhaps I have once again been too optimistic. Is organized religion too inextricably bound to the status quo to save our nation and the world? Perhaps I must turn my faith to the inner spiritual church, the church within the church, as the true *ekklesia* and the hope of the world. But again I am thankful to God that some noble souls from the ranks of organized religion have broken loose from the paralyzing chains of conformity and joined us as active partners in the struggle for freedom. They have left their secure congregations and walked the streets of

Albany, Georgia, with us. They have gone down the highways of the South on tortuous rides for freedom. Yes, they have gone to jail with us. Some have been dismissed from their churches, have lost the support of their bishops and fellow ministers. But they have acted in the faith that right defeated is stronger than evil triumphant. Their witness has been the spiritual salt that has preserved the true meaning of the gospel in these troubled times. They have carved a tunnel of hope through the dark mountain of disappointment.

I hope the church as a whole will meet the challenge of this decisive hour. But even if the church does not come to the aid of justice, I have no despair about the future. I have no fear about the outcome of our struggle in Birmingham, even if our motives are at present misunderstood. We will reach the goal of freedom in Birmingham and all over the nation, because the goal of America is freedom. Abused and scorned though we may be, our destiny is tied up with America's destiny. Before the pilgrims landed at Plymouth, we were here. Before the pen of Jefferson etched the majestic words of the Declaration of Independence across the pages of history, we were here. For more than two centuries our forebears labored in this country without wages: they made cotton king; they built the homes of their masters while suffering gross injustice and shameful humiliation—and yet out of a bottomless vitality they continued to thrive and develop. If the inexpressible cruelties of slavery could not stop us, the opposition we now face will surely fail. We will win our freedom because the sacred heritage of our nation and the eternal will of God are embodied in our echoing demands.

Before closing I feel impelled to mention one other point in your statement that has troubled me profoundly. You warmly commended the Birmingham police force for keeping "order" and "preventing violence." I doubt that you would have so warmly commended the police force if you had seen its dogs sinking their teeth into unarmed, nonviolent Negroes. I doubt that you would so quickly commend the policemen if you were to observe their ugly and inhumane treatment of Negroes here in the city jail; if you were to watch them push and curse old Negro women and young Negro girls; if you were to see them slap and kick old Negro men and young boys; if you were to observe them, as they did on two occasions, refuse to give us food because we wanted to sing our grace together. I cannot join you in your praise of the Birmingham police department.

It is true that the police have exercised a degree of discipline in handling the demonstrators. In this sense they have conducted themselves rather "nonviolently" in public. But for what purpose? To preserve the evil system of segregation. Over the past few years I have consistently preached that nonviolence demands that the means we use must be as pure as the ends we seek. I have tried to make clear that it is wrong to use immoral means to attain moral ends. But now I must affirm that it is just as wrong, or perhaps even more so, to use moral means to preserve immoral ends. Perhaps Mr. Connor and his policemen have been rather nonviolent in public, as was Chief Pritchett in Albany, Georgia, but they have used the moral means of nonviolence to maintain the immoral end of racial injustice. As T. S. Eliot has said. "The last temptation is the greatest treason: To do the right deed for the wrong reason."

I wish you had commended the Negro sit-inners and demonstrators of Birmingham for their sublime courage, their willingness to suffer, and their amazing discipline in the midst of great provocation. One day the South will recognize its real heroes. They will be the James Merediths, with the noble sense of purpose that enables them to face jeering and hostile mobs, and with the agonizing loneliness that characterizes the life of the pioneer. They will be old, oppressed, battered Negro women, symbolized in a seventy-two-year-old woman in Montgomery, Alabama, who rose up with a sense of dignity and with her people decided not to ride segregated buses, and who responded with ungrammatical profundity to one who inquired about her weariness: "My feets is tired, but my soul is at rest." They will be the young high school and college students, the young ministers of the gospel and a host of their elders, courageously and nonviolently sitting in at lunch counters and willingly going to jail for conscience' sake. One day the South will know that when these disinherited children of God sat down at lunch counters, they were in reality standing up for what is best in the American dream and for the most sacred values in our Judaeo-Christian heritage, thereby bringing our nation back to those great wells of democracy which were dug deep by the founding fathers in their formulation of the Constitution and the Declaration of Independence.

Never before have I written so long a letter. I'm afraid it is much too long to take your precious time. I can assure you that it would have been much shorter if I had been writing from a comfortable desk, but what else can one do when he is alone in a narrow jail cell, other than write long letters, think long thoughts, and pray long prayers?

If I have said anything in this letter that overstates the truth and indicates an unreasonable impatience, I beg you to forgive me. If I have said anything that understates the truth and indicates my having a patience that allows me to settle for anything less than brotherhood, I beg God to forgive me.

I hope this letter finds you strong in the faith. I also hope that circumstances will soon make it possible for me to meet each of you, not as an integrationist or a civil-rights leader but as a fellow clergyman and a Christian brother. Let us all hope that the dark clouds of racial prejudice will soon pass away and the deep fog of misunderstanding will be lifted from our fear-drenched communities, and in some not too distant tomorrow the radiant stars of love and brotherhood will shine over our great nation with all their scintillating beauty.

Yours for the cause of Peace and Brotherhood,
MARTIN LUTHER KING, JR.

Possibilities for Writing

1. King's letter is a classic example of refutation, taking arguments made against one's opinions or actions and showing why they are wrong or incomplete. In an essay, note each point made in the statement condemning King's actions that King sets out to refute. How does he go about doing so? How do you respond to his arguments?

2. King is writing here to white moderates who say, in his words, "I agree with you in the goal you seek, but I cannot agree with your methods of direct action." In what ways has he tailored his arguments to such an audience? How does his tone reveal his understanding of this audience?

3. King makes a distinction between "just" and "unjust" laws. How does he define an "unjust" law? Do you agree with his definition? Point to any current examples of laws that you think are unjust, and explain why you feel as you do.

*Maxine Hong Kingston (b. 1940) grew up in Stockton, California, the daughter
of Chinese immigrants in a close-knit Asian community; her first language was
a dialect of Chinese. She graduated from the University of California at
Berkeley and went on to teach high school English in California and Hawaii.
Her award-winning* The Woman Warrior: Memoirs of a Childhood Among
Ghosts *(1976) is an impressionistic remembrance of the stories she grew up with
concerning women in her culture, both real and legendary. Its companion
volume focusing on images of manhood,* China Men, *followed in 1980. Kingston
has also published a novel,* Tripmaster Monkey: His Fake Book *(1989). She is
currently a senior lecturer at her alma mater and was awarded a National
Humanities Medal by President Clinton in 1997.*

Maxine Hong Kingston
On Discovery

"On Discovery" is an unusual piece of writing. An excerpt from Kingston's book
China Men, "On Discovery" tells the story of a man who became a woman.
Encased within Kingston's hybrid factual/fictional prose of the book, as a
whole, is this parable about gender and identity. It's a prose piece that invites
consideration of how gender identity is formed and why it is such a powerful
cultural construct.

Tang Ao's odyssey takes him/her on a journey that could only be imagined,
and one that ends with a shift in how Tang Ao imagines him/her self. In Tang
Ao's transformation from man to woman, Tang Ao undergoes as much an inner,
psychological change as an external one.

In Tang Ao's case, the transformation was neither desired not sought. But
neither was it resisted when it was forced upon Tang Ao. It is a metamorphosis
that Kingston's readers can hardly believe and certainly never forget.

Once upon a time, a man, named Tang Ao, looking for the Gold Mountain, crossed an ocean, and came upon the Land of Women. The women
immediately captured him, not on guard against ladies. When they
asked Tang Ao to come along, he followed; if he had had male companions, he would've winked over his shoulder.

"We have to prepare you to meet the queen," the women said. They
locked him in a canopied apartment equipped with pots of makeup, mir-
rors, and a woman's clothes. "Let us help you off with your armor and
boots," said the women. They slipped his coat off his shoulders, pulled it

down his arms, and shackled his wrists behind him. The women who kneeled to take off his shoes chained his ankles together.

A door opened, and he expected to meet his match, but it was only two old women with sewing boxes in their hands. "The less you struggle, the less it'll hurt," one said, squinting a bright eye as she threaded her needle. Two captors sat on him while another held his head. He felt an old woman's dry fingers trace his ear; the long nail on her little finger scraped his neck. "What are you doing?" he asked. "Sewing your lips together," she joked, blackening needles in a candle flame. The ones who sat on him bounced with laughter. But the old woman did not sew his lips together. They pulled his earlobes taut and jabbed a needle through each of them. They had to poke and probe before puncturing the layers of skin correctly, the hole in the front of the lobe in line with one in back, the layers of skin sliding about so. They worked the needle through—a last jerk for the needle's wide eye ("needle's nose" in Chinese). They strung his raw flesh with silk threads; he could feel the fibers.

The women who sat on him turned to direct their attention to his feet. They bent his toes so far backward that his arched foot cracked. The old ladies squeezed each foot and broke many tiny bones along the sides. They gathered his toes, toes over and under one another like a knot of ginger root. Tang Ao wept with pain. As they wound the bandages tight and tighter around his feet, the women sang foot-binding songs to distract him: "Use aloe for binding feet and not for scholars."

During the months of a season, they fed him on women's food: the tea was thick with white chrysanthemums and stirred the cool female winds inside his body; chicken wings made his hair shine; vinegar soup improved his womb. They drew the loops of thread through the scabs that grew daily over the holes in his earlobes. One day they inserted gold hoops. Every night they unbound his feet, but his veins had shrunk, and the blood pumping through them hurt so much, he begged to have his feet rewrapped tight. They forced him to wash his used bandages, which were embroidered with flowers and smelled of rot and cheese. He hung the bandages up to dry, streamers that drooped and draped wall to wall. He felt embarrassed; the wrapping were like underwear, and they were his.

One day his attendants changed his gold hoops to jade studs and strapped his feet to shoes that curved like bridges. They plucked out each hair on his face, powdered him white, painted his eyebrows like a moth's wings, painted his cheeks and lips red. He served a meal at the queen's court. His hips swayed and his shoulders swiveled because of his shaped feet. "She's pretty, don't you agree?" the diners said, smacking their lips at his dainty feet as he bent to put dishes before them.

In the Women's Land there are no taxes and no wars. Some scholars say that that country was discovered during the reign of Empress Wu (A.D. 694–705), and some say earlier than that, A.D. 441, and it was in North America.

Possibilities for Writing

1. What is Kingston's central idea in "On Discovery"? To what extent is this piece about gender switching? About gender roles? About power?
2. What ironies does Kingston play up in "On Discovery"? Consider both verbal irony and irony of situation—that is, ironic comments and ironic developments in the action.
3. Discuss the following comment by Simone de Beauvoir in relation to "On Discovery": "One is not born a woman; one becomes a woman."

N. Scott Momaday (b. 1934) was born in Lawton, Oklahoma, of Kiowa ancestry and grew up on a reservation in New Mexico. A graduate of the University of New Mexico and of Stanford University, he won a Pulitzer Prize for his first novel, House Made of Dawn *(1968). Author of many genres in addition to fiction, Momaday has published volumes of poetry, including* The Gourd Dancer *(1976), and the memoirs* The Way to Rainy Mountain *(1969) and* The Names *(1976), as well as children's books, essay collections, and plays. He is also an artist whose work has been widely exhibited. For many years a professor at the University of Arizona, Momaday often takes as his subject the history and culture of Native Americans and, in particular, their relationship with the physical environment. His most recent collection is* The Man Made of Words *(1997).*

N. Scott Momaday
The Way to Rainy Mountain

In his autobiographical memoir, *The Way to Rainy Mountain*, N. Scott Momaday celebrates his Kiowa Native American heritage. Momaday describes both a place and a person in this essay from his memoir. He describes Rainy Mountain as a place saturated in the history of the Kiowa people. It is a place every aspect of which bears significance.

But it is not only place that is celebrated in Momaday's essay/memoir. He also memorializes his grandmother, who is, herself, a repository of Kiowa history and culture. Momaday's moving portrait captures her dignity and nobility as an individual and as a representative of her vanishing Kiowa world. In language at once reverential and wonderfully precise, Momaday describes the holy regard that his grandmother held for the sun, an awe and a reverence reflected in the sun dances of Kiowa cultural tradition.

A single knoll rises out of the plain in Oklahoma, north and west of the Wichita Range. For my people, the Kiowas, it is an old landmark, and they gave it the name Rainy Mountain. The hardest weather in the world is there. Winter brings blizzards, hot tornadic winds arise in the spring, and in summer the prairie is an anvil's edge. The grass turns brittle and brown, and it cracks beneath your feet. There are green belts along the rivers and creeks, linear groves of hickory and pecan, willow and witch hazel. At a distance in July or August the steaming foliage seems almost to writhe in fire. Great green and yellow grasshoppers are everywhere in the tall grass, popping up like corn to sting the flesh, and tortoises crawl about on the red earth, going nowhere in the plenty of time. Loneliness is an aspect of the land. All things in the plain are isolate; there is no confusion of objects in the eye, but *one* hill or *one* tree or *one* man. To look upon that landscape in the early morning, with the sun at your back, is to lose the sense of proportion. Your imagination comes to life, and this, you think, is where Creation was begun.

I returned to Rainy Mountain in July. My grandmother had died in the spring, and I wanted to be at her grave. She had lived to be very old and at last infirm. Her only living daughter was with her when she died, and I was told that in death her face was that of a child.

I like to think of her as a child. When she was born, the Kiowas were living the last great moment of their history. For more than a hundred years they had controlled the open range from the Smoky Hill River to the Red, from the headwaters of the Canadian to the fork of the Arkansas and Cimarron. In alliance with the Comanches, they had ruled the whole of the southern Plains. War was their sacred business, and they were among the finest horsemen the world has ever known. But warfare for the Kiowas was preeminently a matter of disposition rather than of survival, and they never understood the grim, unrelenting advance of the U.S. Cavalry. When at last, divided and ill-provisioned, they were driven onto the Staked Plains in the cold rains of autumn, they fell into panic. In Palo Duro Canyon they abandoned their crucial stores to pillage and had nothing then but their lives. In order to save themselves, they surrendered to the soldiers at Fort Sill and were imprisoned in the old stone corral that now stands as a military museum. My grandmother was spared the humiliation of those high gray walls by eight or ten years, but she must have known from birth the affliction of defeat, the dark brooding of old warriors.

Her name was Aho, and she belonged to the last culture to evolve in North America. Her forebears came down from the high country in western Montana nearly three centuries ago. They were a mountain people, a mysterious tribe of hunters whose language has never been positively classified in any major group. In the late seventeenth century they began a long migration to the south and east. It was a journey toward the dawn, and it led to a golden age. Along the way the Kiowas were befriended by the Crows, who gave them the culture and religion of the Plains. They acquired horses, and their ancient nomadic spirit was suddenly free of the ground. They acquired Tai-me, the sacred Sun Dance doll, from that moment the object and symbol of their worship, and so shared in the divinity of the sun. Not least, they acquired the sense of destiny, therefore courage and pride. When they entered upon the southern Plains they had been transformed. No longer were they slaves to the simple necessity of survival; they were a lordly and dangerous society of fighters and thieves, hunters and priests of the sun. According to their origin myth, they entered the world through a hollow log. From one point of view, their migration was the fruit of an old prophecy, for indeed they emerged from a sunless world.

Although my grandmother lived out her long life in the shadow of Rainy Mountain, the immense landscape of the continental interior lay like memory in her blood. She could tell of the Crows, whom she had never seen, and of the Black Hills, where she had never been. I wanted to see in reality what she had seen more perfectly in the mind's eye, and traveled fifteen hundred miles to begin my pilgrimage.

Yellowstone, it seemed to me, was the top of the world, a region of deep lakes and dark timber, canyons and waterfalls. But, beautiful as it is, one might have the sense of confinement there. The skyline in all directions is close at hand, the high wall of the woods and deep cleavages of shade. There is a perfect freedom in the mountains, but it belongs to the eagle and the elk, the badger and the bear. The Kiowas reckoned their stature by the distance they could see, and they were bent and blind in the wilderness.

Descending eastward, the highland meadows are a stairway to the plain. In July the inland slope of the Rockies is luxuriant with flax and buckwheat, stonecrop and larkspur. The earth unfolds and the limit of the land recedes. Clusters of trees, and animals grazing far in the distance, cause the vision to reach away and wonder to build upon the mind. The sun follows a longer course in the day, and the sky is immense beyond all comparison. The great billowing clouds that sail upon it are the shadows that move upon the grain like water, dividing light. Farther down, in the land of the Crows and Blackfeet, the plain is yellow. Sweet clover takes hold of the hills and bends upon itself to cover and seal the soil. There the Kiowas paused on their way; they had come to the place where they must change their lives. The sun is at home on the plains. Precisely there does it have the certain character of a god. When the Kiowas came to the land of the Crows, they could see the dark lees of the hills at dawn across the Bighorn River, the profusion of light on the grain shelves, the oldest deity ranging after the solstices. Not yet would they veer southward to the caldron of the land that lay below; they must wean their blood from the northern winter and hold the mountains a while longer in their view. They bore Tai-me in procession to the east.

A dark mist lay over the Black Hills, and the land was like iron. At the top of a ridge I caught sight of Devil's Tower upthrust against the gray sky as if in the birth of time the core of the earth had broken through its crust and the motion of the world was begun. There are things in nature that engender an awful quiet in the heart of man; Devil's Tower is one of them. Two centuries ago, because they could not do otherwise, the Kiowas made a legend at the base of the rock. My grandmother said:

> Eight children were there at play, seven sisters and their brother. Suddenly the boy was struck dumb; he trembled and began to run upon his hands and feet. His fingers became claws, and his body was covered with fur. Directly there was a bear where the boy had been. The sisters were terrified; they ran, and the bear after them. They came to the stump of a great tree, and the tree spoke to them. It bade them climb upon it, and as they did so it began to rise into the air. The bear came to kill them, but they were just beyond its reach. It reared against the tree and scored the bark all around with its claws. The seven sisters were borne into the sky, and they became the stars of the Big Dipper.

From that moment, and so long as the legend lives, the Kiowas have kinsmen in the night sky. Whatever they were in the mountains, they could be no more. However tenuous their well-being, however much they had suffered and would suffer again, they had found a way out of the wilderness.

My grandmother had a reverence for the sun, a holy regard that now is all but gone out of mankind. There was a wariness in her, and an ancient awe. She was a Christian in her later years, but she had come a long way about, and she never forgot her birthright. As a child she had been to the Sun Dances; she had taken part in those annual rites, and by them she had learned the restoration of her people in the presence of Tai-me. She was about seven when the last Kiowa Sun Dance was held in 1887 on the Washita River above Rainy Mountain Creek. The buffalo were gone. In order to consummate the ancient sacrifice—to impale the head of a buffalo bull upon the medicine tree—a delegation of old men journeyed into Texas, there to beg and barter for an animal from the Goodnight herd. She was ten when the Kiowas came together for the last time as a living Sun Dance culture. They could find no buffalo; they had to hang an old hide from the sacred tree. Before the dance could begin, a company of soldiers rode out from Fort Sill under orders to disperse the tribe. Forbidden without cause the essential act of their faith, having seen the wild herds slaughtered and left to rot upon the ground, the Kiowas backed away forever from the medicine tree. That was July 20, 1890, at the great bend of the Washita. My grandmother was there. Without bitterness, and for as long as she lived, she bore a vision of deicide.

Now that I can have her only in memory, I see my grandmother in the several postures that were peculiar to her: standing at the wood stove on a winter morning and turning meat in a great iron skillet: sitting at the south window, bent above her beadwork, and afterwards, when her vision failed, looking down for a long time into the fold of her hands; going out upon a cane, very slowly as she did when the weight of age came upon her; praying. I remember her most often at prayer. She made long, rambling prayers out of suffering and hope, having seen many things. I was never sure that I had the right to hear, so exclusive were they of all mere custom and company. The last time I saw her she prayed standing by the side of her bed at night, naked to the waist, the light of a kerosene lamp moving upon her dark skin. Her long, black hair, always drawn and braided in the day, lay upon her shoulders and against her breasts like a shawl. I do not speak Kiowa, and I never understood her prayers, but there was something inherently sad in the sound, some merest hesitation upon the syllables of sorrow. She began in a high and descending pitch, exhausting her breath to silence; then again and again—and always the same intensity of effort, of something that is, and is not, like urgency in the human voice. Transported so in the dancing light among the shadows of her room, she seemed beyond the reach of time. But that was illusion; I think I knew then that I should not see her again.

Houses are like sentinels in the plain, old keepers of the weather watch. There, in a very little while, wood takes on the appearance of great age. All colors wear soon away in the wind and rain, and then the wood is burned gray and the grain appears and the nails turn red with rust. The windowpanes are black and opaque; you imagine there is nothing within, and indeed there are many ghosts, bones given up to the land. They stand here and there against the sky, and you approach them for a longer time than you expect. They belong in the distance; it is their domain.

Once there was a lot of sound in my grandmother's house, a lot of coming and going, feasting and talk. The summers there were full of excitement and reunion. The Kiowas are a summer people; they abide the cold and keep to themselves, but when the season turns and the land becomes warm and vital they cannot hold still; an old love of going returns upon them. The aged visitors who came to my grandmother's house when I was a child were made of lean and leather, and they bore themselves upright. They wore great black hats and bright ample shirts that shook in the wind. They rubbed fat upon their hair and wound their braids with strips of colored cloth. Some of them painted their faces and carried the scars of old and cherished enmities. They were an old council of warlords, come to remind and be reminded of who they were. Their wives and daughters served them well. The women might indulge themselves; gossip was at once the mark and compensation of their servitude. They made loud and elaborate talk among themselves, full of jest and gesture, fright and false alarm. They went abroad in fringed and flowered shawls, bright beadwork and German silver. They were at home in the kitchen, and they prepared meals that were banquets.

There were frequent prayer meetings, and great nocturnal feasts. When I was a child I played with my cousins outside, where the lamplight fell upon the ground and the singing of the old people rose up around us and carried away into the darkness. There were a lot of good things to eat, a lot of laughter and surprise. And afterwards, when the quiet returned, I lay down with my grandmother and could hear the frogs away by the river and feel the motion of the air.

Now there is a funeral silence in the rooms, the endless wake of some final word. The walls have closed in upon my grandmother's house. When I returned to it in mourning, I saw for the first time in my life how small it was. It was late at night, and there was a white moon, nearly full. I sat for a long time on the stone steps by the kitchen door. From there I could see out across the land; I could see the long row of trees by the creek, the low light upon the rolling plains, and the stars of the Big Dipper. Once I looked at the moon and caught sight of a strange thing. A cricket had perched upon the handrail, only a few inches away from me. My line of vision was such that the creature filled the moon like a fossil. It had gone there, I thought, to live and die, for there, of all places, was its small definition made whole and eternal. A warm wind rose up and purled like the longing within me.

The next morning I awoke at dawn and went out on the dirt road to Rainy Mountain. It was already hot, and the grasshoppers began to fill the air. Still, it was early in the morning, and the birds sang out of the shadows. The long yellow grass on the mountain shone in the bright light, and a scissortail hied above the land. There, where it ought to be, at the end of a long and legendary way, was my grandmother's grave. Here and there on the dark stones were ancestral names. Looking back once, I saw the mountain and came away.

Possibilities for Writing

1. Momaday traces the migration of the Kiowa from Montana to the Great Plains in terms of both physical landscape and of spiritual development. For him, how are the two related in the rise and fall of Kiowa history and culture? What is the significance of his ending the story of his journey at his grandmother's grave?

2. What does his grandmother represent for Momaday? Why, for example, does he begin his pilgrimage to her grave from Yellowstone, fifteen hundred miles away? How do his memories of her, as he describes them, help develop this image?

3. Explore the ways in which a grandparent or other older relative provides you with ties to your history and culture. Like Momaday, you may wish to develop the influence of a particular place associated with that person as well.

Michel de Montaigne (1533–1592), the father of the modern essay, was born in Perigord, France, to a family of wealthy landowners. He studied law at the University of Guyenne in Bordeaux and during his career served as a local magistrate and later as mayor of Bordeaux. In 1580 he published the first of his collected Essais, which were revised and added to in 1588. These "attempts" or "trials," as he termed them, dealt with a wide range of subjects and were intended as personal, but at the same time universal, reflections on the human condition. Intensely intellectual, the essais are nonetheless written in concrete, everyday language and marked by a great deal of humor. His works were highly influential throughout Europe, not only in terms of their subject matter but also as exemplars of this unique literary form.

Michel de Montaigne
Of Smells

Michel de Montaigne originated a unique style that is at once both personal and reflective. Montaigne's "Of Smells," though one of his shortest essays, exemplifies his characteristic method. It begins with a few general thoughts on the nature of odors that human beings give off. It moves quickly to a series of quotations from Montaigne's reading in classic writers from the past. And it includes a number of observations based on Montaigne's experience—his autobiographical perspective on what he himself has noticed about the way people smell, including the way he himself smells.

The unpretentiousness of this little essay is part of its charm. "Of Smells" wears its learning lightly. And it leans lightly, too, on what Montaigne has experienced in the realm of the olfactory. It never pretends to be anything more than a brief set of notes on what is noteworthy about smell. Montaigne's essay is suggestive without being insistent. It presents opportunities for readers to notice what Montaigne himself has noticed. But it doesn't force the issue; it doesn't argue in any systematic or methodical way. Nonetheless, "Of Smells" makes a good case for the influence of smell in our everyday lives.

It is said of some, as of Alexander the Great, that their sweat emitted a sweet odor, owing to some rare and extraordinary constitution of theirs, of which Plutarch and others seek the cause. But the common make-up of bodies is the opposite, and the best condition they may have is to be free of smell. The sweetness even of the purest breath has nothing more excellent about it than to be without any odor that offends us, as is that of very healthy children. That is why, says Plautus,

A woman smells good when she does not smell.

The most perfect smell for a woman is to smell of nothing, as they say that her actions smell best when they are imperceptible and mute, And perfumes are rightly considered suspicious in those who use them, and thought to be used to cover up some natural defect in that quarter. Whence arise these nice sayings of the ancient poets: To smell good is to stink:

> You laugh at us because we do not smell.
> I'd rather smell of nothing than smell sweet.
>
> MARTIAL

And elsewhere:

> Men who smell always sweet, Posthumus, don't smell good.
>
> MARTIAL

However, I like very much to be surrounded with good smells, and I hate bad ones beyond measure, and detect them from further off than anyone else:

> My scent will sooner be aware
> Where goat-smells, Polypus, in hairy arm-pits lurk,
> Than keen hounds scent a wild boar's lair.
>
> HORACE

The simplest and most natural smells seem to me the most agreeable. And this concern chiefly affects the ladies. Amid the densest barbarism, the Scythian women, after washing, powder and plaster their whole body and face with a certain odoriferous drug that is native to their soil; and having removed this paint to approach the men, they find themselves both sleek and perfumed.

Whatever the odor is, it is a marvel how it clings to me and how apt my skin is to imbibe it. He who complains of nature that she has left man without an instrument to convey smells to his nose is wrong, for they convey themselves. But in my particular case my mustache, which is thick, performs that service. If I bring my gloves or my handkerchief near it, the smell will stay there a whole day. It betrays the place I come from. The close kisses of youth, savory, greedy, and sticky, once used to adhere to it and stay there for several hours after. And yet, for all that, I find myself little subject to epidemics, which are caught by communication and bred by the contagion of the air; and I have escaped those of my time, of which there have been many sorts in our cities and our armies. We read of Socrates that though he never left Athens during many recurrences of the plague which so many times tormented that city, he alone never found himself the worse for it.

The doctors might, I believe, derive more use from odors than they do; for I have often noticed that they make a change in me and work upon my spirits according to their properties; which makes me approve of the idea that the use of incense and perfumes in churches, so ancient and widespread in all nations and religions, was intended to delight us and arouse and purify our senses to make us more fit for contemplation.

I should like, in order to judge of it, to have shared the art of those cooks who know how to add a seasoning of foreign odors to the savor of foods, as was particularly remarked in the service of the king of Tunis, who in our time landed at Naples to confer with the Emperor Charles. They stuffed his foods with aromatic substances, so sumptuously that one peacock and two pheasants came to a hundred ducats to dress them in that manner; and when they were carved, they filled not only the dining hall but all the rooms in his palace, and even the neighboring houses, with sweet fumes which did not vanish for some time.

The principal care I take in my lodgings is to avoid heavy, stinking air. Those beautiful cities Venice and Paris weaken my fondness for them by the acrid smell of the marshes of the one and of the mud of the other.

Possibilities for Writing

1. Trace closely the arc of this brief essay, exploring the sequence of thoughts from beginning to end. Do you find a coherent pattern here? If so, explain the pattern you find. If not, how does this fact affect your reading of the essay?

2. Write an essay of your own titled "Of Smells." Focus on your personal responses to the odors you encounter at home, in public, and in man-made and natural settings, as well as on how our culture seems to define good and bad smells. Don't be afraid to be whimsical.

3. Using Montaigne as a model, write an impressionistic essay on a topic that is common to everyone's experience but that would not normally be thought of as the subject of an essay: hands or feet, say, or tears, or refrigerators, or dust. Use your imagination. Incorporate quotations as you may find them.

George Orwell
Shooting an Elephant

George Orwell's "Shooting an Elephant," one of the most frequently anthologized and analyzed of all modern essays, has achieved the status of a modern classic. The essay describes Orwell's experience in Burma, when he served as a sub-divisional police officer for Burma's colonial master, England. Through an incident that involved his shooting of an elephant, Orwell conveys his ambivalence about the people he supervises and the country he serves.

At the climactic moment of the essay, Orwell describes in harrowing detail the agony of the elephant in its death throes. At this point Orwell has so slowed the pace of the essay as to create a cinematic effect of slow motion, which highlights the elephant's agony and intensifies the emotional effect upon the reader. Then with the narrative drive halted and the harrowing description over, Orwell speculates on the larger significance of this most unusual experience.

In Moulmein, in Lower Burma, I was hated by large numbers of people—the only time in my life that I have been important enough for this to happen to me. I was sub-divisional police officer of the town, and in an aimless, petty kind of way anti-European feeling was very bitter. No one had the guts to raise a riot, but if a European woman went through the bazaars alone somebody would probably spit betel juice over her dress. As a police officer I was an obvious target and was baited whenever it seemed safe to do so. When a nimble Burman tripped me up on the football field and the referee (another Burman) looked the other way, the crowd yelled with hideous laughter. This happened more than once. In the end the sneering yellow faces of young men that met me everywhere, the insults hooted after me when I was at a safe distance, got badly on my nerves. The young Buddhist priests were the worst of all. There were several thousands of them in the town and none of them seemed to have anything to do except stand on street corners and jeer at Europeans.

All this was perplexing and upsetting. For at that time I had already made up my mind that imperialism was an evil thing and the sooner I chucked up my job and got out of it the better. Theoretically—and secretly, of course—I was all for the Burmese and all against their oppressors, the British. As for the job I was doing, I hated it more bitterly than I can perhaps make clear. In a job like that you see the dirty work of Empire at close quarters. The wretched prisoners huddling in the stinking cages of the lock-ups, the grey, cowed faces of the long-term convicts, the scarred buttocks of the men who had been flogged with bamboos—all these oppressed me with an intolerable sense of guilt. But I could get nothing into perspective. I was young and ill-educated and I had had to think out my problems in the utter silence that is imposed on every Englishman in the East. I did not even know that the British Empire is dying, still less did I know that it is a great deal better than the younger empires that are going to supplant it. All I knew was that I was stuck between my hatred of the empire I served and my rage against the evil-spirited little beasts who tried to make my job impossible. With one part of my mind I thought of the British Raj as an unbreakable tyranny, as something clamped down, in *saecula saeculorum* upon the will of prostrate peoples; with another part I thought that the greatest joy in the world would be to drive a bayonet into a Buddhist priest's guts. Feelings like these are the normal by-products of imperialism; ask any Anglo-Indian official, if you can catch him off duty.

One day something happened which in a roundabout way was enlightening. It was a tiny incident in itself, but it gave me a better glimpse than I had had before of the real nature of imperialism—the real motives for which despotic governments act. Early one morning the sub-inspector at a police station the other end of the town rang me up on the 'phone and said that an elephant was ravaging the bazaar. Would I please come and do something about it? I did not know what I could do, but I wanted to see what was happening and I got on to a pony and started out. I took my rifle, an old .44 Winchester and much too small to kill an elephant, but I thought the noise might be useful *in terrorem*. Various Burmans stopped me on the way and told me about the elephant's doings. It was not, of course, a wild elephant, but a tame one which had gone "must." It had been chained up, as tame elephants always are when their attack of "must" is due, but on the previous night it had broken its chain and escaped. Its mahout, the only person who could manage it when it was in that state, had set out in pursuit, but had taken the wrong direction and was now twelve hours' journey away, and in the morning the elephant had suddenly reappeared in the town. The Burmese population had no weapons and were quite helpless against it. It had already destroyed somebody's bamboo hut, killed a cow and raided some fruit-stalls and devoured the stock; also it had met the municipal rubbish van and, when the driver jumped out and took to his heels, had turned the van over and inflicted violences upon it.

The Burmese sub-inspector and some Indian constables were waiting for me in the quarter where the elephant had been seen. It was a very poor quarter, a labyrinth of squalid bamboo huts, thatched with palm-leaf, winding all over a steep hillside. I remember that it was a cloudy, stuffy morning at the beginning of the rains. We began questioning the people as to where the elephant had gone and, as usual, failed to get any definite information. That is invariably the case in the East; a story always sounds clear enough at a distance, but the nearer you get to the scene of events the vaguer it becomes. Some of the people said that the elephant had gone in one direction, some said that he had gone in another, some professed not even to have heard of any elephant. I had almost made up my mind that the whole story was a pack of lies, when we heard yells a little distance away. There was a loud, scandalized cry of "Go away, child! Go away this instant!" and an old woman with a switch in her hand came round the corner of a hut, violently shooing away a crowd of naked children. Some more women followed, clicking their tongues and exclaiming; evidently there was something that the children ought not to have seen. I rounded the hut and saw a man's dead body sprawling in the mud. He was an Indian, a black Dravidian coolie, almost naked, and he could not have been dead many minutes. The people said that the elephant had come suddenly upon him round the corner of the hut, caught him with its trunk, put its foot on his back and ground him into the earth. This was the rainy season and the ground was soft, and his face had scored a trench a foot deep and a couple of yards long. He was lying on his belly with arms crucified and head sharply twisted to one side. His face was coated with mud, the eyes wide open, the teeth bared and grinning with an expression of unendurable agony. (Never tell me, by the way, that the dead look peaceful. Most of the corpses I have seen looked devilish.) The friction of the great beast's foot had stripped the skin from his back as neatly as one skins a rabbit. As soon as I saw the dead man I sent an orderly to a friend's house nearby to borrow an elephant rifle. I had already sent back the pony, not wanting it to go mad with fright and throw me if it smelt the elephant.

The orderly came back in a few minutes with a rifle and five cartridges, and meanwhile some Burmans had arrived and told us that the elephant was in the paddy fields below, only a few hundred yards away. As I started forward practically the whole population of the quarter flocked out of the houses and followed me. They had seen the rifle and were all shouting excitedly that I was going to shoot the elephant. They had not shown much interest in the elephant when he was merely ravaging their homes, but it was different now that he was going to be shot. It was a bit of fun to them, as it would be to an English crowd; besides they wanted the meat. It made me vaguely uneasy. I had no intention of shooting the elephant—I had merely sent for the rifle to defend myself if necessary—and it is always unnerving to have a crowd following you. I marched down the hill, looking and feeling a fool, with the rifle over my shoulder and an ever-growing army of people jostling at my heels. At the bottom, when you got away from the huts, there was a metalled road and beyond that a miry waste of paddy fields a thousand yards across, not yet ploughed but soggy from the first rains and dotted with coarse grass. The elephant was standing eight yards from the road, his left side towards us. He took not the slightest notice of the crowd's approach. He was tearing up bunches of grass, beating them against his knees to clean them and stuffing them into his mouth.

I had halted on the road. As soon as I saw the elephant I knew with perfect certainty that I ought not to shoot him. It is a serious matter to shoot a working elephant—it is comparable to destroying a huge and costly piece of machinery—and obviously one ought not to do it if it can possibly be avoided. And at that distance, peacefully eating, the elephant looked no more dangerous than a cow. I thought then and I think now that his attack of "must" was already passing off; in which case he would merely wander harmlessly about until the mahout came back and caught him. Moreover, I did not in the least want to shoot him. I decided that I would watch him for a little while to make sure that he did not turn savage again, and then go home.

But at that moment I glanced round at the crowd that had followed me. It was an immense crowd, two thousand at the least and growing every minute. It blocked the road for a long distance on either side. I looked at the sea of yellow faces above the garish clothes—faces all happy and excited over this bit of fun, all certain that the elephant was going to be shot. They were watching me as they would watch a conjurer about to perform a trick. They did not like me, but with the magical rifle in my hands I was momentarily worth watching. And suddenly I realized that I should have to shoot the elephant after all. The people expected it of me and I had got to do it; I could feel their two thousand wills pressing me forward, irresistibly. And it was at this moment, as I stood there with the rifle in my hands, that I first grasped the hollowness, the futility of the white man's dominion in the East. Here was I, the white man with his gun, standing in front of the unarmed native crowd—seemingly the leading actor of the piece; but in reality I was only an absurd puppet pushed to and fro by the will of those yellow faces behind. I perceived in this moment that when the white man turns tyrant it is his own freedom that he destroys. He becomes a sort of hollow, posing dummy, the conventionalized figure of a sahib. For it is the condition of his rule that he shall spend his life in trying to impress the "natives," and so in every crisis he has got to do what the "natives" expect of him. He wears a mask, and his face grows to fit it. I had got to shoot the elephant. I had committed myself to doing it when I sent for the rifle. A sahib has got to act like a sahib; he has got to appear resolute, to know his own mind and do definite things. To come all that way, rifle in hand, with two thousand people marching at my heels, and then to trail feebly away, having done nothing—no, that was impossible. The crowd would laugh at me. And my whole life, every white man's life in the East, was one long struggle not to be laughed at.

But I did not want to shoot the elephant. I watched him beating his bunch of grass against his knees, with that preoccupied grandmotherly air that elephants have. It seemed to me that it would be murder to shoot him. At that age I was not squeamish about killing animals, but I had never shot an elephant and never wanted to. (Somehow it always seems worse to kill a *large* animal.) Besides, there was the beast's owner to be considered. Alive, the elephant was worth at least a hundred pounds; dead, he would only be worth the value of his tusks, five pounds, possibly. But I had got to act quickly. I turned to some experienced-looking Burmans who had been there when we arrived, and asked them how the elephant had been behaving. They all said the same thing: he took no notice of you if you left him alone, but he might charge if you went too close to him.

It was perfectly clear to me what I ought to do. I ought to walk up to within, say, twenty-five yards of the elephant and test his behavior. If he charged, I could shoot; if he took no notice of me, it would be safe to leave him until the mahout came back. But also I knew that I was going to do no such thing. I was a poor shot with a rifle and the ground was soft mud into which one would sink at every step. If the elephant charged and I missed him, I should have about as much chance as a toad under a steam-roller. But even then I was not thinking particularly of my own skin, only of the watchful yellow faces behind. For at that moment, with the crowd watching me, I was not afraid in the ordinary sense, as I would have been if I had been alone. A white man mustn't be frightened in front of "natives"; and so, in general, he isn't frightened. The sole thought in my mind was that if anything went wrong those two thousand Burmans would see me pursued, caught, trampled on and reduced to a grinning corpse like that Indian up the hill. And if that happened it was quite probable that some of them would laugh. That would never do. There was only one alternative. I shoved the cartridges into the magazine and lay down on the road to get a better aim.

The crowd grew very still, and a deep, low, happy sigh, as of people who see the theatre curtain go up at last, breathed from innumerable throats. They were going to have their bit of fun after all. The rifle was a beautiful German thing with cross-hair sights. I did not then know that in shooting an elephant one would shoot to cut an imaginary bar running from ear-hole to ear-hole. I ought, therefore, as the elephant was sideways on, to have aimed straight at his ear-hole; actually I aimed several inches in front of this, thinking the brain would be further forward.

When I pulled the trigger I did not hear the bang or feel the kick—one never does when a shot goes home—but I heard the devilish roar of glee that went up from the crowd. In that instant, in too short a time, one would have thought, even for the bullet to get there, a mysterious, terrible change had come over the elephant. He neither stirred nor fell, but every line of his body had altered. He looked suddenly stricken, shrunken, immensely old, as though the frightful impact of the bullet had paralysed him without knocking him down. At last, after what seemed a long time—it might have been five seconds, I dare say—he sagged flabbily to his knees. His mouth slobbered. An enormous senility seemed to have settled upon him. One could have imagined him thousands of years old. I fired again into the same spot. At the second shot he did not collapse but climbed with desperate slowness to his feet and stood weakly upright, with legs sagging and head drooping. I fired a third time. That was the shot that did for him. You could see the agony of it jolt his whole body and knock the last remnant of strength from his legs. But in falling he seemed for a moment to rise, for as his hind legs collapsed beneath him he seemed to tower upward like a huge rock toppling, his trunk reaching skywards like a tree. He trumpeted, for the first and only time. And then down he came, his belly towards me, with a crash that seemed to shake the ground even where I lay.

I got up. The Burmans were already racing past me across the mud. It was obvious that the elephant would never rise again, but he was not dead. He was breathing very rhythmically with long rattling gasps, his great mound of a side painfully rising and falling. His mouth was wide open—I could see far down into caverns of pale pink throat. I waited a long time for him to die, but his breathing did not weaken. Finally I fired my two remaining shots into the spot where I thought his heart must be. The thick blood welled out of him like red velvet, but still he did not die. His body did not even jerk when the shots hit him, the tortured breathing continued without a pause. He was dying, very slowly and in great agony, but in some world remote from me where not even a bullet could damage him further. I felt that I had got to put an end to that dreadful noise. It seemed dreadful to see the great beast lying there, powerless to move and yet powerless to die, and not even to be able to finish him. I sent back for my small rifle and poured shot after shot into his heart and down his throat. They seemed to make no impression. The tortured gasps continued as steadily as the ticking of a clock.

In the end I could not stand it any longer and went away. I heard later that it took him half an hour to die. Burmans were bringing dahs and baskets even before I left, and I was told they had stripped his body almost to the bones by the afternoon.

Afterwards, of course, there were endless discussions about the shooting of the elephant. The owner was furious, but he was only an Indian and could do nothing. Besides, legally I had done the right thing, for a mad elephant has to be killed, like a mad dog, if its owner fails to control it. Among the Europeans opinion was divided. The older men said I was right, the younger men said it was a damn shame to shoot an elephant for killing a coolie, because an elephant was worth more than any damn Coringhee coolie. And afterwards I was very glad that the coolie had been killed; it put me legally in the right and it gave me a sufficient pretext for shooting the elephant. I often wondered whether any of the others grasped that I had done it solely to avoid looking a fool.

Possibilities for Writing

1. Orwell makes the point in his second paragraph that he had come to believe that "imperialism was an evil thing," and he goes on to explain why he believes this both explicitly, through his own thoughts, and implicitly, through the circumstances of the story he tells. In an essay, examine Orwell's views of the evils of imperialism, both for the natives and for the colonizers.

2. Analyze Orwell's essay to consider the sense of ambivalence he felt in his position as part of the imperial police force. What does this ambivalence contribute to the tone of the essay and to Orwell's central point?

3. Orwell describes acting against his better judgment "solely to avoid looking like a fool." Have you ever done anything you believed to be wrong in order to save face, to avoid looking like a fool? Describe such an experience and what it led you to understand about yourself and about the pressure to save face.

Susan Sontag (1933–2004) was one of America's most prominent intellectuals, having been involved with the world of ideas all her life. After studying at the University of California at Berkeley, she earned a B.A. in philosophy from the University of Chicago at the age of eighteen, after which she studied religion at the Union Theological Seminary in New York, then philosophy and literature at Harvard, receiving master's degrees in both fields. Sontag also studied at Oxford and the Sorbonne. From the other side of the desk, she taught and lectured extensively at universities around the world, but for many years she made her academic home at Columbia and Rutgers universities. Sontag's books range widely, and include a collection of stories, I, etcetera *(1978); a play,* Alice in Bed *(1993); and six volumes of essays, including* Against Interpretation *(1966),* Illness as Metaphor *(1978), and* On Photography *(1977). Among her four novels are* The Volcano Lover *(1992), which was a best-seller, and* In America *(2000), which won the National Book Critics Circle Award. In addition, Sontag wrote and directed four feature-length films and was a human rights activist for more than two decades. She was also a MacArthur Fellow.*

Susan Sontag

A Woman's Beauty: Put-Down or Power Source?

In "A Woman's Beauty: Put-Down or Power Source?" Sontag displays her historical interest as well as her interest in current attitudes toward gender roles. In arguing against the dangerous and limiting ideals to which women have subjected themselves (and been subjected by men), Sontag brings to bear a brisk analysis of Greek and Christian perspectives, implicating both in their consequences for contemporary women's obsessive and compulsive efforts to make themselves beautiful.

Unlike many contemporary essays, Sontag's essays lack a strong autobiographical impulse. One might expect such a personal strain in an essay on women's beauty—it certainly would not be out of place—but Sontag assiduously avoids the personal note. But Sontag is less concerned either with her own experience of beauty or with past perspectives on beauty in and of themselves. She is far more interested in how the past can help us understand the present, and how past perspectives affect modern women's fascination with and desire for personal beauty.

For the Greeks, beauty was a virtue: a kind of excellence. Persons then were assumed to be what we now have to call—lamely, enviously— *whole* persons. If it did occur to the Greeks to distinguish between a person's "inside" and "outside," they still expected that inner beauty would be matched by beauty of the other kind. The well-born young Athenians who gathered around Socrates found it quite paradoxical that their hero was so intelligent, so brave, so honorable, so seductive—and so ugly. One of Socrates' main pedagogical acts was to be ugly—and teach those innocent, no doubt splendid-looking disciples of his how full of paradoxes life really was.

They may have resisted Socrates' lesson. We do not. Several thousand years later, we are more wary of the enchantments of beauty. We not only split off—with the greatest facility—the "inside" (character, intellect) from the "outside" (looks); but we are actually surprised when someone who is beautiful is also intelligent, talented, good.

It was principally the influence of Christianity that deprived beauty of the central place it had in classical ideals of human excellence. By limiting excellence (*virtus* in Latin) to *moral* virtue only, Christianity set beauty adrift—as an alienated, arbitrary, superficial enchantment. And beauty has continued to lose prestige. For close to two centuries it has become a convention to attribute beauty to only one of the two sexes: the sex which, however Fair, is always Second. Associating beauty with women has put beauty even further on the defensive, morally.

A beautiful woman, we say in English. But a handsome man. "Handsome" is the masculine equivalent of—and refusal of—a compliment which has accumulated certain demeaning overtones, by being reserved for women only. That one can call a man "beautiful" in French and in Italian suggests that Catholic countries—unlike those countries shaped by the Protestant version of Christianity—still retain some vestiges of the pagan admiration for beauty. But the difference, if one exists, is of degree only. In every modern country that is Christian or post-Christian, women *are* the beautiful sex—to the detriment of the notion of beauty as well as of women.

To be called beautiful is thought to name something essential to women's character and concerns. (In contrast to men—whose essence is to be strong, or effective, or competent.) It does not take someone in the throes of advanced feminist awareness to perceive that the way women are taught to be involved with beauty encourages narcissism, reinforces dependence and immaturity. Everybody (women and men) knows that. For it is "everybody," a whole society, that has identified being feminine with caring about how one *looks*. (In contrast to being masculine—which is identified with caring about what one *is* and *does* and only secondarily, if at all, about how one looks.) Given these stereotypes, it is no wonder that beauty enjoys, at best, a rather mixed reputation.

It is not, of course, the desire to be beautiful that is wrong but the obligation to be—or to try. What is accepted by most women as a flattering idealization of their sex is a way of making women feel inferior to what they actually are—or normally grow to be. For the ideal of beauty is administered as a form of self-oppression. Women are taught to see their bodies in *parts*, and to evaluate each part separately. Breasts, feet, hips, waistline, neck, eyes, nose, complexion, hair, and so on—each in turn is submitted to an anxious, fretful, often despairing scrutiny. Even if some pass muster, some will always be found wanting. Nothing less than perfection will do.

In men, good looks is a whole, something taken in at a glance. It does not need to be confirmed by giving measurements of different regions of the body; nobody encourages a man to dissect his appearance, feature by feature. As for perfection, that is considered trivial—almost unmanly. Indeed, in the ideally good-looking man a small imperfection or blemish is considered positively desirable. According to one movie critic (a woman) who is a declared Robert Redford fan, it is having that cluster of skin-colored moles on one cheek that saves Redford from being merely a "pretty face." Think of the depreciation of women—as well as of beauty—that is implied in that judgment.

"The privileges of beauty are immense," said Cocteau. To be sure, beauty is a form of power. And deservedly so. What is lamentable is that it is the only form of power that most women are encouraged to seek. This power is always conceived in relation to men; it is not the power to do but the power to attract. It is a power that negates itself. For this power is not one that can be chosen freely—at least, not by women—or renounced without social censure.

To preen, for a woman, can never be just a pleasure. It is also a duty. It is her work. If a woman does real work—and even if she has clambered up to a leading position in politics, law, medicine, business, or whatever—she is always under pressure to confess that she still works at being attractive. But in so far as she is keeping up as one of the Fair Sex, she brings under suspicion her very capacity to be objective, professional, authoritative, thoughtful. Damned if they do—women are. And damned if they don't.

One could hardly ask for more important evidence of the dangers of considering persons as split between what is "inside" and what is "outside" than that interminable half-comic half-tragic tale, the oppression of women. How easy it is to start off by defining women as caretakers of their surfaces, and then to disparage them (or find them adorable) for being "superficial." It is a crude trap, and it has worked for too long. But to get out of the trap requires that women get some critical distance from that excellence and privilege which is beauty, enough distance to see how much beauty itself has been abridged in order to prop up the mythology of the "feminine." There should be a way of saving beauty *from* women—and *for* them.

Possibilities for Writing

1. Consider the extent to which you agree (or disagree) with Sontag regarding what she says about the plight of contemporary women with respect to beauty. To what extent are men responsible for women's obsession with beauty? To what extent are women themselves responsible? Explain.

2. Sontag makes a brief historical excursion to consider the place of beauty in classical Greek culture and in early Christian times. How effective is this excursion into history? How important is it for Sontag's argument? And how persuasive is Sontag's use of these references?

3. Do your own little study of women's attitudes to beauty by surveying women you know in varying age groups. Consider both what they say and what they do with regard to the use of beauty products. Write up your findings and your analysis of the significance of beauty for women today.

Jonathan Swift (1667–1745) was born to English parents in Dublin, Ireland, and received a degree from Trinity College there. Unable to obtain a living in Ireland, he worked for some years as a secretary to a nobleman in Surrey, England, during which time he became acquainted with some of the most important literary figures of his day. He eventually returned to Ireland to assume a clerical post but still spent much of his time among the literary set in London. Swift published several volumes of romantic poetry and a wide variety of literary lampoons and political broadsides, but he is best known today for Gulliver's Travels *(1726), a sharp satire of human foibles. Appointed Dean of Dublin's St. Patrick's Cathedral in 1713, Swift was a tireless defender of the Irish in their struggle against England's harsh, sometimes unbearable rule.*

Jonathan Swift
A Modest Proposal

Jonathan Swift's "A Modest Proposal" is among the most famous satires in English. In it Swift—or rather the persona or speaker he creates to make the modest proposal—recommends killing Irish babies at one year of age. The speaker makes this proposal as a way to solve a severe economic problem that occasions great human suffering: the overpopulation of the Irish people, particularly among Irish Catholics.

The essay's power resides partly in Swift's never lifting the mask he wears, portraying his speaker as a man with a serious public service proposal. It resides, too, in the tone of consummate seriousness and scientific objectivity with which it is offered. And it also derives from Swift's use of irony and digression, from his leaving unspoken the proposal's violation of morality. The consummate reasonableness of the speaker and the wonderful summary of benefits his enacted proposal would provide show Swift wearing his mask to the very end of the essay.

It is a melancholy object to those who walk through this great town or travel in the country, when they see the streets, the roads, and cabin doors, crowded with beggars of the female-sex, followed by three, four, or six children, all in rags and importuning every passenger for an alms. These mothers, instead of being able to work for their honest livelihood, are forced to employ all their time in strolling to beg sustenance for their helpless infants, who, as they grow up, either turn thieves for want of work, or leave their dear native country to fight for the Pretender in Spain, or sell themselves to the Barbadoes.

I think it is agreed by all parties that this prodigious number of children in the arms, or on the backs, or at the heels of their mothers, and frequently of their fathers, is in the present deplorable state of the kingdom a very great additional grievance; and therefore whoever could find out a fair, cheap, and easy method of making these children sound, useful members of the commonwealth would deserve so well of the public as to have his statue set up for a preserver of the nation.

But my intention is very far from being confined to provide only for the children of professed beggars; it is of a much greater extent, and shall take in the whole number of infants at a certain age who are born of parents in effect as little able to support them as those who demand our charity in the streets.

As to my own part, having turned my thoughts for many years upon this important subject, and maturely weighed the several schemes of other projectors, I have always found them grossly mistaken in their computation. It is true, a child just dropped from its dam may be supported by her milk for a solar year, with little other nourishment; at most not above the value of two shillings, which the mother may certainly get, or the value in scraps, by her lawful occupation of begging; and it is exactly at one year old that I propose to provide for them in such a manner as instead of being a charge upon their parents or the parish, or wanting food and raiment for the rest of their lives, they shall on the contrary contribute to the feeding, and partly to the clothing, of many thousands.

There is likewise another great advantage in my scheme, that it will prevent those voluntary abortions, and that horrid practice of women murdering their bastard children, alas, too frequent among us, sacrificing the poor innocent babes, I doubt, more to avoid the expense than the shame, which would move tears and pity in the most savage and inhuman breast.

The number of souls in this kingdom being usually reckoned one million and a half, of these I calculate there may be about two hundred thousand couples whose wives are breeders; from which number I subtract thirty thousand couples who are able to maintain their own children, although I apprehend there cannot be so many under the present distresses of the kingdom; but this being granted, there will remain an hundred and seventy thousand breeders. I again subtract fifty thousand for those women who miscarry, or whose children die by accident or disease within the year. There only remain an hundred and twenty

thousand children of poor parents annually born. The question therefore is, how this number shall be reared and provided for, which, as
I have already said, under the present situation of affairs, is utterly
impossible by all the methods hitherto proposed. For we can neither
employ them in handicraft or agriculture; we neither build houses
(I mean in the country) nor cultivate land. They can very seldom pick
up a livelihood by stealing till they arrive at six years old, except where
they are of towardly parts; although I confess they learn the rudiments
much earlier, during which time they can however be looked upon only
as probationers, as I have been informed by a principal gentleman in
the county of Cavan, who protested to me that he never knew above one
or two instances under the age of six, even in a part of the kingdom so
renowned for the quickest proficiency in that art.

I am assured by our merchants that a boy or a girl before twelve
years old is no salable commodity; and even when they come to this age
they will not yield above three pounds, or three pounds and half a crown
at most on the Exchange; which cannot turn to account either to the
parents or the kingdom, the charge of nutriment and rags having been at
least four times that value.

I shall now therefore humbly propose my own thoughts, which I hope
will not be liable to the least objection.

I have been assured by a very knowing American of my acquaintance in London, that a young healthy child well nursed is at a year old
a most delicious, nourishing, and wholesome food, whether stewed,
roasted, baked, or boiled; and I make no doubt that it will equally serve
in a fricassee or a ragout.

I do therefore humbly offer it to public consideration that of the
hundred and twenty thousand children, already computed, twenty
thousand may be reserved for breed, whereof only one fourth part to be
males, which is more than we allow to sheep, black cattle, or swine; and
my reason is that these children are seldom the fruits of marriage, a cir-
cumstance not much regarded by our savages, therefore one male will
be sufficient to serve four females. That the remaining hundred thousand may at a year old be offered in sale to the persons of quality and
fortune through the kingdom, always advising the mother to let them
suck plentifully in the last month, so as to render them plump and fat
for a good table. A child will make two dishes at an entertainment for
friends; and when the family dines alone, the fore or hind quarter will

make a reasonable dish, and seasoned with a little pepper or salt will be very good boiled on the fourth day, especially in winter.

I have reckoned upon a medium that a child just born will weigh twelve pounds, and in a solar year if tolerably nursed increaseth to twenty-eight pounds.

I grant this food will be somewhat dear, and therefore very proper for landlords, who, as they have already devoured most of the parents, seem to have the best title to the children.

Infant's flesh will be in season throughout the year, but more plentiful in March, and a little before and after. For we are told by a grave author, an eminent French physician, that fish being a prolific diet, there are more children born in Roman Catholic countries about nine months after Lent than at any other season; therefore, reckoning a year after Lent, the markets will be more glutted than usual, because the number of popish infants is at least three to one in this kingdom; and therefore it will have one other collateral advantage, by lessening the number of Papists among us.

I have already computed the charge of nursing a beggar's child (in which list I reckon all cottagers, laborers, and four fifths of the farmers) to be about two shillings per annum, rags included; and I believe no gentleman would repine to give ten shillings for the carcass of a good fat child, which, as I have said, will make four dishes of excellent nutritive meat, when he hath only some particular friend or his own family to dine with him. Thus the squire will learn to be a good landlord, and grow popular among the tenants; the mother will have eight shillings net profit, and be fit for work till she produces another child.

Those who are more thrifty (as I must confess the times require) may flay the carcass; the skin of which artificially dressed will make admirable gloves for ladies, and summer boots for fine gentlemen.

As to our city of Dublin, shambles may be appointed for this purpose in the most convenient parts of it, and butchers we may be assured will not be wanting; although I rather recommend buying the children alive, and dressing them hot from the knife as we do roasting pigs.

A very worthy person, a true lover of his country, and whose virtues I highly esteem, was lately pleased in discoursing on this matter to offer a refinement upon my scheme. He said that many gentlemen of this kingdom, having of late destroyed their deer, he conceived that the want of venison might be well supplied by the bodies of young lads and maidens, not exceeding fourteen years of age nor under twelve, so great a number of both sexes in every county being now ready to starve for want of work and service; and these to be disposed of by their parents, if alive, or otherwise by their nearest relations. But with due deference to so excellent a friend and so deserving a patriot, I cannot be altogether in his sentiments; for as to the males, my American acquaintance assured me from frequent experience that their flesh was generally tough and lean, like that of our schoolboys, by continual exercise, and their taste disagreeable; and to fatten them would not answer the charge. Then as to the females, it would, I think with humble submission, be a loss to the public, because they soon would become breeders themselves: and besides, it is not improbable that some scrupulous people might be apt to censure such a practice (although indeed very unjustly) as a little bordering upon cruelty; which, I confess, hath always been with me the strongest objection against any project, how well soever intended.

But in order to justify my friend, he confessed that this expedient was put into his head by the famous Psalmanazar, a native of the island Formosa, who came from thence to London above twenty years ago, and in conversation told my friend that in his country when any young person happened to be put to death, the executioner sold the carcass to persons of quality as a prime dainty; and that in his time the body of a plump girl of fifteen, who was crucified for an attempt to poison the emperor, was sold to his Imperial Majesty's prime minister of state, and other great mandarins of the court, in joints from the gibbet, at four hundred crowns. Neither indeed can I deny that if the same use were made of several plump young girls in this town, who without one single groat to their fortunes cannot stir abroad without a chair, and appear at the playhouse and assemblies in foreign fineries which they never will pay for, the kingdom would not be the worse.

Some persons of a desponding spirit are in great concern about that vast number of poor people who are aged, diseased, or maimed, and I have been desired to employ my thoughts what course may be taken to ease the nation of so grievous an encumbrance. But I am not in the least pain upon that matter, because it is very well known that they are every day dying and rotting by cold and famine, and filth and vermin, as fast as can be reasonably expected. And as to the younger laborers, they are now in almost as hopeful a condition. They cannot get work, and consequently pine away for want of nourishment to a degree that if at any time they are accidentally hired to common labor, they have not strength to perform it; and thus the country and themselves are happily delivered from the evils to come.

I have too long digressed, and therefore shall return to my subject. I think the advantages by the proposal which I have made are obvious and many, as well as of the highest importance.

For first, as I have already observed, it would greatly lessen the number of Papists, with whom we are yearly overrun, being the principal breeders of the nation as well as our most dangerous enemies; and who stay at home on purpose to deliver the kingdom to the Pretender, hoping to take their advantage by the absence of so many good Protestants, who have chosen rather to leave their country than to stay at home and pay tithes against their conscience to an Episcopal curate.

Secondly, the poorer tenants will have something valuable of their own, which by law may be made liable to distress, and help to pay their landlord's rent, their corn and cattle being already seized and money a thing unknown.

Thirdly, whereas the maintenance of an hundred thousand children, from two years old and upwards, cannot be computed at less than ten shillings a piece per annum, the nation's stock will be thereby increased fifty thousand pounds per annum, besides the profit of a new dish introduced to the tables of all gentlemen of fortune in the kingdom who have any refinement in taste. And the money will circulate among ourselves, the goods being entirely of our own growth and manufacture.

Fourthly, the constant breeders, besides the gain of eight shillings sterling per annum by the sale of their children, will be rid of the charge of maintaining them after the first year.

Fifthly, this food would likewise bring great custom to taverns, where the vintners will certainly be so prudent as to procure the best receipts for dressing it to perfection, and consequently have their houses frequented by all the fine gentlemen, who justly value themselves upon their knowledge in good eating; and a skillful cook, who understands how to oblige his guests, will contrive to make it as expensive as they please.

Sixthly, this would be a great inducement to marriage, which all wise nations have either encouraged by rewards or enforced by laws and penalties. It would increase the care and tenderness of mothers toward their children, when they were sure of a settlement for life to the poor babes, provided in some sort by the public, to their annual profit instead of expense. We should see an honest emulation among the married women, which of them could bring the fattest child to the market. Men would become as fond of their wives during the time of their pregnancy as they are now of their mares in foal, their cows in calf, or sows when they are ready to farrow; nor offer to beat or kick them (as is too frequent a practice) for fear of a miscarriage.

Many other advantages might be enumerated. For instance, the addition of some thousand carcasses in our exportation of barreled beef, the propagation of swine's flesh, and improvement in the art of making good bacon, so much wanted among us by the great destruction of pigs, too frequent at our tables, which are no way comparable in taste or magnificence to a well-grown, fat, yearling child, which roasted whole will make a considerable figure at a lord mayor's feast or any other public entertainment. But this and many others I omit, being studious of brevity.

Supposing that one thousand families in this city would be constant customers for infants' flesh, besides others who might have it at merry meetings, particularly weddings and christenings, I compute that Dublin would take off annually about twenty thousand carcasses, and the rest of the kingdom (where probably they will be sold somewhat cheaper) the remaining eighty thousand.

I can think of no one objection that will possibly be raised against this proposal, unless it should be urged that the number of people will be thereby much lessened in the kingdom. This I freely own, and it was indeed one principal design in offering it to the world. I desire the reader will observe, that I calculate my remedy for this one individual kingdom of Ireland and for no other that ever was, is, or I think ever can be upon earth. Therefore let no man talk to me of other expedients: of taxing our absentees at five shillings a pound: of using neither clothes nor household furniture except what is of our own growth and manufacture: of utterly rejecting the materials and instruments that promote foreign luxury: of curing the expensiveness of pride, vanity, idleness, and gaming in our women: of introducing a vein of parsimony, prudence, and temperance: of learning to love our country, in the want of which we differ even from Laplanders and the inhabitants of Topinamboo: of quitting our animosities and factions, nor acting any longer like the Jews, who were murdering one another at the very moment their city was taken: of being a little cautious not to sell our country and conscience for nothing: of teaching landlords to have at least one degree of mercy toward their tenants: lastly, of putting a spirit of honesty, industry, and skill into our shopkeepers; who, if a resolution could now be taken to buy only our native goods, would immediately unite to cheat and exact upon us in the price, the measure, and the goodness, nor could ever yet be brought to make one fair proposal of just dealing, though often and earnestly invited to it.

Therefore I repeat, let no man talk to me of these and the like expedients, till he hath at least some glimpse of hope that there will ever be some hearty and sincere attempt to put them in practice.

But as to myself, having been wearied out for many years with offering vain, idle, visionary thoughts, and at length utterly despairing of success, I fortunately fell upon this proposal, which, as it is wholly new, so it hath something solid and real, of no expense and little trouble, full in our own power, and whereby we can incur no danger in disobliging England. For this kind of commodity will not bear exportation, the flesh being of too tender a consistence to admit a long continuance in salt, although perhaps I could name a country which would be glad to eat up our whole nation without it.

After all, I am not so violently bent upon my own opinion as to reject any offer proposed by wise men, which shall be found equally innocent, cheap, easy, and effectual. But before something of that kind shall be advanced in contradiction to my scheme, and offering a better, I desire the author or authors will be pleased maturely to consider two points. First, as things now stand, how they will be able to find food and raiment for an hundred thousand useless mouths and backs. And secondly, there being a round million of creatures in human figure throughout this kingdom, whose sole subsistence put into a common stock would leave them in debt two millions of pounds sterling, adding those who are beggars by profession to the bulk of farmers, cottagers, and laborers, with their wives and children who are beggars in effect; I desire those politicians who dislike my overture, and may perhaps be so bold to attempt an answer, that they will first ask the parents of these mortals whether they would not at this day think it a great happiness to have been sold for food at a year old in the manner I prescribe, and thereby have avoided such a perpetual scene of misfortunes as they have since gone through by the oppression of landlords, the impossibility of paying rent without money or trade, the want of common sustenance, with neither house nor clothes to cover them from the inclemencies of the weather, and the most inevitable prospect of entailing the like or greater miseries upon their breed forever.

I profess, in the sincerity of my heart, that I have not the least personal interest in endeavoring to promote this necessary work, having no other motive than the public good of my country, by advancing our trade, providing for infants, relieving the poor, and giving some pleasure to the rich. I have no children by which I can propose to get a single penny; the youngest being nine years old, and my wife past childbearing.

Possibilities for Writing

1. Throughout "A Modest Proposal," Swift uses language that dehumanizes the Irish people. Point out examples of such language, and explain their effect both in terms of Swift's satire and his underlying purpose.

2. Though Swift never fully drops his mask, he does make a number of veiled appeals toward sympathy for the Irish and legitimate suggestions for alleviating their predicament. Citing the text, examine when and where he does so. How can you recognize his seriousness?

3. Write a "modest proposal" of your own in which you offer an outrageous solution to alleviate some social problem. Make sure that readers understand that your proposal is satirical and that they recognize your real purpose in writing.

Amy Tan (b. 1952) grew up in Oakland, California, her parents having immigrated from China only shortly before her birth. She graduated from San Francisco State University with degrees in English and linguistics and began her writing career in the business world, drafting presentations, marketing materials, and producing various corporate publications. Tan began pursuing fiction writing as a break from the stress of her job, and in 1987, after years of literary workshops, she produced The Joy Luck Club, *a group of interrelated stories about four Chinese immigrant mothers and their assimilated, second-generation daughters. It was an immediate success both with critics and readers and was followed by* The Kitchen's God's Wife *(1991),* The Hundred Secret Senses *(1995),* The Bonesetter's Daughter *(2001), and* Saving Fish from Drowning *(2005) all dealing with similar themes of family and culture.*

Amy Tan
Mother Tongue

In "Mother Tongue," Amy Tan describes the various kinds of English she uses—from the "broken" English she uses in speaking with her mother, to the formal and sophisticated English she employs in public settings. Tan plays upon the meaning of the term "mother tongue," referring both to English as one's native language and to the English her own mother uses, that is, her mother's English, which is not her mother's "mother tongue."

For Amy Tan herself, English is a variety of tongues. English is more than a single and monolithic way of using the language. Tan finds in her mother's "broken" English, for example, a powerful self-presence, even though the mother's use of English is riddled with grammatical errors and idiomatic incongruities. Part of the pleasure of Tan's essay is the way the writer plays off various kinds of English against one another. Part of the essay's power lies in its invitation to see how English provides multiple possibilities for conveying ideas and expressing oneself. An additional but related aspect of Tan's essay is its revelation of culturally conflicting perspectives—and how language, in this case English, both reflects and exacerbates them.

I am not a scholar of English or literature. I cannot give you much more than personal opinions on the English language and its variations in this country or others.

I am a writer. And by that definition, I am someone who has always loved language. I am fascinated by language in daily life. I spend a great deal of my time thinking about the power of language—the way it can evoke an emotion, a visual image, a complex idea, or a simple truth. Language is the tool of my trade. And I use them all—all the Englishes I grew up with.

Recently, I was made keenly aware of the different Englishes I do use. I was giving a talk to a large group of people, the same talk I had already given to half a dozen other groups. The nature of the talk was about my writing, my life, and my book, *The Joy Luck Club*. The talk was going along well enough, until I remembered one major difference that made the whole talk sound wrong. My mother was in the room. And it was perhaps the first time she had heard me give a lengthy speech, using the kind of English I have never used with her. I was saying things like "The intersection of memory upon imagination" and "There is an aspect of my fiction that relates to thus-and-thus"—a speech filled with carefully wrought grammatical phrases, burdened, it suddenly seemed to me, with nominalized forms, past perfect tenses, conditional phrases, all the forms of standard English that I had learned in school and through books, the forms of English I did not use at home with my mother.

Just last week, I was walking down the street with my mother, and I again found myself conscious of the English I was using, the English I do use with her. We were talking about the price of new and used furniture and I heard myself saying this: "Not waste money that way." My husband was with us as well, and he didn't notice any switch in my English. And then I realized why. It's because over the twenty years we've been together I've often used that same kind of English with him, and sometimes he even uses it with me. It has become our language of intimacy, a different sort of English that relates to family talk, the language I grew up with.

So you'll have some idea of what this family talk I heard sounds like, I'll quote what my mother said during a recent conversation which I videotaped and then transcribed. During this conversation, my mother was talking about a political gangster in Shanghai who had the same last name as her family's, Du, and how the gangster in his early years wanted to be adopted by her family, which was rich by comparison. Later, the gangster became more powerful, far richer than my mother's family, and one day showed up at my mother's wedding to pay his respects. Here's what she said in part:

"Du Yusong having business like fruit stand. Like off the street kind. He is Du like Du Zong—but not Tsung-ming Island people. The local people call putong, the river east side, he belong to that side local people. That man want to ask Du Zong father take him in like become own family. Du Zong father wasn't look down on him, but didn't take seriously, until that man big like become a mafia. Now important person, very hard to inviting him. Chinese way, came only to show respect, don't stay for dinner. Respect for making big celebration, he shows up. Mean gives lots of respect. Chinese custom. Chinese social life that way. If too important won't have to stay too long. He come to my wedding. I didn't see, I heard it. I gone to boy's side, they have YMCA dinner. Chinese age I was nineteen."

You should know that my mother's expressive command of English belies how much she actually understands. She reads the *Forbes* report, listens to *Wall Street Week*, converses daily with her stockbroker, reads all of Shirley MacLaine's books with ease—all kinds of things I can't begin to understand. Yet some of my friends tell me they understand 50 percent of what my mother says. Some say they understand 80 to 90 percent. Some say they understand none of it, as if she were speaking pure Chinese. But to me, my mother's English is perfectly clear, perfectly natural. It's my mother tongue. Her language, as I hear it, is vivid, direct, full of observation and imagery. That was the language that helped shape the way I saw things, expressed things, made sense of the world.

Lately, I've been giving more thought to the kind of English my mother speaks. Like others, I have described it to people as "broken" or "fractured" English. But I wince when I say that. It has always bothered me that I can think of no other way to describe it other than "broken," as if it were damaged and needed to be fixed, as if it lacked a certain wholeness and soundness. I've heard other terms used, "limited English," for example. But they seem just as bad, as if everything is limited, including people's perceptions of the limited English speaker.

I know this for a fact, because when I was growing up, my mother's "limited" English limited *my* perception of her. I was ashamed of her English. I believed that her English reflected the quality of what she had to say. That is, because she expressed them imperfectly her thoughts were imperfect. And I had plenty of empirical evidence to support me: the fact that people in department stores, at banks, and at restaurants did not take her seriously, did not give her good service, pretended not to understand her, or even acted as if they did not hear her.

My mother has long realized the limitations of her English as well. When I was fifteen, she used to have me call people on the phone to pretend I was she. In this guise, I was forced to ask for information or even to complain and yell at people who had been rude to her. One time it was a call to her stockbroker in New York. She had cashed out her small portfolio and it just so happened we were going to go to New York the next week, our very first trip outside California. I had to get on the phone and say in an adolescent voice that was not very convincing, "This is Mrs. Tan."

And my mother was standing in the back whispering loudly, "Why he don't send me check, already two weeks late. So mad he lie to me, losing me money."

And then I said in perfect English, "Yes, I'm getting rather concerned. You had agreed to send the check two weeks ago, but it hasn't arrived."

Then she began to talk more loudly. "What he want, I come to New York tell him front of his boss, you cheating me?" And I was trying to calm her down, make her be quiet, while telling the stockbroker, "I can't tolerate any more excuses. If I don't receive the check immediately, I am going to have to speak to your manager when I'm in New York next week." And sure enough, the following week there we were in front of this astonished stockbroker, and I was sitting there red-faced and quiet, and my mother, the real Mrs. Tan, was shouting at his boss in her impeccable broken English.

We used a similar routine just five days ago, for a situation that was far less humorous. My mother had gone to the hospital for an appointment, to find out about a benign brain tumor a CAT scan had revealed a month ago. She said she had spoken very good English, her best English, no mistakes. Still, she said, the hospital did not apologize when they said they had lost the CAT scan and she had come for nothing. She said they did not seem to have any sympathy when she told them she was anxious to know the exact diagnosis, since her husband and son had both died of brain tumors. She said they would not give her any more information until the next time and she would have to make another appointment for that. So she said she would not leave until the doctor called her daughter. She wouldn't budge. And when the doctor finally called her daughter, me, who spoke in perfect English—lo and behold—we had assurances the CAT scan would be found, promises that a conference call on Monday would be held, and apologies for any suffering my mother had gone through for a most regrettable mistake.

I think my mother's English almost had an effect on limiting my possibilities in life as well. Sociologists and linguists probably will tell you that a person's developing language skills are more influenced by peers. But I do think that the language spoken in the family, especially in immigrant families which are more insular, plays a large role in shaping the language of the child. And I believe that it affected my results on achievement tests, IQ tests, and the SAT. While my English skills were never judged as poor, compared to math, English could not be considered my strong suit. In grade school I did moderately well, getting perhaps B's, sometimes B-pluses, in English and scoring perhaps in the sixtieth or seventieth percentile on achievement tests. But those scores were not good enough to override the opinion that my true abilities lay in math and science, because in those areas I achieved A's and scored in the ninetieth percentile or higher.

This was understandable. Math is precise; there is only one correct answer. Whereas, for me at least, the answers on English tests were always a judgment call, a matter of opinion and personal experience. Those tests were constructed around items like fill-in-the-blank sentence completion, such as "Even though Tom was ____, Mary thought he was ____." And the correct answer always seemed to be the most bland combinations of thoughts, for example, "Even though Tom was shy, Mary thought he was charming," with the grammatical structure "even though" limiting the correct answer to some sort of semantic opposites, so you wouldn't get answers like, "Even though Tom was foolish, Mary thought he was ridiculous." Well, according to my mother, there were very few limitations as to what Tom could have been and what Mary might have thought of him. So I never did well on tests like that.

The same was true with word analogies, pairs of words in which you were supposed to find some sort of logical, semantic relationship—for example, "*Sunset* is to *nightfall* as ____ is to ____." And here you would be presented with a list of four possible pairs, one of which showed the same kind of relationship: *red* is to *stoplight*, *bus* is to *arrival*, *chills* is to *fever*, *yawn* is to *boring*. Well, I could never think that way. I knew what the tests were asking, but I could not block out of my mind the images already created by the first pair, "*sunset* is to *nightfall*"—and I would see a burst of colors against a darkening sky, the moon rising, the lowering of a curtain of stars. And all the other pairs of words—red, bus, stoplight, boring—just threw up a mass of confusing images, making it impossible for me to sort out something as logical as saying: "A sunset precedes nightfall" is the same as "a chill precedes a fever." The only way I would have gotten that answer right would have been to imagine an associative situation, for example, my being disobedient and staying out past sunset, catching a chill at night, which turns into feverish pneumonia as punishment, which indeed did happen to me.

I have been thinking about all this lately, about my mother's English, about achievement tests. Because lately I've been asked, as a writer, why there are not more Asian Americans represented in American literature. Why are there few Asian Americans enrolled in creative writing programs? Why do so many Chinese students go into engineering? Well, these are broad sociological questions I can't begin to answer. But I have noticed in surveys—in fact, just last week—that Asian students, as a whole, always do significantly better on math achievement tests than in English. And this makes me think that there are other Asian-American students whose English spoken in the home might also be described as "broken" or "limited." And perhaps they also have teachers who are steering them away from writing and into math and science, which is what happened to me.

Fortunately, I happen to be rebellious in nature and enjoy the challenge of disproving assumptions made about me. I became an English major my first year in college, after being enrolled as pre-med. I started writing nonfiction as a freelancer the week after I was told by my former boss that writing was my worst skill and I should hone my talents toward account management.

But it wasn't until 1985 that I finally began to write fiction. And at first I wrote using what I thought to be wittily crafted sentences, sentences that would finally prove I had mastery over the English language. Here's an example from the first draft of a story that later made its way into *The Joy Luck Club*, but without this line: "That was my mental quandary in its nascent state." A terrible line, which I can barely pronounce.

Fortunately, for reasons I won't get into today, I later decided I should envision a reader for the stories I would write. And the reader I decided upon was my mother, because these were stories about mothers. So with this reader in mind—and in fact she did read my early drafts—I began to write stories using all the Englishes I grew up with: the English I spoke to my mother, which for lack of a better term might be described as "simple"; the English she used with me, which for lack of a better term might be described as "broken"; my translation of her Chinese, which could certainly be described as "watered down"; and what I imagined to be her translation of her Chinese if she could speak in perfect English, her internal language, and for that I sought to preserve the essence, but neither an English nor a Chinese structure. I wanted to capture what language ability tests can never reveal: her intent, her passion, her imagery, the rhythms of her speech, and the nature of her thoughts.

Apart from what any critic had to say about my writing, I knew I had succeeded where it counted when my mother finished reading my book and gave me her verdict: "So easy to read."

Possibilities for Writing

1. Tan's focus here is on the "different Englishes" she uses. What are these, and what occasions her shift from one to another? Consider, as well, her feelings about these various "Englishes" and about her mother's fractured English. In what ways are these both limiting and liberating for communication?

2. Tan is pleased when her mother's verdict on her first novel was that it was "So easy to read." Do you find Tan's style in this essay "easy to read"? In an essay, evaluate her style, quoting from the text to support your viewpoint.

3. How does your language and that of your peers differ from that of a different generation of speakers—your parents, say, or your children? How does the language you use in formal situations differ from that you use in less formal ones? In an essay, describe the different sorts of "Englishes" you encounter in your life.

Henry David Thoreau (1817–1862) was born in Concord, Massachusetts, where he spent most of his life. A graduate of Harvard, he was an early protégé of Ralph Waldo Emerson, whom he served for several years as an assistant and under whose tutelage he began to write for publication. Thoreau was philosophically a strict individualist and antimaterialist, and in 1845 he retired for two years to an isolated cabin on Walden Pond, near Concord, where he lived in comparative solitude, studying the natural world, reading, and keeping a journal that would become the basis for Walden *(1854), a lyrical but deeply reasoned account of his experiences there and what they meant to him, as well as four later volumes. His work has influenced generations of writers, thinkers, and even political movements in terms of determining what constitutes true human and natural value.*

Henry David Thoreau

Why I Went to the Woods

In this excerpt from the second chapter of *Walden*, Thoreau explains why he "went to the woods," that is, why he took a sabbatical from civilization to get away from it all for a while. (Thoreau spent two years and two weeks at Walden pond, where he built himself a cabin, grew his own food, and subsisted simply, as an experiment to see how little he would really need to live.) Essentially, Thoreau wanted time to read, write, and think. He wanted to make time for nature. And he wanted to test himself, to see just how much he could simplify his life, to determine how much time he could save to do what he really wanted to do with every minute of every day.

The appeal of Thoreau's central idea and fundamental ideal is especially acute for twenty-first century America, where people strive to accomplish as much as they can as fast as they can so as to accumulate everything they think they need. Thoreau postulates an opposite ideal: to see how little we really require to live our lives, with an appreciation for what is truly essential and a respect for the rhythms of the natural world.

I went to the woods because I wished to live deliberately, to front only the essential facts of life, and see if I could not learn what it had to teach, and not, when I came to die, discover that I had not lived. I did not wish to live what was not life, living is so dear; nor did I wish to practice resignation, unless it was quite necessary. I wanted to live deep and suck out all the marrow of life, to live so sturdily and Spartan-like as to put to rout all that was not life, to cut a broad swath and shave close, to drive life into a corner, and reduce it to its lowest terms, and, if it proved to be mean, why then to get the whole and genuine meanness of it, and publish its meanness to the world; or if it were sublime, to know it by experience, and be able to give a true account of it in my next excursion. For most men, it appears to me, are in a strange uncertainty about it, whether it is of the devil or of God, and have *somewhat hastily* concluded that it is the chief end of man here to "glorify God and enjoy him forever."

Still we live meanly, like ants; though the fable tells us that we were long ago changed into men; like pygmies we fight with cranes; it is error upon error, and clout upon clout, and our best virtue has for its occasion a superfluous and evitable wretchedness. Our life is frittered away by detail. An honest man has hardly need to count more than his ten fingers, or in extreme cases he may add his ten toes, and lump the rest. Simplicity, simplicity, simplicity! I say, let your affairs be as two or three, and not a hundred or a thousand; instead of a million count half a dozen, and keep your accounts on your thumb-nail. In the midst of this chopping sea of civilized life, such are the clouds and storms and quicksands and thousand-and-one items to be allowed for, that a man has to live, if he would not founder and go to the bottom and not make his port at all, by dead reckoning, and he must be a great calculator indeed who succeeds. Simplify, simplify. Instead of three meals a day, if it be necessary eat but one; instead of a hundred dishes, five; and reduce other things in proportion. Our life is like a German Confederacy, made of up petty states, with its boundary forever fluctuating, so that even a German cannot tell you how it is bounded at any moment. The nation itself, with all its so-called internal improvements, which, by the way are all external and superficial, is just such an unwieldy and overgrown establishment, cluttered with furniture and tripped up by its own traps, ruined by luxury and heedless expense, by want of calculation and a worthy aim, as the million households in the lands; and the only cure for it, as for them, is in a rigid economy, a stern and more than Spartan simplicity of life and elevation of purpose. It lives too fast. Men think that it is essential that the *Nation* have commerce, and export ice, and talk through a telegraph, and ride thirty miles an hour, without a doubt, whether *they* do or not; but whether we should live like baboons or like men, is a little uncertain. If we do not get our sleepers, and forge rails, and devote days and nights to the work, but go to tinkering upon our *lives* to improve *them*, who will build railroads? And if railroads are not built, how shall we get to heaven in season? But if we stay at home and mind our business, who will want railroads? We do not ride on the rail-road; it rides upon us. Did you ever think what those sleepers are that underlie the railroad? Each one is a man, an Irishman, or a Yankee man. The rails are laid on them, and they are covered with sand, and the cars run smoothly over them. They are sound sleepers, I assure you. And every few years a new lot is laid down and run over; so that, if some have the pleasure of riding on a rail, others have the misfortune to be ridden upon. And when they run over a man that is walking in his sleep, a supernumerary sleeper in the wrong position, and wake him up, they suddenly stop the cars, and make a hue and cry about it, as if this were an exception. I am glad to know that it takes a gang of men for every five miles to keep the sleepers down and level in their beds as it is, for this is a sign that they may sometimes get up again.

Why should we live with such hurry and waste of life? We are determined to be starved before we are hungry. Men say that a stitch in time saves nine, and so they take a thousand stitches to-day to save nine tomorrow. As for *work*, we haven't any of any consequence. We have the Saint Vitus' dance, and cannot possibly keep our heads still. If I should only give a few pulls at the parish bell-rope, as for a fire, that is, without setting the bell, there is hardly a man on his farm in the outskirts of Concord, notwithstanding that press of engagements which was his excuse so many times this morning, nor a boy, nor a woman, I might almost say, but would foresake all and follow that sound, not mainly to save property from the flames, but, if we will confess the truth, much more to see it burn, since burn it must, and we, be it known, did not set it on fire—or to see it put out, and have a hand in it, if that is done as handsomely; yes, even if it were the parish church itself. Hardly a man takes a half-hour's nap after dinner, but when he wakes he holds up his head and asks, "What's the news?" as if the rest of mankind had stood his sentinels. Some give directions to be waked every half-hour, doubtless for no other purpose; and then, to pay for it, they tell what they have dreamed. After a night's sleep the news is as indispensable as the breakfast. "Pray tell me anything new that has happened to a man anywhere on this globe"—and he reads it over his coffee and rolls, that a man has had his eyes gouged out this morning on the Wachito River; never dreaming the while that he lives in the dark unfathomed mammoth cave of this world, and has but the rudiment of an eye himself.

For my part, I could easily do without the post-office. I think that there are very few important communications made through it. To speak critically, I never received more than one or two letters in my life—I wrote this some years ago—that were worth the postage. The penny-post is, commonly, an institution through which you seriously offer a man that penny for his thoughts which is so often safely offered in jest. And I am sure that I never read any memorable news in a newspaper. If we read of one man robbed, or murdered, or killed by accident, or one house burned, or one vessel wrecked, or one steamboat blown up, or one cow run over on the Western Railroad, or one mad dog killed, or one lot of grasshoppers in the winter—we never need read of another. One is enough. If you are acquainted with the principle, what do you care for a myriad instances and applications? To a philosopher all *news*, as it is called, is gossip, and they who edit and read it are old women over their tea. Yet not a few are greedy after this gossip. There was such a rush, as I hear, the other day at one of the offices to learn the foreign news by the last arrival, that several large squares of plate glass belonging to the establishment were broken by the pressure—news which I seriously think a ready wit might write a twelvemonth, or twelve years, beforehand with sufficient accuracy. As for Spain, for instance, if you know how to throw in Don Carlos and the Infanta, and Don Pedro and Seville and Granada, from time to time in the right proportions—they may have changed the names a little since I saw the papers—and serve up a bullfight when other entertainments fail, it will be true to the letter, and give us as good an idea of the exact state or ruin of things in Spain as the most succinct and lucid reports under this head in the newspapers; and as for England, almost the last significant scrap of news from that quarter was the revolution of 1649; and if you have learned the history of her crops for an average year, you never need attend to that thing again, unless your speculations are of a merely pecuniary character. If one may judge who rarely looks into the newspapers, nothing new does ever happen in foreign parts, a French revolution not excepted.

What news! how much more important to know what that is which was never old! "Kieou-he-yu (great dignitary of the state of Wei) sent a man to Khoung-tseu to know his news. Khoung-tseu caused the messenger to be seated near him, and questioned him in these terms: What is your master doing? The messenger answered with respect: My master desires to diminish the number of his faults, but he cannot come to the end of them. The messenger being gone, the philosopher remarked: What a worthy messenger! What a worthy messenger!" The preacher, instead of vexing the ears of drowsy farmers on their day of rest at the end of the week—for Sunday is the fit conclusion of an ill-spent week, and not the fresh and brave beginning of a new one—with this one other draggle-tail of a sermon, should shout with thundering voice, "Pause! Avast! Why so seeming fast, but deadly slow?"

Shams and delusions are esteemed for soundless truths, while reality is fabulous. If men would steadily observe realities only, and not allow themselves to be deluded, life, to compare it with such things as we know, would be like a fairy tale and the Arabian Nights' Entertainments. If we respected only what is inevitable and has a right to be, music and poetry would resound along the streets. When we are unhurried and wise, we perceive that only great and worthy things have any permanent and absolute existence, that petty fears and petty pleasures are but the shadow of the reality. This is always exhilarating and sublime. By closing the eyes and slumbering, and consenting to be deceived by shows, men establish and confirm their daily life of routine and habit everywhere, which still is built on purely illusory foundations. Children, who play life, discern its true law and relations more clearly than men, who fail to live it worthily, but who think that they are wiser by experience, that is, by failure. I have read in a Hindoo book, that "there was a king's son, who, being expelled in infancy from his native city, was brought up by a forester, and, growing up to maturity in that state, imagined himself to belong to the barbarous race with which he lived. One of his father's ministers having discovered him, revealed to him what he was, and the misconception of his character was removed, and he knew himself to be a prince. So soul," continues the Hindoo philosopher, "from the circumstances in which it is placed, mistakes its own character, until the truth is revealed to it by some holy teacher and then it knows itself to be *Brahme.*" I perceive that we inhabitants of New England live this mean life that we do because our vision does not penetrate the surface of things. We think that that *is* which *appears* to be. If a man should walk through this town and see only the reality, where, think you, would the "Milldam" go to? If he should give us an account of the realities he beheld there, we should not recognize the place in his description. Look at the meetinghouse, or a courthouse, or a jail, or a shop, or a dwelling-house, and say what that thing really is before a true gaze, and they would all go to pieces in your account of them. Men esteem truth remote, in the outskirts of the system, behind the farthest star, before Adam and after the last man. In eternity there is indeed something true and sublime. But all these times and places and occasions are now and here. God himself culminates in the present moment, and will never be more divine in the lapse of all the ages. And we are enabled to apprehend at all what is sublime and noble only by the perpetual instilling and drenching of the reality that surrounds us. The universe constantly and obediently answers to our conceptions; whether we travel fast or slow, the track is laid for us. Let us spend our lives in conceiving then. The poet or the artist never yet had so fair and noble a design but some of his posterity at least could accomplish it.

Let us spend one day as deliberately as Nature, and not be thrown off the track by every nutshell and mosquito's wing that falls on the rails. Let us rise early and fast, or breakfast, gently and without perturbation; let company come and let company go, let the bells ring and the children cry—determined to make a day of it. Why should we knock under and go with the stream? Let us not be upset and overwhelmed in that terrible rapid and whirlpool called a dinner, situated in the meridian shallows. Weather this danger and you are safe, for the rest of the way is downhill. With unrelaxed nerves, with morning vigor, sail by it, looking another way, tied to the mast like Ulysses. If the engine whistles, let it whistle till it is hoarse for its pains. If the bell rings, why should we run? We will consider what kind of music they are like. Let us settle ourselves and work and wedge our feet downward through the mud and slush of opinion, and prejudice, and tradition, and delusion, and appearance, that alluvion which covers the globe, through Paris and London, through New York and Boston and Concord, through Church and State, through poetry and philosophy and religion, till we come to a hard bottom and rocks in place, which we can call *reality*, and say, This is, and no mistake; and then begin, having a *point d'appui*, below freshet and frost and fire, a place where you might found a wall or a state, or set a lamppost safely, or perhaps a gauge, not a Nilometer, but a Realometer, that future ages might know how deep a freshet of shams and appearances had gathered from time to time. If you stand right fronting and face to face to a fact, you will see the sun glimmer on both its surfaces, as if it were a cimeter, and feel its sweet edge dividing you through the heart and marrow, and so you will happily conclude your mortal career. Be it life or death, we crave only reality. If we are really dying, let us hear the rattle in our throats and feel cold in the extremities; if we are alive, let us go about our business.

Time is but the stream I go afishing in. I drink at it; but while I drink I see the sandy bottom and detect how shallow it is. Its thin current slides away but eternity remains. I would drink deeper; fish in the sky, whose bottom is pebbly with stars. I cannot count one. I know not the first letter of the alphabet. I have always been regretting that I was not as wise as the day I was born. The intellect is a cleaver; it discerns and rifts its way into the secret of things. I do not wish to be any more busy with my hands than is necessary. My head is hands and feet. I feel all my best faculties concentrated in it. My instinct tells me that my head is an organ for burrowing, as some creatures use their snout and fore paws, and with it I would mine and burrow my way through these hills. I think that the richest vein is somewhere hereabouts; so by the divining-rod and thin rising vapors, I judge; and here I will begin to mine.

Possibilities for Writing

1. Analyze the recommendations that Thoreau is making here. What are his general recommendations? What are his specific recommendations? How might these recommendations be applied to life as it is lived in the twenty-first century?

2. Thoreau's writing is characterized by extensive use of metaphor. Choose several of these to analyze in detail. How well does metaphor contribute to clarifying Thoreau's ideas?

3. Throughout the essay, Thoreau includes what are for him statements of observed truth—for example, "Our life is frittered away by detail" and "I perceive that we . . . live this mean life that we do because our vision does not penetrate the surface of things." Choose one of these ideas that you find interesting as the basis for an essay of your own.

James Thurber (1894–1961), one the country's premiere humorists, was born in Columbus, Ohio, and educated at Ohio State University, where he wrote for the school newspaper. After working as a reporter for the Columbus Dispatch *and later a Paris-based correspondent for the* Chicago Tribune, *in 1927 he joined the staff of the* New Yorker, *a magazine with which he would be associated for the rest of his life (as a freelancer from 1936). His stylish wit marked by psychological insight, Thurber produced droll short stories, a comic play about college life, and a number of works of gentle satire on various subjects. He is probably best remembered today for his cartoons and drawings, of which there are many collections. These often depict hapless middle-aged men besieged by the demands of domineering wives and beset by the petty irritations of everyday life.*

James Thurber

University Days

In "University Days," the American humorist James Thurber writes comically about his college experience at Ohio State University. Thurber entertains and amuses while conveying his sense of frustration and bemusement at what he experienced and observed there.

Thurber arranges this excerpt from his autobiography, *My Life and Hard Times*, as a series of linked stories. In an anecdote about his botany class, Thurber describes his frustration at not being able to see what he is supposed to see through a microscope, and what, presumably, his fellow classmates see. He structures the botany anecdote to allow for the hope of success, only to dash that hope with comic deflation. Through stories about gym and journalism and military drill, Thurber creates a comic persona that is, paradoxically, both blind and insightful. In showing readers what Thurber the character didn't see, Thurber the writer shows us some things we can smile about.

His anecdote about economics class shifts the focus from Thurber himself to another hapless student—a Polish football player, Bolenciecwz, who serves as a comic stereotype of the intellectually challenged but lovable oversized athlete. His professors and fellow students together help Bolenciecwz to just scrape by academically so as to retain his athletic eligibility. A large part of the humor of this anecdote lies in the variety of ways students and professor hint at the answer to a question Bolenciecwz is asked in class—what goes "choo-choo"; "toot-toot"; "chuffa, chuffa"—and the delay in Bolenciecwz's finally realizing that the answer is "a train."

I passed all the other courses that I took at my university, but I could never pass botany. This was because all botany students had to spend several hours a week in a laboratory looking through a microscope at plant cells, and I could never see through a microscope. I never once saw a cell through a microscope. This used to enrage my instructor. He would wander around the laboratory pleased with the progress all the students were making in drawing the involved and, so I am told, interesting structure of flower cells, until he came to me. I would just be standing there. "I can't see anything," I would say. He would begin patiently enough, explaining how anybody can see through a microscope, but he would always end up in a fury, claiming that I could *too* see through a microscope but just pretended that I couldn't. "It takes away from the beauty of flowers anyway," I used to tell him. "We are not concerned with beauty in this course," he would say. "We are concerned solely with what I may call the *mechanics* of flowers." "Well," I'd say, "I can't see anything." "Try it just once again," he'd say, and I would put my eye to the microscope and see nothing at all, except now and again a nebulous milky substance—a phenomenon of maladjustment. You were supposed to see a vivid, restless clockwork of sharply defined plant cells. "I see what looks like a lot of milk," I would tell him. This, he claimed, was the result of my not having adjusted the microscope properly, so he would readjust it for me, or rather, for himself. And I would look again and see milk.

I finally took a deferred pass, as they called it, and waited a year and tried again. (You had to pass one of the biological sciences or you couldn't graduate.) The professor had come back from vacation brown as a berry, bright-eyed, and eager to explain cell-structure again to his classes. "Well," he said to me, cheerily, when we met in the first laboratory hour of the semester, "we're going to see cells this time, aren't we?" "Yes, sir," I said. Students to right of me and to left of me and in front of me were seeing cells; what's more, they were quietly drawing pictures of them in their notebooks. Of course, I didn't see anything.

"We'll try it," the professor said to me, grimly, "with every adjustment of the microscope known to man. As God is my witness, I'll arrange this glass so that you see cells through it or I'll give up teaching. In twenty-two years of botany, I—" He cut off abruptly for he was beginning to quiver all over, like Lionel Barrymore, and he genuinely wished to hold onto his temper; his scenes with me had taken a great deal out of him.

So we tried it with every adjustment of the microscope known to man. With only one of them did I see anything but blackness or the familiar lacteal opacity, and that time I saw, to my pleasure and amazement, a variegated constellation of flecks, specks, and dots. These I hastily drew. The instructor, noting my activity, came back from an adjoining desk, a smile on his lips and his eyebrows high in hope. He looked at my cell drawing. "What's that?" he demanded, with a hint of a squeal in his voice. "That's what I saw" I said. "You didn't, you didn't, you *didn't!*" he screamed, losing control of his temper instantly, and he bent over and squinted into the microscope. His head snapped up. "That's your eye!" he shouted. "You've fixed the lens so that it reflects! You've drawn your eye!"

Another course that I didn't like, but somehow managed to pass, was economics. I went to that class straight from the botany class, which didn't help me any in understanding either subject. I used to get them mixed up. But not as mixed up as another student in my economics class who came there direct from a physics laboratory. He was a tackle on the football team, named Bolenciecwcz. At that time Ohio State University had one of the best football teams in the country, and Bolenciecwcz was one of its outstanding stars. In order to be eligible to play it was necessary for him to keep up in his studies, a very difficult matter, for while he was not dumber than an ox he was not any smarter. Most of his professors were lenient and helped him along. None gave him more hints in answering questions or asked him simpler ones than the economics professor, a thin, timid man named Bassum. One day when we were on the subject of transportation and distribution, it came Bolenciecwcz's turn to answer a question. "Name one means of transportation," the professor said to him. No light came into the big tackle's eyes. "Just any means of transportation," said the professor. Bolenciecwcz sat staring at him. "That is," pursued the professor, "any medium, agency, or method of going from one place to another." Bolenciecwcz had the look of a man who is being led into a trap. "You may choose among steam, horse-drawn, or electrically propelled vehicles," said the instructor. "I might suggest the one which we commonly take in making long journeys across land." There was a profound silence in which everybody stirred uneasily, including Bolenciecwcz and Mr. Bassum. Mr. Bassum abruptly broke this silence in an amazing manner. "Choo-choo-choo," he said, in a low voice, and turned instantly scarlet. He glanced appealingly around the room. All of us, of course, shared Mr. Bassum's desire that Bolenciecwcz should stay abreast of the class in economics, for the Illinois game, one of the hardest and most important of the season, was only a week off. "Toot, toot, too-tooooooot!" some student with a deep voice moaned, and we all looked encouragingly at Bolenciecwcz. Somebody else gave a fine imitation of a locomotive letting off steam. Mr. Bassum himself rounded off the little show. "Ding, dong, ding, dong," he said, hopefully. Bolenciecwcz was staring at the floor now, trying to think, his great brow furrowed, his huge hands rubbing together, his face red.

"How did you come to college this year, Mr. Bolenciecwcz?" asked the professor. "*Chuffa* chuffa, *chuffa* chuffa."

"M'father sent me," said the football player.

"What on?" asked Bassum.

"I git an 'lowance," said the tackle, in a low, husky voice, obviously embarrassed.

"No, no," said Bassum. "Name a means of transportation. What did you *ride* here on?"

"Train," said Bolenciecwcz.

"Quite right," said the professor. "Now, Mr. Nugent, will you tell us—"

If I went through anguish in botany and economics—for different reasons—gymnasium work was even worse. I don't even like to think about it. They wouldn't let you play games or join in the exercises with your glasses on and I couldn't see with mine off. I bumped into professors, horizontal bars, agricultural students, and swinging iron rings. Not being able to see, I could take it but I couldn't dish it out. Also, in order to pass gymnasium (and you had to pass it to graduate) you had to learn to swim if you didn't know how. I didn't like the swimming pool, I didn't like swimming, and I didn't like the swimming instructor, and after all these years I still don't. I never swam but I passed my gym work anyway, by having another student give my gymnasium number (978) and swim across the pool in my place. He was a quiet, amiable blond youth, number 473, and he would have seen through a microscope for me if we could have got away with it, but we couldn't get away with it. Another thing I didn't like about gymnasium work was that they made you strip the day you registered. It is impossible for me to be happy when I am stripped and being asked a lot of questions. Still, I did better than a lanky agricultural student who was cross-examined just before I was. They asked each student what college he was in—that is, whether Arts, Engineering, Commerce, or Agriculture. "What college are you in?" the instructor snapped at the youth in front of me. "Ohio State University," he said promptly.

It wasn't that agricultural student but it was another a whole lot like him who decided to take up journalism, possibly on the ground that when farming went to hell he could fall back on newspaper work. He didn't realize, of course, that that would be very much like falling back full-length on a kit of carpenter's tools. Haskins didn't seem cut out for journalism, being too embarrassed to talk to anybody and unable to use a typewriter, but the editor of the college paper assigned him to the cow barns, the sheep house, the horse pavilion, and the animal husbandry department generally. This was a genuinely big "beat," for it took up five times as much ground and got ten times as great a legislative appropriation as the College of Liberal Arts. The agricultural student knew animals, but nevertheless his stories were dull and colorlessly written. He took all afternoon on each of them, on account of having to hunt for each letter on the typewriter. Once in a while he had to ask somebody to help him hunt. "C" and "L," in particular, were hard letters for him to find. His editor finally got pretty much annoyed at the farmer-journalist because his pieces were so uninteresting. "See here, Haskins," he snapped at him one day, "why is it we never have anything hot from you on the horse pavilion? Here we have two hundred head of horses on this campus—more than any other university in the Western Conference except Purdue—and yet you never get any real lowdown on them. Now shoot over to the horse barns and dig up something lively." Haskins shambled out and came back in about an hour; he said he had something. "Well, start it off snappily," said the editor. "Something people will read." Haskins set to work and in a couple of hours brought a sheet of typewritten paper to the desk; it was a two-hundred-word story about some disease that had broken out among the horses. Its opening sentence was simple but arresting. It read: "Who has noticed the sores on the tops of the horses in the animal husbandry building?"

Ohio State was a land grant university and therefore two years of military drill was compulsory. We drilled with old Springfield rifles and studied the tactics of the Civil War even though the World War was going on at the time. At 11 o'clock each morning thousands of freshmen and sophomores used to deploy over the campus, moodily creeping up on the old chemistry building. It was good training for the kind of warfare that was waged at Shiloh but it had no connection with what was going on in Europe. Some people used to think there was German money behind it, but they didn't dare say so or they would have been thrown in jail as German spies. It was a period of muddy thought and marked, I believe, the decline of higher education in the Middle West.

As a soldier I was never any good at all. Most of the cadets were glumly indifferent soldiers, but I was no good at all. Once General Littlefield, who was commandant of the cadet corps, popped up in front of me during regimental drill and snapped, "You are the main trouble with this university!" I think he meant that my type was the main trouble with the university but he may have meant me individually. I was mediocre at drill, certainly—that is, until my senior year. By that time I had drilled longer than anybody else in the Western Conference, having failed at military at the end of each preceding year so that I had to do it all over again. I was the only senior still in uniform. The uniform which, when new, had made me look like an interurban railway conductor, now that it had become faded and too tight made me look like Bert Williams in his bellboy act. This had a definitely bad effect on my morale. Even so, I had become by sheer practice little short of wonderful at squad maneuvers.

One day General Littlefield picked our company out of the whole regiment and tried to get it mixed up by putting it through one movement after another as fast as we could execute them: squads right, squads left, squads on right into line, squads right about, squads left front into line, etc. In about three minutes one hundred and nine men were marching in one direction and I was marching away from them at an angle of forty degrees, all alone. "Company, halt!" shouted General Littlefield. "That man is the only man who has it right!" I was made a corporal for my achievement.

The next day General Littlefield summoned me to his office. He was swatting flies when I went in. I was silent and he was silent too, for a long time; I don't think he remembered me or why he had sent for me, but he didn't want to admit it. He swatted some more flies, keeping his eyes on them narrowly before he let go with the swatter. "Button up your coat!" he snapped. Looking back on it now I can see that he meant me although he was looking at a fly, but I just stood there. Another fly came to rest on a paper in front of the general and began rubbing its hind legs together. The general lifted the swatter cautiously. I moved restlessly and the fly flew away. "You startled him!" barked General Littlefield, looking at me severely. I said I was sorry. "That won't help the situation!" snapped the General, with cold military logic. I didn't see what I could do except offer to chase some more flies toward his desk, but I didn't say anything. He stared out the window at the faraway figures of co-eds crossing the campus toward the library. Finally, he told me I could go. So I went. He either didn't know which cadet I was or else he forgot what he wanted to see me about. It may have been that he wished to apologize for having called me the main trouble with the university; or maybe he had decided to compliment me on my brilliant drilling of the day before and then at the last minute decided not to. I don't know. I don't think about it much any more.

Possibilities for Writing

1. Thurber here describes several different incidents from his college days. Consider each as a separate anecdote, and analyze the source of its humor individually. Who—or what—is the "butt" of each story, and how, in your opinion, does this determine the success of its comic effect?

2. Analyze the comic persona Thurber creates here. Is he always in on the joke? How does Thurber achieve this effect?

3. Relate some of your own comic experiences in high school, college, or both to suggest some of the absurdity found in any educational environment. Change names as you see fit, and don't be afraid to exaggerate a bit.

E. B. White (1899–1985) was born to wealthy parents in Mount Vernon, New York, a suburb of Manhattan. At Cornell University, he was editor of the campus newspaper, and he early settled on a career in journalism. In 1927 he joined the staff of the newly formed New Yorker *magazine and contributed greatly to the sophisticated, sharply ironic tone of the publication. He relocated his family to rural Maine in 1933 and left the* New Yorker *in 1937 to write a monthly column for* Harper's. *These more serious and emotionally felt essays were collected in* One Man's Meat *(1942), and White published two more major essay collections in 1954 and 1962. He is also the author of several popular children's books, including* Stuart Little *(1945) and* Charlotte's Web *(1952). Considered a peerless stylist, White also edited and expanded* The Elements of Style *by Willard Strunk, Jr.*

E. B. White

Once More to the Lake

E. B. White's "Once More to the Lake" describes a visit to a Maine Lake that White makes with his family, which evokes memories of the annual trip he made there when he was a young boy. Reflecting on his recent trip in the context of the time he spent at the lake as a youth, White creates a lyrical remembrance of the place and a speculative essay about the passage of time, about change and changelessness, and about mortality.

One of the most striking features of the essay is the way White describes himself, his father, and his son. White explains, for example, how, as he watched his son doing the things he did when he was a boy at the lake—preparing the fishing tackle box, running the boat's outboard motor, casting his fishing line—White felt that he was "living a dual existence." Inhabiting the essay's present as the adult father of his son, White sees himself in his son as the boy he had been when his father occupied the paternal role that White himself later occupies. "It gave me," he writes "a creepy sensation." Just how creepy we only understand with White's culminating realization at the end of the essay.

One summer, along about 1904, my father rented a camp on a lake in Maine and took us all there for the month of August. We all got ringworm from some kittens and had to rub Pond's Extract on our arms and legs night and morning, and my father rolled over in a canoe with all his clothes on; but outside of that the vacation was a success and from then on none of us ever thought there was any place in the world like that lake in Maine. We returned summer after summer—always on August 1 for one month. I have since become a salt-water man, but sometimes in summer there are days when the restlessness of the tides and the fearful

cold of the sea water and the incessant wind that blows across the afternoon and into the evening make me wish for the placidity of a lake in
the woods. A few weeks ago this feeling got so strong I bought myself a
couple of bass hooks and a spinner and returned to the lake where we
used to go, for a week's fishing and to revisit old haunts.

I took along my son, who had never had any fresh water up his nose
and who had seen lily pads only from train windows. On the journey
over to the lake I began to wonder what it would be like. I wondered
how time would have marred this unique, this holy spot—the coves and
streams, the hills that the sun set behind, the camps and the paths
behind the camps. I was sure that the tarred road would have found it
out, and I wondered in what other ways it would be desolated. It is
strange how much you can remember about places like that once you
allow your mind to return into the grooves that lead back. You remember one thing, and that suddenly reminds you of another thing. I guess
I remembered clearest of all the early mornings, when the lake was cool
and motionless, remembered how the bedroom smelled of the lumber it
was made of and of the wet woods whose scent entered through the
screen. The partitions in the camp were thin and did not extend clear to
the top of the rooms, and as I was always the first up I would dress
softly so as not to wake the others, and sneak out into the sweet out-
doors and start out in the canoe, keeping close along the shore in the
long shadows of the pines. I remembered being very careful never to rub
my paddle against the gunwale for fear of disturbing the stillness of the
cathedral.

The lake had never been what you would call a wild lake. There were
cottages sprinkled around the shores, and it was in farming country
although the shores of the lake were quite heavily wooded. Some of the
cottages were owned by nearby farmers, and you would live at the shore
and eat your meals at the farmhouse. That's what our family did. But
although it wasn't wild, it was a fairly large and undisturbed lake and
there were places in it that, to a child at least, seemed infinitely remote and
primeval.

I was right about the tar: it led to within half a mile of the shore. But
when I got back there, with my boy, and we settled into a camp near a
farmhouse and into the kind of summertime I had known, I could tell that
it was going to be pretty much the same as it had been before—I knew it,
lying in bed the first morning, smelling the bedroom and hearing the boy

sneak quietly out and go off along the shore in a boat. I began to sustain
the illusion that he was I, and therefore, by simple transposition, that I
was my father. This sensation persisted, kept cropping up all the time we
were there. It was not an entirely new feeling, but in this setting it grew
much stronger. I seemed to be living a dual existence. I would be in the
middle of some simple act, I would be picking up a bait box or laying
down a table fork, or I would be saying something, and suddenly it would
be not I but my father who was saying the words or making the gesture.
It gave me a creepy sensation.

We went fishing the next morning. I felt the same damp moss covering
the worms in the bait can, and saw the dragonfly alight on the tip of my
rod as it hovered a few inches from the surface of the water. It was the
arrival of this fly that convinced me beyond any doubt that everything
was as it always had been, that the years were a mirage and that there
had been no years. The small waves were the same, chucking the rowboat
under the chin as we fished at anchor, and the boat was the same boat,
the same color green and the ribs broken in the same places, and under
the floorboards the same fresh-water leavings and débris—the dead hel-
gramite, the wisps of moss, the rusty discarded fishhook, the dried blood
from yesterday's catch. We stared silently at the tips of our rods, at the
dragonflies that came and went. I lowered the tip of mine into the water,
tentatively, pensively dislodging the fly, which darted two feet away,
poised, darted two feet back, and came to rest again a little farther up the
rod. There had been no years between the ducking of this dragonfly and
the other one—the one that was part of memory. I looked at the boy, who
was silently watching his fly, and it was my hands that held his rod, my
eyes watching. I felt dizzy and didn't know which rod I was at the end of.

We caught two bass, hauling them in briskly as though they were
mackerel, pulling them over the side of the boat in a businesslike manner
without any landing net, and stunning them with a blow on the back of
the head. When we got back for a swim before lunch, the lake was
exactly where we had left it, the same number of inches from the dock,
and there was only the merest suggestion of a breeze. This seemed an
utterly enchanted sea, this lake you could leave to its own devices for a
few hours and come back to, and find that it had not stirred, this constant and trustworthy body of water. In the shallows, the dark, water-
soaked sticks and twigs, smooth and old, were undulating in clusters on
the bottom against the clean ribbed sand, and the track of the mussel

was plain. A school of minnows swam by, each minnow with its small individual shadow, doubling the attendance, so clear and sharp in the sunlight. Some of the other campers were in swimming, along the shore, one of them with a cake of soap, and the water felt thin and clear and unsubstantial. Over the years there had been this person with the cake of soap, this cultist, and here he was. There had been no years.

Up to the farmhouse to dinner through the teeming, dusty field, the road under our sneakers was only a two-track road. The middle track was missing, the one with the marks of the hooves and the splotches of dried, flaky manure. There had always been three tracks to choose from in choosing which track to walk in; now the choice was narrowed down to two. For a moment I missed terribly the middle alternative. But the way led past the tennis court, and something about the way it lay there in the sun reassured me; the tape had loosened along the backline, the alleys were green with plantains and other weeds, and the net (installed in June and removed in September) sagged in the dry noon, and the whole place steamed with midday heat and hunger and emptiness. There was a choice of pie for dessert, and one was blueberry and one was apple, and the waitresses were the same country girls, there having been no passage of time, only the illusion of it as in a dropped curtain— the waitresses were still fifteen; their hair had been washed, that was the only difference—they had been to the movies and seen the pretty girls with the clean hair.

Summertime, oh, summertime, pattern of life indelible, the fade-proof lake, the woods unshatterable, the pasture with the sweetfern and the juniper forever and ever, summer without end; this was the background, and the life along the shore was the design, the cottagers with their innocent and tranquil design, their tiny docks with the flagpole and the American flag floating against the white clouds in the blue sky, the little paths over the roots of the trees leading from camp to camp and the paths leading back to the outhouses and the can of lime for sprinkling, and at the souvenir counters at the store the miniature birchbark canoes and the postcards that showed things looking a little better than they looked. This was the American family at play, escaping the city heat, wondering whether the newcomers in the camp at the head of the cove were "common" or "nice," wondering whether it was true that the people who drove up for Sunday dinner at the farmhouse were turned away because there wasn't enough chicken.

It seemed to me, as I kept remembering all this, that those times and those summers had been infinitely precious and worth saving. There had been jollity and peace and goodness. The arriving (at the beginning of August) had been so big a business in itself, at the railway station the farm wagon drawn up, the first smell of the pine-laden air, the first glimpse of the smiling farmer, and the great importance of the trunks and your father's enormous authority in such matters, and the feel of the wagon under you for the long ten-mile haul, and at the top of the last long hill catching the first view of the lake after eleven months of not seeing this cherished body of water. The shouts and cries of the other campers when they saw you, and the trunks to be unpacked, to give up their rich burden. (Arriving was less exciting nowadays, when you sneaked up in your car and parked it under a tree near the camp and took out the bags and in five minutes it was all over, no fuss, no loud wonderful fuss about trunks.)

Peace and goodness and jollity. The only thing that was wrong now, really, was the sound of the place, an unfamiliar nervous sound of the outboard motors. This was the note that jarred, the one thing that would sometimes break the illusion and set the years moving. In those other summertimes all motors were inboard; and when they were at a little distance, the noise they made was a sedative, an ingredient of summer sleep. They were one-cylinder and two-cylinder engines, and some were make-and-break and some were jump-spark, but they all made a sleepy sound across the lake. The one-lungers throbbed and fluttered, and the twin-cylinder ones purred and purred, and that was a quiet sound, too. But now the campers all had outboards. In the daytime, in the hot mornings, these motors made a petulant, irritable sound; at night, in the still evening when the afterglow lit the water, they whined about one's ears like mosquitoes. My boy loved our rented outboard, and his great desire was to achieve single-handed mastery over it, and authority, and he soon learned the trick of choking it a little (but not too much), and the adjustment of the needle valve. Watching him I would remember the things you could do with the old one-cylinder engine with the heavy flywheel, how you could have it eating out of your hand if you got really close to it spiritually. Motorboats in those days didn't have clutches, and you would make a landing by shutting off the motor at the proper time and coasting in with a dead rudder. But there was a way of reversing them, if you learned the trick, by cutting the switch and putting it on again exactly on the final dying revolution of the flywheel, so that it would kick back against compression and begin reversing. Approaching a dock in a strong following breeze, it was difficult to slow up sufficiently by the ordinary coasting method, and if a boy felt he had complete mastery over his motor, he was tempted to keep it running beyond its time and then reverse it a few feet from the dock. It took a cool nerve, because if you threw the switch a twentieth of a second too soon you would catch the flywheel when it still had speed enough to go up past center, and the boat would leap ahead, charging bull-fashion at the dock.

We had a good week at the camp. The bass were biting well and the sun shone endlessly, day after day. We would be tired at night and lie down in the accumulated heat of the little bedrooms after the long hot day and the breeze would stir almost imperceptibly outside and the smell of the swamp drift in through the rusty screens. Sleep would come easily and in the morning the red squirrel would be on the roof, tapping out his gay routine. I kept remembering everything, lying in bed in the mornings—the small steamboat that had a long rounded stern like the lip of a Ubangi, and how quietly she ran on the moonlight sails, when the older boys played their mandolins and the girls sang and we ate doughnuts dipped in sugar, and how sweet the music was on the water in the shining night, and what it had felt like to think about girls then. After breakfast we would go up to the store and the things were in the same place—the minnows in a bottle, the plugs and spinners disarranged and pawed over by the youngsters from the boys' camp, the Fig Newtons and the Beeman's gum. Outside, the road was tarred and cars stood in front of the store. Inside, all was just as it had always been, except there was more Coca-Cola and not so much Moxie and root beer and birch beer and sarsaparilla. We would walk out with the bottle of pop apiece and sometimes the pop would backfire up our noses and hurt. We explored the streams, quietly, where the turtles slid off the sunny logs and dug their way into the soft bottom; and we lay on the town wharf and fed worms to the tame bass. Everywhere we went I had trouble making out which was I, the one walking at my side, the one walking in my pants.

One afternoon while we were there at that lake a thunderstorm came up. It was like the revival of an old melodrama that I had seen long ago with childish awe. The second-act climax of the drama of the electrical disturbance over a lake in America had not changed in any important respect. This was the big scene, still the big scene. The whole thing was so familiar, the first feeling of oppression and heat and a general air around camp of not wanting to go very far away. In midafternoon (it was all the same) a curious darkening of the sky, and a lull in everything that had made life tick; and then the way the boats suddenly swung the other way at their moorings with the coming of a breeze out of the new quarter, and the premonitory rumble. Then the kettle drum, then the snare, then the bass drum and cymbals, then crackling light against the dark, and the gods grinning and licking their chops in the hills. Afterward the calm, the rain steadily rustling in the calm lake, the return of light and hope and spirits, and the campers running out in joy and relief to go swimming in the rain, their bright cries perpetuating the deathless joke about how they were getting simply drenched, and the children screaming with delight at the new sensation of bathing in the rain, and the joke about getting drenched linking the generations in a strong indestructible chain. And the comedian who waded in carrying an umbrella.

When the others went swimming, my son said he was going in, too. He pulled his dripping trunks from the line where they had hung all through the shower and wrung them out. Languidly, and with no thought of going in, I watched him, his hard little body, skinny and bare, saw him wince slightly as he pulled up around his vitals the small, soggy, icy garment. As he buckled the swollen belt, suddenly my groin felt the chill of death.

Possibilities for Writing

1. Analyze White's essay to focus on its themes of change and changelessness. To what extent, might White say, is change itself changeless?

2. White is justly noted for his writing style, particularly his attention to concrete yet evocative descriptive detail. Choose several passages that appeal to you, and examine White's use of language in them. How would you characterize White's style?

3. Describe a place that holds a personal sense of history for you. It may be a place you have returned to after a long absence, as the lake is for White, or a place that simply holds many memories. Focus on your responses to and feelings about the place both in the past and from your present perspective.

Virginia Woolf (1882–1941) was born Virginia Stephen into one of London's most prominent literary families. Essentially self-educated in her father's vast library, by her early twenties Woolf was publishing reviews and critical essays in literary journals. Her first novel appeared in 1915, but it was the publication of Mrs. Dalloway *in 1925 and* To the Lighthouse *in 1927 that established her reputation as an important artistic innovator. Four more novels followed, and her criticism and essays were collected in* The Common Reader *(1925, 1932),* Three Guineas *(1938), and* The Death of the Moth and Other Essays *(1942), edited posthumously by her husband after her tragic suicide. Her* Collected Essays *(1967) numbers four volumes. Woolf is also remembered for* A Room of One's Own *(1929), an early feminist consideration of the difficulties facing women writers.*

Virginia Woolf
The Death of the Moth

In her classic essay "The Death of the Moth," Virginia Woolf writes memorably about a moth she chances to see while gazing out her window on a sunny September morning. Watching the moth fly within a small square of window pane, Woolf speculates about the life force that animates the moth and about the myriad forms of life she notices in the fields. With his seemingly unflagging energy, the moth represents for Woolf, the pure energy of "life itself."

Woolf begins with seeing, with careful description of the moth based on attentive observation. The essay moves quickly, however, to speculation, as Woolf reflects on the moth's significance. At first Woof pities the pathetic little moth with its severely circumscribed and limited life. But as she watches it longer, she begins to analogize the life of the moth with human life. Her attitude shifts toward respect for the moth's attempts to live its brief life as exuberantly as it can.

Moths that fly by day are not properly to be called moths; they do not excite that pleasant sense of dark autumn nights and ivy-blossom which the commonest yellow-underwing asleep in the shadow of the curtain never fails to rouse in us. They are hybrid creatures, neither gay like butterflies nor sombre like their own species. Nevertheless the present specimen, with his narrow hay-coloured wings, fringed with a tassel of the same colour, seemed to be content with life. It was a pleasant morning, mid-September, mild, benignant, yet with a keener breath than that of the summer months. The plough was already scoring the field opposite the window, and where the share had been, the earth was pressed flat and gleamed with moisture. Such vigour came rolling in from the fields and the down beyond that it was difficult to keep the eyes strictly turned upon the book. The rooks too were keeping one of their annual festivities; soaring round the tree tops until it looked as if a vast net with thousands of black knots in it had been cast up into the air; which, after a few moments sank slowly down upon the trees until every twig seemed to have a knot at the end of it. Then, suddenly, the net would be thrown into the air again in a wider circle this time, with the utmost clamour and vociferation, as though to be thrown into the air and settle slowly down upon the tree tops were a tremendously exciting experience.

The same energy which inspired the rooks, the ploughmen, the horses, and even, it seemed, the lean bare-backed downs, sent the moth fluttering from side to side of his square of the window-pane. One could not help watching him. One was, indeed, conscious of a queer feeling of pity for him. The possibilities of pleasure seemed that morning so enormous and so various that to have only a moth's part in life, and a day moth's at that, appeared a hard fate, and his zest in enjoying his meagre opportunities to the full, pathetic. He flew vigorously to one corner of his compartment, and, after waiting there a second, flew across to the other. What remained for him but to fly to a third corner and then to a fourth? That was all he could do, in spite of the size of the downs, the width of the sky, the far-off smoke of houses, and the romantic voice, now and then, of a steamer out at sea. What he could do he did. Watching him, it seemed as if a fibre, very thin but pure, of the enormous energy of the world had been thrust into his frail and diminutive body. As often as he crossed the pane, I could fancy that a thread of vital light became visible. He was little or nothing but life.

Yet, because he was so small, and so simple a form of the energy that was rolling in at the open window and driving its way through so many narrow and intricate corridors in my own brain and in those of other human beings, there was something marvellous as well as pathetic about him. It was as if someone had taken a tiny bead of pure life and decking it as lightly as possible with down and feathers, had set it dancing and zig-zagging to show us the true nature of life. Thus displayed one could not get over the strangeness of it. One is apt to forget all about life, seeing it humped and bossed and garnished and cumbered so that it has to move with the greatest circumspection and dignity. Again, the thought of all that life might have been had he been born in any other shape caused one to view his simple activities with a kind of pity.

After a time, tired by his dancing apparently, he settled on the window ledge in the sun, and, the queer spectacle being at an end, I forgot about him. Then, looking up, my eye was caught by him. He was trying to resume his dancing, but seemed either so stiff or so awkward that he could only flutter to the bottom of the window-pane; and when he tried to fly across it he failed. Being intent on other matters I watched these futile attempts for a time without thinking, unconsciously waiting for him to resume his flight, as one waits for a machine, that has stopped momentarily, to start again without considering the reason of its failure. After perhaps a seventh attempt he slipped from the wooden ledge and fell, fluttering his wings, on to his back on the window sill. The helplessness of his attitude roused me. It flashed upon me that he was in difficulties; he could no longer raise himself; his legs struggled vainly. But, as I stretched out a pencil, meaning to help him to right himself, it came over me that the failure and awkwardness were the approach of death. I laid the pencil down again.

The legs agitated themselves once more. I looked as if for the enemy against which he struggled. I looked out of doors. What had happened there? Presumably it was midday, and work in the fields had stopped. Stillness and quiet had replaced the previous animation. The birds had taken themselves off to feed in the brooks. The horses stood still. Yet the power was there all the same, massed outside indifferent, impersonal, not attending to anything in particular. Somehow it was opposed to the little hay-coloured moth. It was useless to try to do anything. One could only watch the extraordinary efforts made by those tiny legs against an oncoming doom which could, had it chosen, have submerged an entire city, not merely a city, but masses of human beings; nothing, I knew, had any chance against death. Nevertheless after a pause of exhaustion the legs fluttered again. It was superb this last protest, and so frantic that he succeeded at last in righting himself. One's sympathies, of course, were all on the side of life. Also, when there was nobody to care or to know, this gigantic effort on the part of an insignificant little moth, against a power of such magnitude, to retain what no one else valued or desired to keep, moved one strangely. Again, somehow, one saw life, a pure bead. I lifted the pencil again, useless though I knew it to be. But even as I did so, the unmistakable tokens of death showed themselves. The body relaxed, and instantly grew stiff. The struggle was over. The insignificant little creature now knew death. As I looked at the dead moth, this minute wayside triumph of so great a force over so mean an antagonist filled me with wonder. Just as life had been strange a few minutes before, so death was now as strange. The moth having righted himself now lay most decently and uncomplainingly composed. O yes, he seemed to say, death is stronger than I am.

Possibilities for Writing

1. The moth in Woolf's essay becomes a potent symbol for life and then also for death more generally. How does Woolf manage to do this? Point to specific passages in the essay that directly or by implication tie the moth to the world beyond itself.

2. For all its concreteness, this essay is quite philosophical. How would you characterize Woolf's conception of the universe, based on the ideas that this essay provokes?

3. In order to explore your feelings about an abstract concept—love, courage, greed, humility, loss, or another of your choice—construct an essay, as Woolf does, around a central symbol. Describe your symbol in primarily concrete terms so that the concept itself becomes concrete.

Credits

Index

Additional Titles of Interest

Allison, Dorothy, *Bastard Out of Carolina*

Alvarez, Julia, *How the Garcia Girls Lost Their Accent*

Austen, Jane, *Persuasion*

Austen, Jane, *Pride and Prejudice*

Austen, Jane, *Sense and Sensibility*

Bloom, Harold, *Shakespeare: The Invention of the Human*

Brontë, Charlotte, *Jane Eyre*

Brontë, Emily, *Wuthering Heights*

Burke, Edmund, *Reflections on the Revolution in France*

Cather, Willa, *My Antonia*

Cather, Willa, *O Pioneers!*

Cellini, Benvenuto, *The Autobiography of Benvenuto Cellini*

Chapman, Abraham, *Black Voices*

Chesnutt, Charles W., *The Marrow of Tradition*

Chopin, Kate, *The Awakening and Selected Stories*

Conrad, Joseph, *Heart of Darkness*

Conrad, Joseph, *Nostromo: A Tale of the Seaboard*

Coraghessan Boyle, T., *The Tortilla Curtain*

Defoe, Daniel, *The Life and Adventures of Robinson Crusoe*

Descartes, René, *Discourse on Method and Meditations*

Descartes, René, *Meditations and Other Metaphysical Writings*

Detocqueville, *Democracy in America*

Dickens, Charles, *Hard Times*

Douglass, Frederick, *Narrative of the Life of Frederick Douglass: An American Slave*

DuBois, W. E. B., *Souls of Black Folk*

Equiano, Olaudah, *The Interesting Narrative and Other Writings*

Gore, Al, *Earth in the Balance: Ecology and the Human Spirit*

Grossman, Lawrence K., *Electronic Republic*

Hawthorne, Nathaniel, *The Scarlet Letter: A Romance*

Hutner, Gordon, *Immigrant Voices: Twenty-Four Narratives on Becoming an American*

Jacobs, Harriet, *Incidents in the Life of a Slave Girl*

Jen, Gish, *Typical American*

King, Martin Luther, Jr., *Why We Can't Wait*

Lewis, Sinclair, *Babbit*

Machiavelli, *The Prince*

Marx, Karl, *The Communist Manifesto*

Mill, Stuart John, *On Liberty*

More, Sir Thomas, *Utopia and Other Essential Writings*

Orwell, George, *1984*

Paine, Thomas, *Common Sense*

Plato, *The Republic*

Postman, Neil, *Amusing Ourselves to Death*

Rose, Mike, *Lives on the Boundary*

Rossiter, *The Federalist Papers*

Rousseau, Jean-Jaques, *The Social Contract*

Shelley, Mary, *Frankenstein*

Sinclair, Upton, *The Jungle*

St. Augustine, *The Confessions of St. Augustine*

Steinbeck, John, *Of Mice and Men*

Stevenson, Robert Louis, *The Strange Case of Dr. Jekyll and Mr. Hyde*

Stoker, Bram, *Dracula*

Stowe, Harriet Beecher, *Uncle Tom's Cabin*

Swift, Jonathan, *Gulliver's Travels*

Taulbert, Clifton L., *Once Upon a Time When We Were Colored*

Thoreau, Henry David, *Walden: Or, Life in the Woods* and *On the Duty of Civil Disobedience*

Truth, Sojourner, *The Narrative of Sojourner Truth*

Woolf, Virginia, *Jacob's Room*

Zola, Emile, *Germinal*